NARROWBOAT DREAMS

A Journey North by England's Waterways

STEVE HAYWOOD

summersdale

NARROWBOAT DREAMS

Summersdale Publishers Ltd
46 West Street
Chichester
West Sussex
PO19 1RP
UK

www.summersdale.com

Printed and bound in Great Britain

ISBN: 978-1-84024-670-4

For Marian Ellen Haywood

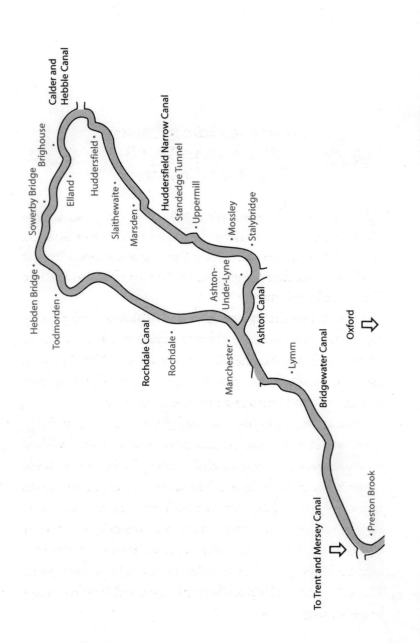

Calder and Hebble Canal

Brighouse

Sowerby Bridge

Elland

Huddersfield

Slaithewaite

Marsden

Hebden Bridge

Todmorden

Huddersfield Narrow Canal

Standedge Tunnel

Uppermill

Mossley

Stalybridge

Ashton-Under-Lyne

Rochdale Canal

Rochdale

Ashton Canal

Manchester

Lymm

Oxford

Bridgewater Canal

To Trent and Mersey Canal

Preston Brook

Understanding Locks – More than You'll Ever Need to Know

*T*he concept of a lock isn't a difficult one to grasp or they wouldn't rent boats out to beginners and let them loose on the canal five minutes later. But if you've never seen a lock, it can be a bit confusing and some of the terms I use to describe them may be off-putting.

In which case the following short explanation and glossary might help. On the other hand it might not help at all. In which case don't take the slightest notice of it. You'll pick up the terminology in the book the same way you'd pick up how to work a lock if you'd just rented out that boat.

Locks are basically just a way of getting boats up or down a hill, which is a major consideration when you're building a canal across a mountain chain. Some locks can be **wide locks**, some **narrow locks**. The wide ones have more **gates** and are bigger and heavier, but both work by the same basic principle. They take water from the **summit**, the top of the canal, and feed it into the lock by a system of cast iron ratchets and cogs which is called the **paddle** or **lock gear**. This is because it lifts **paddles** in the gate which allows water to get through them.

If a lock is **in your favour** as you are approaching it means the water-level in the lock is at the same level you're on. If it is **against you** it will be at a higher or lower level, depending on which direction you're travelling, uphill or downhill. Either way you'll have to moor your boat. Then you will either **empty** or **fill** the lock to the same level you are at by raising the **paddles** on the **gate** using a tool called a **lock-key** or **windlass**. This engages with a **spindle** which you **wind up**. Sometimes if the paddles are stiff and heavy it is a **bastard** and you will find yourself **cursing**, asking **why you ever thought being on a canal could be any fun**.

When the water in the lock gets to the same level you are at, you push open the gates by using the **lock-beams**. These are the counterbalances which extend from the lock-gates and look so much like conveniently-placed benches that even if you didn't know what they were, you'd find yourself naturally sitting on them while you waited for the lock to **empty** or **fill**. If the **gates** are heavy this too can be a **bastard** and you will find yourself **cursing** some more especially at your **husband** or **wife** whose **ridiculous idea** it probably was to come on this **stupid holiday**.

The section of canal between one lock and another is called a **pound**, or on a river, a **reach**. A series of locks together is called a **flight**.

The only other bit of jargon you might want to get to grips with is **British Waterways** though this is a term incomprehensible even to those of us who've been cruising the canals for years. They're supposed to maintain the waterways but you'll soon find this is a **joke** – another term you will need to be familiar with if you intend to do much boating.

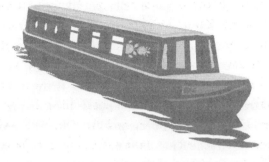

One

*W*hy do these sorts of madnesses always begin in pubs? Is it just that simple equation of beer + lack of inhibition = fruitcake idea? Or is there another reason for it? Perhaps that day it was something to do with being in London. Something to do with the fact that it's the biggest city in the country, the capital, but a place nobody at all really comes from. Everyone in London comes from somewhere else, don't they? London's just the place they end up.

One way or another, there I was that Sunday in the Hare and Billet, sitting at that corner table next to the fireplace where you can look out at the kites flapping over the heath. It was a good day for kites; a brisk wind coming upriver from the estuary and the bright, early-spring sunshine beginning to settle on Greenwich Park. Claire had been talking about her folks' place down in Devon. They live on a little farm nestled in the folds of the fields, hidden behind high hedges. They make clotted cream, for God's sake! It's so idyllic, you can hardly believe it. In fact, if I hadn't been there myself *I* wouldn't believe it. That sort of thing just doesn't seem real when you're sitting in a pub on Blackheath, so high above the rest of London it's as if you're perched on the rim of the city.

Then Tom started going on about the west coast of bloody Ireland and the area between Donegal and Sligo. Fly-fishing for trout in the lakes and rivers round there. Casting for mackerel from storm-tossed little boats. It made me want to weep with envy. Instead I became bitter, the way you can do on a surfeit of Greene King. Don't they do anything in Ireland except fish? Or wax lyrical about the old country?

I bought him a drink; I had to. Not only was it was my round; getting him to use his mouth to swallow beer was the only way of shutting him up.

Eventually, wiping his lips, he said, 'You're from up country, aren't you, Steve? Where is it again?'

It was the question I'd been dreading.

My problem, you see, is that I don't come from anywhere. Well, not anywhere you'd notice.

I was actually born in the East Midlands. And that's the problem in two succinct words: East and Midlands. For anyone living in the South, the East Midlands isn't really anywhere. People have a vague idea that it's somewhere up North, part of what they see as an industrial wasteland of dark satanic mills and wind-swept moorland, a place where they eat the blood-filled inner tubes of bicycle tyres, and where a night on the tiles means clog dancing on the roof of the local working men's club.

Yet to anyone actually from the North, the East Midlands counts as the South. It's a London suburb like East Acton, on the far reaches of some tube line they've never heard of. And they treat us with the same contempt they reserve for anyone who lives nearer to France than Tyneside.

What makes it worse is that even people who come from the Midlands view the East Midlands as off the map. Midlanders – *real* Midlanders – come from places like Dudley and West Brummitch where they beat metal for a living and wean their babies on pork scratchings. If you're from the *real* Midlands you speak in an accent so thick that when you ask for a Cornetto it comes out sounding like an arse cream.

My part of the Midlands – Leicestershire – isn't like that at all. With its gentle, undulating hills, and red-brick villages scattered across the countryside, it's more like an honorary bit of the Home Counties: not the Midlands at all really, but a chunk of Sussex or Kent inadvertently misplaced sometime during the upheavals of the Ice Age. They may love us for our fatty food – we make pork pies, after all, we make Stilton, we are the crisp capital of Europe and produce more packets of cheese and onion than any other place in the world – but we are hated for our hunting and our frock-coated landed gentry who ponce about as if the world belongs to them because, of course, in this part of the country most of it still does.

I got the idea that afternoon in the Hare and Billet with Tom and Claire. And once inside my head I couldn't get it out. A week or two later I was still chewing it over and, one night over dinner, I finally raised the matter with Em. We were having one of those evenings. One of those evenings generally begins after a bad day with a bottle or two of Bishops Finger. Then if things don't improve we move onto a glass of something red, blackcurrantish and generally around 13.5 per cent alcohol. By this stage, if we're not so entirely pickled that we can't string two words together, we might drift into some sort of desultory conversation.

'It puts me in a unique position,' I pontificated. 'Coming from the East Midlands, I mean. It gives me a dispassionate view of both parts of the country, north and south.'

Em is used to me sounding off like this – especially after drink has been taken. It makes me hard going. Or 'as boring as bat shit' as she prefers to put it.

'You mean, coming from where you do, you can be equally rude about all parts of England,' she laughed. 'And even Ireland, Scotland and Wales if circumstances demand it.'

'No, I'm being serious,' I said, marshalling the one or two brain cells that had survived the battle for the ridge at Cabernet Sauvignon. 'There's a real problem here. The North and the South are like two separate countries. We already speak different languages; soon it'll be passport control at Stafford or border police on the A1. Maybe it's always been that way, but it's more noticeable nowadays, isn't it? We've always been a country divided, but now we're two halves without a function. The North doesn't make things like it used to; and with Brussels, Strasbourg and Washington calling all the shots, London and the South doesn't even take the decisions any more like it once did…'

Now, if this speech sounds somewhat too well rehearsed for a bloke in the condition I was, well… you'd be right. The fact is there was a sub-text to what I was saying. Em and I, you see, are the owners of a fifty-seven-foot six-inch narrowboat, and when the inconveniences of urban life become a little too much, I'm in the habit of taking off on it to explore the 3,000 miles of canals and rivers that compose Britain's inland waterways' network. I justify these jaunts on the basis that I'm researching some vague project of one sort or another.

It keeps me off the streets. And sometimes it's even true.

What it means though, is that I have to leave Em at home in London, doing the sort of tedious things that being at home entails. Things like going into work every day to earn us money. When I'm away everything's down to her and as a result she doesn't have things done for her that she very much likes having done. Things like home maintenance, for instance. This is one of those things that falls under the heading of 'Stuff Steve is Responsible For' and can be anything from decorating that upstairs room (the one I haven't touched since we moved in fifteen years ago), to working on the patio I started four years before and somehow never got around to finishing. At the best of times I am not very good at home maintenance. Away from home I have found that I am useless at it.

So I have to be very careful about raising the idea of one of my waterways projects. Especially one of the sort I'd been chewing over – one that would take me north to the furthest reaches of the canal system, about as far away as it is possible to get from London on the inland waterways. But momentous changes had been taking place up there: two derelict canals had been restored, brought back from the dead after half a century of disuse. I couldn't wait to get up there and explore them. In waterways terms, it was like opening up Eastern Europe after the fall of the Berlin Wall.

In fact, it was more astonishing than that – which may seem an exaggeration, except that as a baby boomer I grew up in the Cold War when you couldn't help but be aware of the struggle that was taking place between us, the West (good guys, upholders of peace, freedom and liberty) and them, the Commie bastards (vodka-drinking warmongers in furry hats who wanted to subjugate the world). Yet because I'd been so well brainwashed there wasn't a scintilla of doubt in my mind – not one iota of uncertainty – that sooner or later good would prevail over evil and we would eventually win this Wagnerian battle of moral ideology.

Yet if you'd have told me that the stagnant old ditch at the bottom of my granddad's garden in Loughborough would become the hub of a new leisure business which would come to dwarf the country's heavy industries like coal-mining, engineering and textiles… well, I'd have laughed in your face. Part of the Grand Union linking London to Birmingham, it might once have been – a sort of M1 of its day, I guess. But at the stage I was old enough to begin to take interest, it had become almost impassable, reduced to a stinking channel of reed-covered mud, strewn with old bikes and half-submerged oil drums. Yet I was fascinated with it, obsessed you might say; and despite being constantly warned by my mum and dad not to go anywhere near the place on account of the thousands of kids they told me had been drowned there, there was nothing I liked more than playing around the old lock just down from the town wharf.

I used to spend hours there, swinging on the gates and staring down into the chasm of the lock chamber, transfixed by the black, oily water clinging to the walls. I remember the first time it struck me what locks were for, and the first time I realised that by twisting the spindles on the gear that operated them, I could lift the greasy paddles an inch or two, releasing a satisfying a torrent of water for as long as my wrists could take the strain. Occasionally I'd be rewarded with the rare sight of passing traffic. Some of it was no doubt the last of that old breed of working boat that had carried coal along this canal for a couple of centuries and longer; some, I guess, was the first of the new generation of holiday craft, pioneers of the new leisure age. The details, sadly, I forget, but I do recall clearly the wonder I felt as it began to dawn on me that this canal wasn't just a one-off, but part of a whole network that covered the whole country.

What intrigued me was how they all linked up. And where they all went.

Growing up in Leicestershire I was never far from the waterways. When I was young we lived in a small village called Shepshed where the long-abandoned Charnwood Canal skirts the cemetery where most of my family are buried, and where until relatively recently, just outside the village, a single hump-backed canal bridge still stood stranded in the middle of a flat, ploughed field as a surreal monument to an industrial artery that had once carried coal from these parts to feed an empire that stretched across the world. Later on, we lived over the other side of the county, close to the River Soar, which was deep and wide and sometimes fast-flowing, and where you could make rafts out of pallets and rent rowing boats at Barrow.

My parents must have been sick with worry that I might drown. But what could they have done? I was at that stage all kids go through when the water is like a magnet. Whatever dire warnings they issued, I took no notice of, and I was always getting a clip around the ear from my dad for my pains – something that must have had more of a psychological effect on me than I care to admit, since many years later, when I first got a boat of my own and invited him to visit, I remember flinching whenever he moved, convinced that it was only a matter of time before I'd cop it again for *still* ignoring him.

Getting my own boat was something that was bound to happen; something in my genes, I guess. My interest in waterways survived my university years when I was tempted by new diversions involving women and beer, and sometimes, when I got lucky, both together. I got lucky with Em. She was from London and one of the few women I knew who could tell the difference between Adnams and Shepherd Neame. She'd also taken a holiday on a narrowboat once, and encouraged me to do the same one year when I'd got time on my hands and no idea how to use it. It wasn't long before we tied the knot.

No, I don't mean we got married. Our commitment to each other was far more enduring than this. What I mean is that we bought our first boat together.

Though the word 'boat' in this context is somewhat misleading.

Canal boats in those days generally meant plastic cruisers of one sort or another, though there was a smattering of other craft around: former lifeboats with lengths of canvas tacked across their bows to afford their owners some protection from the elements, or dodgy-looking DIY constructions made out of marine ply and looking for all the world like floating garden sheds. There were a lot of old working 'flats' as well – low-sided tubs like shallow steel trays, built for industrial use but given a new lease of life by having some sort of superstructure tacked onto them. This was invariably made out of cheap tongue-and-groove which always warped and stained however often it was varnished.

What narrowboats there were at this time were either full-length, former working boats, seventy feet long and more, or cut-down versions of the same, some of them converted to a basic standard by the nascent hire companies that were beginning to spring up all over the place. Appearing too were occasional purpose-built steel narrowboats, constructed specifically for the leisure market. Among these were boats built in my part of the world – in Market Harborough in Leicestershire – by a man called Sam Springer who used to knock them together out of old gasometers he picked up on the cheap and flattened by laying on his workshop floor and driving over them in his ex-army Land Rover.

Sam saw a gap in the market before anyone else and he switched from his old business of making oil tanks. These, he figured, were just square steel boxes designed not to let liquid out. What were canal boats except differently shaped steel boxes designed not to let liquid in? True, he made one or two concessions to design. He put a pointy bit on the front, for example, and he put a bit of a deck on the back. But basically Sam's early boats were just long, thin boxes.

However, even though Springers were inexpensive, they were well beyond what Em and I could afford. The boat we bought was a Springer replica. A tribute boat, I suppose you could call it. It was thirty feet long and had been knocked together by an amateur so that it wasn't really like anything else you'd ever seen floating before. For a start it hadn't got a bow as such. The bloke who made it was a welder who used to work on Saudi pipelines; his steelwork could have survived a nuclear explosion. Unfortunately he didn't know a lot about marine design. What this meant in practice was that when he'd finished constructing the sides of the boat he just bent them round at the front so as not to let the water in.

Bows on boats are supposed to be elegant, graceful and stylish. They are supposed to cut through the water effortlessly like a knife. Ours didn't. Instead we ploughed the water. We pushed it in front of us like a bulldozer so that wherever we went there was always a foot-high wave preceding us like a tsunami causing chaos along the banks. The sides of the boat were even worse. Well, you've heard of a dog's leg, haven't you? This was a dog's dinner. This was 100 per cent Winalot.

If that wasn't bad enough, there was one other small matter which was to prove inconvenient in taking this first hesitant step in the new world of leisure cruising. The fact was, the boat hadn't got an engine. Quite why it hadn't got an engine, I can't clearly remember – though it may have had something to do with my grandfather. The boat, you see, was on sale at a gravel pit in Derbyshire near where he lived. I rang him up to ask him if he'd have a look over it for us. When he called back, he'd bought it.

'But it… er… hasn't got an engine,' I said, when I eventually saw it for myself. I could have said a lot of other things about its failings, but this was the most obvious of them. Well, it was obvious to me. Somehow he'd missed it. He was never a man for detail.

Eventually we fitted it with a crap engine we bought from the classifieds of the *Derby Evening Telegraph* for no better reason than it only cost thirty quid, which was all we had left after we paid for the boat. It was a single cylinder engine which worked by a process of controlled explosions, and we used it to drive a propeller no bigger than your hand, which we ran through a gearbox designed for a high-revving petrol engine.

A slow-firing diesel engine? A high-revving petrol gear box? A propeller the size of a toy? Frankly, you don't need a degree in mechanical engineering to see that this set-up lacked that fine sense of precision which once made us the world's leading industrial nation.

It hadn't got any starter so we used to get it going by holding a loose wire onto the battery. This could be an alarming experience if you weren't used to it. The battery would spark like the flintlock of an old pistol and the engine would kick into life with a sound of hand grenades exploding in your head. Engaging forward gear – which you did with a bit of old pipe sticking through the deck – it began to whine like a dentist's drill, so that after about an hour, holes started appearing in your skull from the sound it was making.

Mind you, it rarely ran for as long as an hour. More often than not after a few minutes there'd be the fearsome screech of metal grinding or bolts exploding and the whole thing would stop dead. I used to think it was better that way. When the engine didn't run, I mean. That way you didn't find yourself relying on it to get you anywhere. If you did, it would invariably let you down.

Once we were cruising down the Avon after a violent storm and it gave out at the head of a weir leaving us hanging onto a safety chain until someone rescued us. Another time we were doing a ninety-degree turn at a junction and it packed up on us without warning, sending us crashing into the wall of a wharf.

The notch in the concrete is still there to this day.

We bought the boat at Shardlow off the Trent, and to get onto the main canal system we had to come down the river and turn against the flow, a manoeuvre fraught with such uncertainty that on our maiden voyage friends insisted on accompanying us along the bank as far as the junction for fear we'd get swept to our deaths. This was a nice gesture, but quite what they planned doing if we had got swept to our deaths was never clear to me. Ensured our bodies were recovered, I guess. It wasn't something I wanted to dwell on too much.

For all its problems, we cruised that boat for more than a decade and travelled the system from one end of the country to the other, frequently to places where, in those days, the appearance of a pleasure boat was a rarity.

And this was the other reason I felt drawn to go to the North. Because in one of our trips in this boat many years before, we'd crossed the Pennines on the 127-mile Leeds and Liverpool Canal which connects the North Sea on the east coast to the Irish Sea on the west. It had been a tremendous adventure for a couple of kids. Since then we'd travelled the world, both for work and pleasure. Yet we hadn't been back to the Pennines. Now, with all the restoration that had happened, there were two new routes across England's central mountain spine.

I couldn't wait to get to them.

That weekend Em and I went walking in the countryside. One of the advantages of living in south-east London is that you can easily get away from the city and be in deepest Kent inside an hour. We'd walked from the ancient village of Sutton Valence along a greensand escarpment to the settlement of Ulcombe, where a little beyond the church, high on the ridge, we sat on a bench thoughtfully positioned for walkers against the natural shelter of a cobnut platt which acted as a windbreak. It was a bitterly cold day, but bright with sharp spring sunshine; and so clear we could see the whole length of the Low Weald to where the land rose up again in a series of gentle woodland slopes.

It had been a typical Sunday walk, through a typical English landscape – the sort of thing thousands of us do every week. At Sutton Valence, a place we'd not visited before, we stumbled on the old gabled grammar school which incorporates some sixteenth-century almshouses; and just around the corner, delaying our start still further, we unexpectedly came across the ruins of a small twelfth-century Norman castle. The remains of its keep had been taken over by a flock of doves and at our arrival they flapped about distractedly showering feathers, affronted by the presence of these lumbering two-legged beasts disturbing their tranquillity.

The Church of All Saints at Ulcombe was a gem. Another Norman structure constructed of ragstone, Kent's most important building stone, it's bigger than you'd expect in a village of this size because a college of priests was established there by Archbishop Stephen Langton around the time of Magna Carta. There were clumps of snowdrops dotted around the back of the churchyard, and tucked among the gravestones at the front where they could catch the warmth were a few shy primroses cautiously peeping out at the sun. Dominating the frontage was an enormous yew tree estimated to be 2,300 years old – older than the Christ the church was built to celebrate.

'England is such an astonishing country,' I said to Em, after we'd been inside to look at some medieval wall paintings that had somehow survived the years. 'Wherever you are, there's always something to see, and however much you see, there's always more.'

She threw me a suspicious look. Maybe she'd realised by now I was after something.

So it was that I first raised my idea of a trip to the newly opened northern canals, a discussion that continued later over roast beef and Yorkshire pudding in a local pub. I said the journey would give me a fresh perspective on England; I said it would give me a new way of seeing the past. After all, wasn't our contemporary history an industrial history? And didn't that start in the North, fired by a revolution which really was as momentous as the one that had brought down the Berlin Wall? A revolution centred on canals, an Industrial Revolution that really *did* change the world.

But life's a funny old business, and when you start something you don't always know where it's going to lead you. I hadn't planned for this journey to be a voyage of discovery in any metaphysical sense. Far from it. I'd already had my fiftieth birthday and I'd been through that process of setting myself challenges as a puny gesture of defiance to the onset of middle age. I didn't want to pitch myself against the forces of nature. That sort of thing bored me. There was something futile in the gesture of stamping your foot at God as if you were a defiant child and he some imperious father who wouldn't let you stay out late at the party.

Yet in coming up with this idea, though I didn't know it, I was biting off more than I could chew, planning something which would take me to the edge of my physical limits. Paradoxically, for one not interested in this sort of thing, it

CHAPTER ONE

would prove to be more of a challenge than I could ever have imagined. More of a challenge than I wanted, in fact.

But hey! Why should this be such a surprise? Others might climb Everest with a piano, row across the Atlantic on a tea tray or walk to the South Pole on stilts. But most of us aren't going to do anything like this, are we? We've got mortgages. We've got families. And anyhow we know that journeys are in the mind, not on the map. My nemesis would arrive in the most peculiar of places and in the oddest of ways. In a gentle valley in West Yorkshire, for instance, on a towpath where families picnicked and the elderly went for a gentle afternoon stroll. Or in the early morning travelling through Manchester with only drunks and vagrants for company. Or late at night in Lancashire with every flickering shadow of twilight fuelling my fertile imagination. In all of these places I would get pretty close to the end of my tether.

And like most journeys worth doing, it would change me for ever.

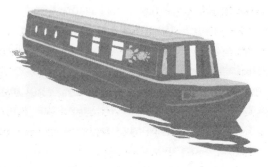

Two

So there I am, splayed out, one leg on the floor and the other perched over the edge of the dining room table in a manner reminiscent of some snooker player preparing to pot a black.

Imagine it.

This is not some contortion to reach the salt. Nor is it some form of bizarre sexual practice involving exotic foodstuffs. What I am actually doing is reading a map – or at least attempting to read one. It is one of those fold-up maps that once you've opened them never actually fold back the same way again. When you try, they're all over the place so that eventually you lose patience and finish up wrapping them back up any way they will go. This, of course, means that the next time you come to use them, they're even more unmanageable than before. Now, not only will they not fold back properly, they won't fold out either. They rip. They tear. They tangle and finish up looking like a hopeless attempt at origami. They develop creases which give them the texture of reptile skins so that they begin to look less like maps than some repulsive iguana from a jungle swamp.

At times like this it's easy to let your imagination run away with you. Maps spread across a table seem to develop a life of their own. It's as if they've got it in for you. They are forever slithering and sliding about, wrapping themselves around you, looking for an opportunity to do you mischief. Reading a map, it is impossible to relax, even for a moment. You constantly have to be on your guard.

This is the state I am in, looking at this map. It is a map of the waterways, covered in long fronds of green, red and blue which represent different categories of canal and river. Perversely this makes it look even more like a creature from the swamp, as if I am looking through its skin and seeing its blood system laid out like a diagram from a biology textbook. Not that this deters me. I am made of sterner stuff than to be intimidated by a map, and I am fighting back. Against all odds I have managed to subdue the beast. I have secured one of its corners with a heavy glass candlestick. The other I have restrained temporarily with my leg, hence the snooker pose. Now I manage to weigh it down with a mug of tea I poured earlier in the day and totally forgot to drink.

This, unfortunately, is the very moment that Em comes home from work. She is in stealth-bomber mode, creeping into the house so soundlessly that the first I am aware of her presence is when I hear her voice an inch or two behind me asking what on earth I think I am doing. From her tone it is clear she thinks that whatever it is, it's something unwholesome. So much for love and trust.

My nerves are already shot to pieces struggling with the map. The shock of her appearing out of the blue like this just about does for me. I jump involuntarily and suddenly find myself hovering in mid-air. At the same time the map seems to detonate. Suddenly it is all over the place and the mug and candlestick which had been securing it lie smashed in fragments on the floor. Everything is awash with cold Typhoo.

It hasn't been a particularly good day so far. Believe me, it isn't getting any better.

'I am trying to plan my route,' I say eventually, recovering myself. 'For my trip to the North, you remember?'

'Anyone would think you were some sort of polar explorer the way you're going about it,' she says sceptically, heading off to the kitchen in search of some happy juice. 'The dustpan's under the stairs,' she shouts helpfully. 'The floorcloth's in here.'

But what other way are you supposed to go about planning a journey except by consulting a map? I suppose I could do what I've done in the past – what a lot of people cruising the canals do – and make no plans at all, exploring one waterway because it looks pretty, or deciding not to go up another because it doesn't. But I have done this sort of careless wandering too often, and though the sense of freedom you get travelling this way is a delight, and something everyone should experience at least once in their life, it's no way for a grown-up to act. Adults shouldn't meander around the country aimlessly, without direction or purpose. Adults should have goals and targets. They should know exactly what they're doing and… well, just do it.

CHAPTER TWO

I know what I am doing. I am going to boldly go where no man has gone before. I am going to explore the previously derelict canals of the North. Places like Stalybridge, where a newly built section of canal cuts through the very centre of town, and where they built a brand new town square to welcome it. Places like Standedge where Britain's highest, longest and deepest tunnel is open to boats once more after being closed for a generation. Places like Huddersfield where the route of the old canal was built over so they had to burrow under parts of the town to accommodate it again.

Em comes back into the room clutching an enormous balloon glass of something red. Trust me, it's not Ribena. By now I have finished cleaning up the chaos caused by her arrival home. I have also somehow succeeded in stabilising the map without having to resort to six-inch nails through the table. We both stand for a moment surveying it suspiciously, though it now seems innocuous and lifeless. It is as if the creature within it has reverted to the deep once more and we are left staring at the water into which it has sunk, for with its new patina of sand-coloured tea stains, the map looks like nothing more than a muddy edge of a swamp.

Em says, 'Well, it's hardly much of a choice, is it?' There is a note of derision in her voice. She, remember, has been at work all day. She is a Mistress of the Universe, righting wrongs where she finds them, brandishing the virtuous sword of truth and justice on behalf of the charity for which she works. For her, a decision about which way to cruise north on a boat is not one she's going to spend much time agonising about.

'I mean, you can only go two ways, can't you?' she goes on, sweeping her arm across the map a couple of times in the way of some general deploying a force on a battlefield. 'You can either go this way,' she announces, 'or that.'

'This way,' as she calls it, is the Trent and Mersey Canal which goes to the North from the River Trent at its junction with the River Soar in Nottinghamshire. It leads to Manchester and Liverpool, and it's a slow route, heavily locked and not particularly attractive; though if you want, you can go part of the way by making a detour through Shropshire and into the Cheshire Plain, pottering through countryside so pretty it makes you want to weep.

'That way', by comparison, isn't pretty at all. Far from it. It is a faster route – think railway lines, think electrified East Coast route – but it is downright ugly. What is more, it is hazardous too. It involves going down the Trent itself, through Nottingham and onto the tidal reaches of the river towards the Humber where the only thing you see for days on end are mudbanks lined by massive heaps of rock waiting to lure you to your death. After any sort of rain, even a modest shower, the River Trent can become like a theme park water-ride, flushing you out to the North Sea with all the speed of a lavatory pan.

But even when it's dry, the tidal Trent's not to be trusted. It's as bad in a drought, take it from me. On our previous trip to the North all those years ago, Em and I travelled downstream during a glorious summer when there hadn't been rain for weeks. This was just as well really since we were cruising in the boat with the crap engine, and had conditions been any more challenging it would have been a kamikaze mission as opposed to what it was, which was merely a stupid one. That year the river was placid, as still as a millpond. We relaxed. We cracked open a couple of beers. We toasted the passing water skiers and began to enjoy the ride.

This was a mistake.

Not far below Newark where the Lincolnshire flatlands begin to stretch out like a prairie, and where the river widens so that you can barely see the other side, we suddenly heard the awful sound of our hull grinding against the gravel of the riverbed. Before we could react, the bow reared out of the water, almost tossing us off the boat which swung to one side, and then to the other – us hanging on for dear life – until it ground to a halt mid-stream, our hull completely out of the water on a submerged island. Nothing we could do would get us off. No amount of pulling or pushing would help: no amount of revving the engine.

It got worse.

We were so badly stranded that when the tide went out we were left so high and dry that we could – and did – climb off the boat and go for a walk. Every day, in fact. Twice a day sometimes. Well, we had to do *something*, didn't we? We were trapped there for nearly two weeks before we were rescued and it was a major operation to do it. They had to send two massive tugs out to us in the early hours of the morning, when the spring tides were at their highest. They wrapped a massive ship rope around us and it was a toss up whether they'd get us off the gravel or rip us in half first.

Em was right about the routes, but the decision was even simpler than she'd said. Theoretically there might have been two ways north, but in reality there was only one. I was going to be travelling single-handed most of the time, after all. A tidal river is no place for go-it-alone heroes. I didn't want to get stranded again. There was no way I was going anywhere near the River Trent.

We keep our boat in Banbury in Oxfordshire. This is something of a historical accident, since years ago the boat with the crap engine broke down there and we were stuck. Before that we moored for years at a place called Bedworth, near Coventry. It broke down there as well. Thinking about it, our mooring before that had been in Leamington Spa where the engine had given up the ghost yet again.

In fact, looking back, the way in which we explored Britain's inland waterways network had more to do with the unreliability of that engine than it did any sort of forward-planning.

Mind you, there have been advantages in letting chance decide things like this. Left to ourselves we'd no doubt have berthed the boat for preference in some rural arcadia, some gentle pasture sweeping down to the water's edge. Or in some tiny picturesque hamlet (God knows, there are enough of them around the English waterways) where boaters gather of an evening in front of roaring log fires in bars serving foaming pints of real ale.

It would have been idyllic, yes. But boring. Very boring.

As it was, we made something of a speciality of mooring in places so grotty that most people would have baulked at staying there overnight, let alone for years on end. In Leamington, for instance, we pulled up one wet night opposite the gasworks, adjacent to the main road into town. And stayed there for most of the 1970s. At Bedworth, we moored at a place that was more like a scrapyard than a boatyard, and where the nearest pub was on a council estate where you could be more confident of seeing a fight than getting a decent pint of bitter. The compensation was that we met people we'd never have met any other way, and we made friends we've kept in touch with ever since.

Both moorings were remarkable places; both, in different ways, encapsulated the age. Leamington was a like a leftover fragment of hippydom, a block of San Francisco's Haight-Ashbury transferred to urban Warwickshire. At the core were about half a dozen boats, a close-knit community of people you'd probably nowadays call new-agers; except that in those days – the old age – they didn't merit any special title. They were – we were! – just young people doing the sort of things young people did in the days before everyone under the age of thirty started selling their souls for an iPod.

There was Ian, a dopehead whose one ambition in life was to go to Brazil and open a brothel. He lived on a small cruiser and his mother used to look after his marijuana, measuring it out to him by the day so he wouldn't be tempted to smoke too much. He was a recovering alcoholic who'd turned to drugs to keep him off the drink. Alcohol turned him nasty, made him violent – though I never saw him like that. I only ever saw him stoned which made him gentle, almost childlike. My overriding memory of him is one afternoon when he was worrying about whether or not he'd harm the fish as he harvested what he swore were hallucinogenic lily tubers.

On the next boat to his, living with his Trotskyist Irish girlfriend, was Malcolm, a junior doctor who was training in

Birmingham. Moored next to him were Bob and Judy – she small and pretty, hair as straight as the fronds of a willow tree; he as tall as the tree itself, his hair a riot of blond Viking curls cascading to his shoulders. The two of them brought up a family of girls on the canal. Eventually the pure weight of oestrogen on their boat threatened to sink it, and they moved into a house where the same boat is still moored at the bottom of their garden.

In Bedworth the scrapyard we moored at was called Charity Dock, and our stay there pretty well accounted for the 1980s. The place was unbelievably squalid, ankle deep in oil and running with rats. But this was filth with a long and illustrious history. The same family had run the yard for generations, so long that if you look in the books, you'll find that there was once a particular style of traditional canalboat 'roses and castles' painting which was associated with the place. Even the fighting in the Furnace round the corner was in the best traditions of the waterways, for despite the way we romanticise the past nowadays, brawls between boatmen were common in years gone by. And the fact is, most of the blokes fighting in the pub were of waterways stock. They were either the children or grandchildren of boat families who'd been stranded locally in the icy winter of 1963 when the canal froze over and no traffic moved for months; and when eventually the waterways' authorities made the whole lot of them redundant, taking away not just their livelihoods, but also their boats which were their homes too. It was the end of two centuries of commercial canal carrying.

The old boatmen themselves were long past fighting by the time we washed up in Bedworth – or Bed'uth, as we soon learned to pronounce it. Even so, they hadn't lost their love for the cut. Canal water ran in their veins. They'd been thrown on the mercy of the council after they'd been made homeless, and despite living 'on the land' as they put it, they were drawn to the water 'like pigs to shit', as one of them once said to me. Most days there'd be one or two of them hanging around the dry dock where Joe Gilbert, who ran the place, worked. He was one of the few people in the country who could repair old wooden boats, and he was always messing about on some job he wouldn't finish until months after he'd promised, proving the old waterways adage that the only boatbuilder who ever finished on time was Noah – but only because he had an incentive.

One of the old boatmen, John Saxon, had bought a working boat of his own and adapted it for pleasure cruising. But John was the exception. He was younger than the rest, young enough to have had another career as a lorry driver after he came off the water. Most of the blokes kicking about the yard were old men by this stage: small taciturn men with strong features and skin the texture of leather. You could tell them a mile off. You could tell them by their doleful faces, and their sharp appraising eyes. You could tell them by their thick Black Country accents, like treacle dripping off a spoon.

'Yer doing that wrong,' one of them said to me one day when I was splicing a rope, or painting a door, or some such thing, I forget what. We'd been moored at the yard three or four years at this point, and I'd seen him around many times, though we'd only ever nodded to each other before. That day he stood watching me for what seemed an eternity before he said anything. For him, speaking to a stranger was impertinent, you see. It was rude. It was something you only did under extreme circumstances. Whatever it was I was doing that day, it must have irritated him intensely for him to have mentioned it at all. Or perhaps he'd seen me around the yard often enough to feel he knew me now. One way or another, I took it as a compliment that he spoke; it implied a form of acceptance.

And whatever job I was doing that day, I never did get to finish it. Once the ice had been broken, and he'd said his piece, we got talking. You always *do* get talking on the cut. He started chatting about the past and eventually began telling me about the work he'd done. He'd carried coal from local pits to power stations, and he was a fund of stories.

Stories about the characters he'd worked with – eccentrics every one. I remember him telling me about a lockkeeper who ran a black market in ration books after the war, and about a 'Number One' – a man who owned his own boat – who made more money poaching than he did carrying freight. There were stories about drinking in pubs after a day's work, about how so-and-so would always want to fight after a few pints, and so-and-so would always want to sing. But most of all, stories about his day-to-day life. About the relentless unremitting toil of it all. Loading up at the pit, travelling to wherever, hour after hour, day after day, never mind the rain, never mind the wind. Shovel off and unload, and then another ticket back again to load once more, summer after summer, winter after winter, your life not your own. The best these boat families could hope for was to support themselves and their kids, and keep all their bellies full.

I wouldn't have missed the stories for the world, let alone for a poncey mooring in some country hamlet somewhere.

Or worse, in one of those boatyards like car parks they've been building recently which are like suburban housing estates with everyone out on a Sunday morning polishing their brass.

I feel the same about Banbury, where we are now. The South Oxford Canal on which the town is located is one of the prettiest on the system. It follows the valley of the River Cherwell along the edge of the Cotswolds where charming honeystone villages line its course. But do we moor in one? Do we moor in a nice part of Banbury even? No chance! We moor in a cul-de-sac off the cut where an oxbow was cut off when they built the ring road. We moor parallel to the workshops of a Citroën garage, underneath the towering megalith of the General Foods factory which belches out thick plumes of smoke day and night like a burning oil well.

Pretty? Well, no, not exactly. But we wouldn't have it any other way. What is important in a mooring is the people you moor with. And in their own ways those in the arm at Banbury are as much eccentrics as those the old boatman told me about all those years ago. One of them is off the boats herself, born on a boat to a family of working boat people. Her son is an employee of British Waterways, who run the canals, thus keeping alive a family tradition of working on the cut. But there are other people there too from backgrounds equally remarkable. One's father was an equerry to the royal family; another's was a traveller, working the shows and fairgrounds.

This is unusual in today's world. Today we are only ever comfortable within separate homogeneous communities: we live in places where people like us live, we work with people like us and socialise with them in our spare time. If we are poor we never meet the well-off, and if we are well-off, the rich will have nothing to do with us. We are a united kingdom, but despite what we pretend to ourselves, we are divided as much as we ever were by geography, class and money, by religion and race. On the canals – at least until recently – there was a remarkable diversity about everything, boats and people alike…

'I'm sorry, what did you say?' I said to Em.

'I asked you if you were all right.'

'All right? Of course I'm all right. What on earth made you think I wasn't?'

'Because your eyes went funny. The way they do when you're just about to get on your high horse and start preaching. They go mad and staring, so I can see the whites all the way round…'

I ignored her and went off to get myself a glass of wine. This was so she wouldn't have to drink alone. I am thoughtful this way.

When I came back, she said, 'When are you planning to start out, then?'

'Next week, Monday, Tuesday maybe. I thought I'd go up to Banbury this weekend and get things sorted out.'

'For the examination, you mean?'

I stared at her. The examination? What on earth was she on about? I left school years ago. I wasn't doing my GCSEs.

Then it struck me. Oh God, she meant the test! I'd mentioned it to her months before and in typical fashion she'd remembered. I – equally typically – had forgotten about it entirely, even though it put the trip I was planning in jeopardy.

The test! The bloody test! How could I have forgotten?

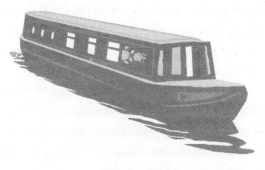

Three

*U*ntil recently getting on the water was an easy enough business. First of all you bought a boat, which didn't need to be expensive. Then you sent a modest cheque to the British Waterways Board who were overjoyed to receive it since they did very little to deserve it except try to close canals which you'd have preferred to keep open.

Nowadays, apart from the cost of boats, which has gone through the roof, your biggest problem getting onto the waterways is likely to be your door handles. Or your taps. Or some other modest domestic accoutrement – all of which you'll find, like as not, is regulated by some clause of an esoteric European directive, or a subsection of a parliamentary bill passed by half a dozen MPs one wet Friday when they were impatient to get back to their constituencies.

Believe me, the bureaucracy on the waterways has got out of hand.

I got a sense of the way things were shaping up some twenty-odd years ago when I received a curious padded envelope in the post from the BWB. It was long and thin and slightly pliable, the dimension of a large letterbox. When I opened it up, I could scarcely believe what I found. I ran to the bottom of the stairs and shouted excitedly up to Em who was making the bed or something.

'You've gotta come down and see this,' I yelled. 'It's unbelievable. Absolutely extraordinary!'

The package contained two cheap aluminium plates. On them were some numbers: 6399 were ours, if my memory serves me correctly. They were number plates, boat number plates.

The future, you see, had arrived.

Recounting this story to people over the years, the commonest reaction I get is not surprise that number plates for boats were introduced so recently, but disbelief that they hadn't been introduced a lot earlier. In fact, so conditioned are people who've only recently come to the canals to the regulation they've found there, it's actually hard for some of them to believe there ever was a time when you could wander with impunity, anonymous and unrecognised, around the watery highways and byways of this country.

But as late as the 1960s, the waterways were a secret world, their existence known only to enthusiasts, industrial archaeologists, and the sort of holidaymaker who'd otherwise take the family rambling up Kinder Scout or across the North Yorkshire Moors. Then they were discovered by a generation of students for whom the isolation proved the perfect environment to experiment with questionable substances, and play psychedelic music very loudly. The cheapness of renting boats and the availability of beer in pubs that were often somewhat cavalier with their opening times also played well in their favour.

On the whole, canals in those days were ignored by the contemporary world. You could cruise for days without seeing another boat and when you did it could be startling, as it must have been for one Victorian explorer to stumble across another in the middle of the African jungle. On a boat, the canals belonged to you; England belonged to you. You could spend weeks – months! – pottering through some of the most hauntingly beautiful countryside, your only company the wildlife around you or the fishermen you'd inevitably pass wherever you went.

Even in the centre of cities you somehow didn't feel part of the present. In places like Birmingham or Manchester, the canals were separated from the town, tucked away down alleyways or behind the crumbling facades of derelict factories, cut off, isolated. I remember once needing some milk, a stone's throw from New Street station. But the canal was below street level, with no way of getting up to the shops which were so close I could virtually hear what people were saying to each other in the queue.

Today if you're interested in canals you're considered a bit of an anorak. In those days, they thought you were mad, only a stage removed from Care in the Community. Where I worked, people used to fix their faces into a frozen smile and shuffle away sheepishly whenever the subject of inland waterways came up in conversation. Eventually I learnt not to take this personally. There are some things in life – like your sexual proclivities and your toilet habits – that are best not shared, even with friends.

Not that I'm saying some system of boat identification *shouldn't* have been introduced, if only as a way of getting us to make some modest contribution towards the upkeep of the waterways. Revenue from boaters in this early period before the hire-boat industry was properly established, and before the idea of private boating had really taken root, wasn't just low – it was all but non-existent. Not surprising really. Boats move about. Without any way of identifying them, it wasn't exactly easy to hunt them down for outstanding debts. And yet the canals were desperate for investment. They were shallow, overgrown and in places completely derelict, and though there was some notion they might someday be used for leisure purposes, no one had much of an idea of how that was going to happen, or what it might amount to once it had. Certainly no one in their wildest dreams predicted the phenomenal growth of recent years which has made canals so astonishingly popular, valued among other things for environmental and conservation reasons that wouldn't have been dreamed of then.

Even so, in terms of the development of contemporary pleasure-boating, something was lost by that decision to introduce number plates – something critical in terms of the relationship of the people who used canals to the people who operated them. From that moment on they – whoever 'they' were – knew who you were. They knew where you lived; they knew how to find you. And somehow, part of that sense of being separate and disconnected from modern life, which drew so many of us to the cut in those days, was inexorably destroyed.

From then on it was downhill all the way. Licence plates were just the beginning. A whole host of rules followed; one edict after another with all the monotonous regularity of a leaking lock gate. There was regulation about where you could and couldn't moor, and for how long. Regulation about the insurance you had to have. Regulation about the information you had to have displayed on your boat.

Then they introduced a set of safety standards for anyone building new boats, and before long this became a set of standards for all boats, regardless of when they were built. This system lasted a few years until we got used to it. Then, they changed it. A while later – presumably because they thought we were getting too complacent – they changed it again, and then continued to refine it over the next few years until we didn't know where we were. Finally in 2002 they introduced what they called the Boat Safety Scheme – a sort of MoT of the water.

Now (becoming predictable, isn't it?) they've changed this. Recently, after years of making the rules tighter than the belt on a boaters' beer belly, they've relented altogether and made most of them advisory – though why they couldn't have done this before we spent thousands of pounds adapting our engines, cutting holes in our bulkheads, and doing all the thousand and one other things they required of us, I don't know.

I mean, I'm not a technical man. If something was dangerous last year, why has it suddenly become safe now? And why is some stuff still subject to sanction when it patently has nothing to do with safety at all?

Take my diesel tank filler, for instance. This has to be clearly marked 'Diesel' to differentiate it from my water tank filler which has to be clearly marked 'Water'. Now what on earth has this got to do with safety, I want to know? If I put diesel on my Typhoo, then surely that's my business. I'll tell you one thing for sure – I won't do it twice. And as for water in my diesel tank? It's the safest thing I could do. I'd never be able go anywhere.

Don't get me wrong, I'm not an unreasonable sort of fellow. I don't want a boat blowing up next to me in a lock. Of course I can see the need for regulating things like gas where there's potentially a real danger. But regulation designed to prevent the stupidity of people putting diesel into their water tanks? They'll never stop it, don't they realise? People are stupid. Regulation doesn't help.

The trouble with this sort of 'safety' nonsense is that it chips away at the sense of freedom you get on the waterways. And this above all else is what we value most about them. The fact is, you don't go boating to be regulated. You go to be left alone. Sadly though, you can't avoid bureaucracy on the canals nowadays because everyone's at it.

Moor in any boatyard and there'll be a list of dos and don'ts as long as your arm that you'll have to sign up to before they'll accept you. Stop in any town centre and the lampposts are all but bending under the weight of signs telling you what you can and can't do. Even in little villages, miles from anywhere, there'll be a welter of notices reminding you you're in a residential area and 'requesting your co-operation' with regard to the noise you make, or the way you dispose of your rubbish or the place you let your dog off its lead…

Em interrupted me.

'You're doing it again,' she said. 'That thing with your eyes – when they go all white and starey. It's creepy.'

I ignored her. 'I can't stop thinking about the damn test,' I said. 'Until you mentioned it, I'd completely forgotten about it. I'll have to ring Pete, see if he's got any suggestions.'

Pete is the guy who has the arm at Banbury where we moor and, as such, he's our landlord. When I called, he did, as I'd hoped, have a solution to the problem. It was in the form of a bloke I'll call Alf, a boat safety scheme examiner who, unbeknown to me, had been coming up to the arm for more than a year now to do tests.

'What's he like?' I asked, somewhat apprehensively, remembering my last examination four years before. This had been done by a guy who might just as well have worn the uniform of the Waffen SS judging by his attitude to rules. Every one of them had been interpreted to its strict letter. It had cost me a fortune.

'Alf's OK,' Pete said. 'He's a stickler for the things that matter, but he turns a blind eye to the silly stuff. He takes more of a commonsense approach to his job.'

This was what I wanted to hear. By the end of the day I'd made an appointment, and a week or two afterwards I was on the Westway above London's Notting Hill, on that familiar asphalt path to freedom, otherwise known as the M40.

The departure had not been an easy one. In fact I'd planned to leave a few days before in order to give myself time to prepare for the test; but in inimitable fashion we had some problem in the crumbling old pile we call home. I can't remember now whether it was something structural like a leaking pipe, or whether – more likely – one of the domestic appliances on which nowadays we've all come to rely so absolutely had gone on the blink. After all, most of ours were at least two years old.

So I had to delay for a while – and then after that, there were other problems to do with the family or work or the car or the cat, or just my own creeping reluctance to be involved in this whole testing process. I mean, why should I have to tailor the start of my trip for this nonsense? Why should I have to be a part of it?

One way or another, it was only on the morning of my appointment that I finally got it together to leave for Banbury; and such was the state of the traffic that day I only arrived at the boat half an hour or so before I was scheduled to see Alf. It didn't leave me a lot of time. In fact, hardly any time at all. But at least I could remedy a few of the basic things I knew would inevitably mean I'd fail the examination. That water tank filler, for instance. I had bought a shiny new brass plate embossed with the word 'Water'. I could stick that on with a squirt of silicon; screw it down later after Alf had gone.

Imagine my dismay when I arrived and found him standing on my deck with such enthusiasm to start work he was like the school swot on the first day of term. He had turned up early and had a wide, welcoming smile on his face that was supposed to be friendly. I found it more threatening than a 12-bore shotgun.

I was in a tricky position. The fact is – affable or not – at that moment I'd have preferred him anywhere than on the boat. We shook hands. We exchanged pleasantries. He told me he had driven down from Birmingham where he'd already done one test that morning. I began to drop hints about the café at Tesco over the road. Given his busy morning, perhaps he'd like a cup of tea, or a bacon butty? No, he didn't want breakfast; he'd already had breakfast; if it was all right with me, he'd rather crack on.

Well... erm... what about a bit of a break then? Did he want five minutes with his feet up for the sake of his digestion, perhaps a smoke? No, no, he didn't smoke, but even if he did, he'd got a busy day ahead and, begging my pardon, could he get on with it? What about a morning paper then; did he want a paper? He could get a paper at the supermarket; they'd still have some left. A *Mirror* perhaps? A *Sun*? Maybe a copy of *The Times* if he was that way inclined?

He looked at me, a mixture of incredulity and impatience in his eyes. I'd only met him ten minutes before, but I could read him like a book. Are you listening to a word I'm saying, his demeanour seemed to suggest. Or are you completely off your trolley?

All this was getting me nowhere and I finally decided that I might as well be straight with him. I told him outright what my problem was, and said that it was hardly worth him doing the test if I couldn't do a few jobs beforehand because I was bound to fail.

'Oh don't bother with all that sort of rubbish,' he said dismissively. 'Let's look at the serious stuff like your gas and your engine. That's where there could be real problems. Where you could kill yourself – or worse, kill other people.'

An hour or so later, he emerged from fiddling in the bilges, his face slightly smeared with grease. 'Well, that all seems OK,' he said. 'There's a few minor things you need to do, but I'll trust you to clear those up after I've gone.'

He sat down and began to write out my certificate. This was the 'ticket' to say I had passed the examination. I couldn't believe it.

'So... the engine...?' I began.

blems at all, though you need to just put an extra ᴄ ᴜp on the fuel line.' He searched around in his pocket and took one out. 'Here, have this.'

'And the gas?'

'Couldn't be better, the pressure is perfect and your pipework's as sound as a bell.'

After he'd gone I sat staring at the certificate where he had left it on the cabin table, scarcely daring to pick it up for fear it might disintegrate in my hands. I hadn't believed for one moment that it could all be so easy. I'd imagined hundreds of pounds worth of work like I'd had on my last examination; I'd imagined being in dock for months on end, the boat useless for anything.

And this, I realised now, somewhat perversely, had been a strange comfort to me. Somehow, while this examination was still pending, my trip to the North, which I'd talked about so much and planned for so long, wasn't a real trip at all but just one of those ideas you comfort yourself with when life's a bit dull or difficult. One of those plans you make but never put into effect, making you feel you're doing things when you're not.

Now, with the certificate in front of me, there was absolutely nothing stopping me going. That very day if I wanted to.

If I'd needed more encouragement, I was about to get it. At that moment the mobile rang. It was Em.

'If you're serious about this trip, then I think you should put the radio on,' she said, a slight note of gravity in her voice. 'I've just heard on the news that there are some problems in Oldham. They're talking about firebombs...'

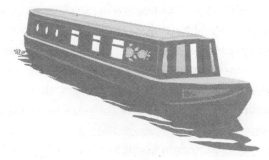

Four

Arthur Ransome, who wrote *Swallows and Amazons* and knew a bit about this sort of thing, got it absolutely right. He said of houses that they were just badly built boats, so firmly aground you couldn't think of moving them.

I know what he means. Anyone who has a boat knows what he means. There's something about the mobility of a boat – especially a boat you can live on – that appeals to something deep and fundamental inside us. It's the idea that you can just pack up your home and take it with you wherever you want, something that must be connected with our primeval past when we were hunter-gatherers, travelling every day as we followed food, our homes on our backs.

But it's a childhood thing too. It's to do with camping trips with mum and dad, the Cubs or the Brownies; it's to do with the excitement of summer holidays when even putting up a tent in the garden was an adventure. It's to do with the films we saw then, and the stories we absorbed, about gypsies in their brightly-painted vardos, and cowboys and covered

ening up the West, everyone on the move, no one
...u anywhere, every hill on the horizon and every bend in
the road a new world waiting to be explored. It's that thing we
had about 'gentlemen of the road' – as we used to call tramps
then. People who spent their lives meandering in carefree
abandon, sleeping in barns or under hedges, their errant lives
untrammelled and unregulated by the petty restrictions which
limited the rest of us.

There's a heady freedom about not having a home, because
then, paradoxically, *everywhere* becomes your home – wherever
you lay your hat, as they say. Yet you don't lose that sense of
liberation if you have a home that moves. You get the best
of both worlds: the chance to wander about, but to sleep
in your own bed too. Caravans, I'm told, can give you the
same feeling – though their drawback is that they are linked
inexorably to roads. And in the twenty-first century roads are
busy, noisy hellholes where everyone's going somewhere only
to come back again immediately afterwards. On the canals,
the water road is tranquil and calming, and nobody's actually
travelling anywhere properly – just, like me, pretending to go
on journeys to give some purpose to their wanderings.

After the surveyor had left, after Em had called, there was
nothing stopping me from getting off. All I had to do was turn
the key and start the engine; all I had to do was throw off the
frail ropes by which I was tethered to land, and the world – as
they say – was my oyster. Or at least my freshwater mussel.

Why then was it was another year before I left? I think
getting the certificate with so little hassle had unbalanced me.
Not content with having a decent boat – by which I mean a

boat that worked, a boat that didn't leak and had an engine that functioned – I now had to have a *perfect* boat. The paintwork on the roof started me off. I'd noticed it was looking a bit ropey and I thought that since the forecasts were predicting a spell of dry weather, I'd spend a couple of days touching it up.

Touching it up! Touching it up? What sort of mad fool was I? What drugs had I been on?

You don't 'touch up' a steel narrowboat. It isn't an Edwardian watercolour. Painting a narrowboat properly (rather than just coating it with paint so as to provide better conditions for nurturing rust later) is a serious job for which hairy-arsed professionals with tattooed arms the size of my thigh get to earn shedloads of money and drink lots of beer. The old paintwork has to be scoured down to bright steel, the rust has to be obliterated inch by inch with all the savage determination of Kim and Aggie, those queens of clean on Channel 4 who make us all feel so guilty for not dusting our houses properly.

The fact is, there's a lot of paintwork on a narrowboat – even if you're only doing the roof. *Justice* is nearly sixty feet long and almost seven feet wide. By the workings of my dreadful maths, that's about 400-odd square feet, even allowing for the decks – which, actually, wasn't an allowance I could make since the more I looked at them, the more it became apparent that they needed repainting too.

To handle that much work is a major project. It requires commitment, and determination, and power tools like angle-grinders, which – for those not familiar with such things – are implements designed to drive a steel brush, the main function of which is to deposit splinters in any exposed area of flesh before the motor expires with a whimper after a couple of hours use. This leaves you no alternative but to fuel the already overheated Chinese economy by buying another. It also leaves you looking like Pin-cushion-Head in *Hellraiser* which is no way to be seen out in public.

Touch up the roof of a narrowboat. I must have been mad. I *was* mad. But like all mad people, there was method in my madness. I thought, you see, that I would just attend to those bits of roof where the old paint had lifted, places where I could see telltale signs of corrosion. I thought I could get away with doing one or two patches here and there – the big one that was up the back, those two smaller ones at the front, that sort of thing. Except that what I didn't realise until I'd started to probe the offending areas was that what I could see was just the tip of the iceberg. It wasn't just that bits of the roof were rusty; under the surface *all* of it was rusty. It's just that most of it wasn't showing yet.

There was nothing for it. I had to roll up my sleeves and get on with it. Two weeks, and five or six angle-grinders later, I had arms like a porcupine and a beard like Desperate Dan. I was also in danger of spontaneously combusting with all the white spirit I'd been using to keep myself clean. But the roof had the sheen of silver, so perfect and unblemished and bright that to look at in the sunshine you needed wraparound Ray-Bans.

Of course, that's the very point it chose to rain. It rained for three days solid, and afterwards, when I came to survey the results, I found that all my perfect preparation had gone to waste; and in place of the lustrous metallic shine I had worked so hard to achieve was a fine rust like coffee dust. I found it very confusing. This is because the General Foods factory, under whose shadow I was moored, is owned by Kraft which produces coffee by the ton for brands like Kenco, Maxwell House and Birds. The rust could have been coffee dust. Indeed, it's not unusual to wake up in Banbury with coffee dust across your boat. In fact, it happens most mornings because the company seems to burn surplus stock at night through its eructing chimneys, leaving deposits of the stuff all over the place. This, I guess, could be useful if you liked instant coffee and had run out. You could probably rustle up a decent cup by washing down your windows in hot water.

One way or another, coffee or rust, it meant that I had to start my preparation again – though this time I did what I should have done from the outset and primed the steel as I went along. This way – after a few more angle-grinders and another gallon or two of white spirit – I succeeded in achieving a half-decent finish. OK, the roof might have been a lot brighter than the rest of the boat, which had faded over the years to a pale imitation of its original colour. And true, the effect of this new and garish roof might have been to make the rest of the boat seem a bit scruffy, if not downright tatty. But hell, what did I care? By now I'd learnt my lesson. *Justice* was more than ten years old. Once it *had* been a posh boat, the sort of gleaming vision of the traditional canal boat you see on tourist brochures aimed at Americans. But those days were long gone, and much water had passed under many bridges, most of which I'd contrived to scrape.

Besides, perfection is not for this life but the next; I was just being naive striving for it. Once again I prepared to throw off my fetters – or at least my mooring ropes: those loosely knotted ties that were the only things standing between me and freedom. I made up my mind to leave the following day. This was a momentous decision after so many weeks of procrastination; the more so because I'd finally worked out the route I was going to take and could no longer use that as an excuse not to go. I had decided to head to the Huddersfield Narrow Canal by way of Manchester. Once there I would cross the Pennines to Huddersfield before returning back over the hills on the Rochdale Canal. Both these Pennine routes had only just opened for navigation after long and expensive restorations. I wouldn't exactly be exploring them, but it was as close to exploration as a man with hair as white as mine was ever going to get.

It was all systems go. I was all set. Or at least I was until I looked in the gas locker. The gas locker, as its name suggests, is an enclosure in the bow where we lock our bottles of gas. It is damp and dark. It is covered with canal mud which gets in where the excess gas is supposed to drain out. It is populated with spiders the size of small birds.

I'd gone into the gas locker to change a gas bottle and what I saw horrified me. Apart from the soil composition and the resident wildlife, the sides of the locker were so rusty they crumbled in my hand. I couldn't leave it like that, could I? It was only a day's job to paint it. Or at least that's what I thought until I started clearing it out and rubbing it down. Then it became a two-day job. And then a three-day one. Finally, it finished up taking the rest of the summer and most of the following spring. Then, just as I was finishing it off and thinking once again about setting off for Manchester, I discovered the space under the back deck. The space under the back deck is the boat equivalent of the attic in a house. It is the repository of everything you can't bear to throw away, or can't be bothered to take to the tip. This, too, was so scaly with rust it was like a Chieftain tank with dandruff. Out came the angle-grinder again. By now I'd gone through about a couple of dozen of the things. In fact, most of the space under the back deck was filled with burnt-out angle-grinders.

'Now don't take this the wrong way,' said Em when we spoke on the phone that night. 'But don't you think you might have become a teensy-weensy bit paranoid about this rust thing?'

The next day I raised the matter with Pete, the landlord.

'Don't take this the wrong way,' I said. 'But do you think I might have become a teensy-weensy bit paranoid about this rust thing?'

For a moment or two he said nothing. Then he started sucking his teeth in a way that left me wondering why people always suck their teeth just before they tell you something difficult.

'Now you come to mention it,' he hesitated, 'it does seem to be something you've been a bit... erm... a bit concerned about recently.'

'To the point of paranoia?'

'That might be stating the case a little strongly.'

'Maybe a bit obsessional, then? Would you say that?'

Pete nodded his head in the direction of my hand. We were standing on the towpath, leaning against his boat. When I looked I found myself picking at the paintwork.

'Some might say that,' he agreed without exactly saying it himself. 'Oh, and by the way, that's dried coffee dust you're fiddling with.'

So I packed up immediately, and set off straight away, that very moment. I didn't even bother stocking up with food. I didn't even bother saying goodbye to anyone. As I passed under the ring road and through Banbury's northern industrial suburbs, past the Alcan factory and the field where a hundred or so rabbits had come out to feed in the early evening sunshine, I felt a great weight lift off me. I was so much happier to be finally on the move with the promise of months of cruising ahead.

The throb of my engine soon settled into its regular hypnotic rhythm, a contented heartbeat which would be the soundtrack to my summer. Cruising the boat, rather than painting it, I didn't have to worry about getting steel needles in my arm every few seconds, or fret about the declining quality of internationally produced power tools. I could even smell again, which was a relief after a month showering every night in white spirit.

At Bourton Lock, Irene came out from the cottage to pass the time of day.

'You seem unusually joyful,' she said.

'I am ecstatic,' I replied, 'Like a kid going on holiday. It's that gypsy thing, you know – that sense of freedom and independence. It's exhilarating. The empty canal, the weeks stretching ahead, the sunny summer days and the balmy evenings with the shadows lengthening across the countryside...'

She nodded in the general direction of my arm where a few stray needles still awaited extraction. 'Enjoy yourself,' she said. 'But if I were you, I'd ease up on the drugs.'

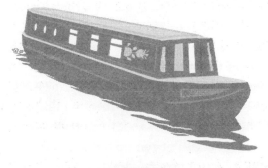

Five

*B*eyond Banbury the canal snakes north with all the doggedness of a drunkard trying to find his way home after a good night out. This is because the Oxford Canal is a contour canal. It winds about all over the place following the profile of the landscape. For the original canal builders this meant they could avoid the cost of constructing unnecessary locks, but on some sections – especially the 11-mile summit pound – all this twisting about makes cruising a surreal experience.

You see what appears to be another boat coming towards you on some parallel canal. Except that it's not a parallel canal at all, but the same canal bending around you in a great, arching loop which then veers off again in the other direction before swinging back on itself once more. Finally it dawns on you that the boat you're looking at isn't coming towards you at all: that it's actually going *away* from you, travelling the same direction as you.

Take it from me, all this circuitous weaving and wiggling can be bewildering. There's a radio mast halfway across the summit which seems to be on your right-hand side. But the next time you notice it, it's on your left. Then it suddenly pops up behind you like some kid playing catch-me in the woods. It keeps doing this for what seems hours until you feel dizzy. You can't seem to get away from it. It stands dominating the countryside, mocking your attempts to escape it.

It certainly doesn't do to be impatient on this section of the Oxford. The canal's shallow and if you try cutting the bends you'll ground yourself, or run up the bank. You just have to live with the constant geographical contortion of it all which means that when you're steering, you're always scything your tiller from side to side as if you're cutting a path through an overgrown thicket. After an hour you lose all sense of direction. After two hours you lose your mind. Left? Right? Up? Down? Who cares? I mean, it's not as if you're actually going anywhere, is it?

At the 435-foot Wormleighton Hill it gets farcical. It takes you two hours to go round it on a boat. If you were to cut across the fields, you could walk it in ten minutes without breaking into a sweat.

The nature of the Oxford summit means you constantly have to keep your wits about you. But in truth, even if you crammed your pockets to overflowing with wits, or strapped wits on your back, or stuffed them in your socks, it wouldn't make the slightest difference. With the canal meandering about like this, you can never be in total control. If you meet an oncoming boat at a narrow bridge hole or on a bend – and sod's law dictates that that is exactly what you will do – then there's bound to be a collision, and there's nothing you can do about it except console yourself that narrowboats are made of quarter-inch steel, and that the worst that can happen to them is that they'll bounce off each other like a couple of dodgems at the fair.

But there are other boats on the canal apart from narrowboats. There are frail canoes. There are wooden rowing boats. There are craft called cruisers. These are made of the same white plastic they use to make yogurt pots, and they are powered by engines that sound as if they are food mixers. Unless you're an egg, this may not seem particularly threatening; but believe me, these things are so light they go like bats out of hell. They fair fly along the canal. Meeting one of them on a bend, you'll slice straight through it. What is more, you won't even know you've sliced through it until you moor up later in the day and find a stain on the bow and the crew clinging to your gunnels in terror.

Oh, what fun those early canal-builders must have, surveying the fruits of their labour from their seats in Paradise! They must think we're crazy playing around in these ditches they built as industrial arteries to carry coal. They must think we're daft treating them as holiday destinations, sunbathing on the locksides and having barbecues on the towpath. They would turn in their graves at the idea of it. Towpaths, after all, weren't built as dining rooms. They were designed for horses to tow boats, and for centuries horses – being horses – did what horses do after you feed them oats and hay and whatnot.

Makes you want your sausages cooked more thoroughly when you think about it, doesn't it?

The boats today would tickle people from the past too, since a modern narrowboat isn't that much different to how canal boats have always been. They're just the same old cigar tubes they always were – built that way because they have to be able to fit into narrow locks (though why on earth the locks were built that size in the first place no one really knows). It's a preposterous shape which makes for a preposterous lifestyle. Nowadays boats may have baths and showers and washing machines and televisions, but you still have to live linear, everything in a long line. The bedroom leads into the bathroom which leads into the lounge. Or there's a narrow corridor which runs the full length of the boat and cuts down on the already restricted seven-foot width. One way or another, on a narrowboat everything is cramped and sideways; everything is small or reduced. Everything is, well… narrow.

You'd think it was impossible to function in such a space, let alone live in it with any comfort. Yet, it's not true. Narrowboats are the cosiest and most secure places in the world. Give me a storm raging outside, or one of those flat, drizzly days we call summer when the world's covered in a damp pall, and there's nowhere else I'd rather be. That's because with the curtains closed, the rain hammering on the roof, and the fire blazing away in the cast-iron stove, there *is* no better place to be. It's a womb, a refuge, a hideout. It's like the dens we used to build ourselves as kids, a respite from the world, but a world in itself.

Anyway, a lot of modern boats are 'replica boats', built with washers to imitate original rivets, or with so-called 'traditional' back cabins – reproductions of the tiny eight-foot-long space in which a Victorian boatman would live with his wife and family. Nowadays they're mainly used as spare bedrooms to impress friends who come down for the weekend to get away from town. Or for showing off to the rest of us on summer evenings when their owners throw open the doors for us all to see inside. It's a way people have of establishing their credentials as waterways' purists. There's a lot of this on the canals recently: people wanting to establish their credentials by boasting about their boats. Personally, I get embarrassed when they do. People should keep their credentials to themselves. Credentials shouldn't be flashed around willy nilly. Not only is it snobbish, it's unseemly too.

The picturesque village of Braunston, beyond the summit of the Oxford Canal where the Grand Union branches off north towards Leicester, is the centre of a lot of this sort of nonsense. It used to be the acknowledged capital of the canal world, the base for major waterways haulage companies and the boatyards that serviced them. Once it was a bustling focus of canal trade, but after the Second World War the trade melted away and Braunston reverted to being a sleepy, somewhat fusty backwater stuck in a cul-de-sac of the contemporary world.

This is no bad fate for any village. Essentially it's what most canal villages are, and they don't seem any the worse for it. Just out-of-the-way sleepy hamlets. Maybe

a street or two of cottages, sometimes a pub, and if you're lucky the occasional shop or post office. Braunston though had different ideas. Braunston had ambition. With the revitalisation of the canals in the 1980s Braunston began to reinvent itself.

Tucked away in the heart of Northamptonshire, at that point where you've left the South but you're not quite in the North, it's convenient for motorways, which makes it accessible for anyone wanting to moor a boat there. Braunston always was a mooring centre, even in its commercial heyday. Now, in this burgeoning Leisure Age, it set about re-establishing its reputation as the canal capital by developing itself as *the* mooring centre. New marinas were built with rows and rows of jetties, like floating caravan sites, designed to cram in more and more craft. And marinas begat new marinas, which in turn begat more yet. Today there must be getting on for a dozen of them in and around the Braunston area. And more are planned. Soon there won't be room between the marinas, and this part of the country will turn into a massive inland lake.

Mercifully, most boat-owners round Braunston are disinclined to risk taking their boats out onto the canal. Perhaps it's the difficulty of getting them out on the open canal, or perhaps it's just that the open canal isn't so open round here when they do. Maybe it's just that having bought boats, so many people discover that they don't actually like boating – though this shouldn't necessarily preclude anyone from enjoying the canals. Boats have to be maintained. They have to be polished and their brasses cleaned. If you like this sort of thing, then Braunston's the place for you. Go there any weekend and it's full of folk buffing up their boats to an ever more lustrous shine. It's a competitive sport with them. They go at it as if they're trying to break Olympic records.

The concentration of so many boats in such a small area does cause problems though. Normally, when you're talking about the waterways, the juxtaposition of the adjective 'busy' with the noun 'canal' is very rare. Canals are generally places of great quietude, lonely places where by day you hear the wind rustle over the fields and by night the owls shrieking in the woods. They are places of serenity, of peacefulness; places where you can take a step back and ruminate quietly on the world and its follies.

But there are one or two places where the canal is busy – and Braunston is probably the worst of them. It's so bad that, if it keeps going the way it is, it will soon be the first stretch of waterway to gridlock. It sometimes seems like that already on sunny Bank Holidays, when everyone's struggling to get into the place, or get out of it, trying to negotiate the difficult T-junction there, or queuing for its short flight of locks. As bad as the M25 when they're doing roadworks. Worse really, because at least on the M25 you expect hold-ups; whereas on the canals, however many times a voice in your head keeps telling you that they're building more boats than the system can handle, and that eventually it's all going to all go pear-shaped, it still comes as a bit of a shock to realise that in some places it actually has.

It's a mercy most people don't take their boats out. I wouldn't want to think how chaotic it would be if they did.

Strictly speaking, since I was travelling northwards up the Oxford Canal towards Coventry I didn't actually have to stop in Braunston at all. But dusk was beginning to fall and supplies were low, so I found a convenient mooring on the turn; and with a thirst on me that could have emptied a reservoir, I tied up and went up to the pub.

There I fell into conversation with this bloke I know. I've known him off and on for years, though I couldn't tell you his name to save my life. Thankfully, he can't remember my name either so to avoid embarrassment we get by calling each other 'mate'. This is typical of blokes in pubs. It happens because we drink so much we can't even remember our own names, let along anyone else's.

He was impressed when I told him I was going to Huddersfield.

'Huddersfield?' he said, gurgling into his beer. 'Huddersfield!'

I'd have felt more flattered if I hadn't known from previous conversations that he hadn't the first idea of the geography of the UK, having only left Braunston a dozen or so times in his entire life, one of them when the Queen was visiting Northampton. He hadn't got much idea about canals either, despite living in a place renowned as a canal centre.

He said, 'You can get a boat up there, can you?'

I resisted the temptation to become facetious. It would have been too easy to have told him that no, there wasn't a canal that went to Huddersfield but that didn't matter since I was intending to haul *Justice* out of the water and manhandle her across the mountains like bloody Fitzcarraldo. Instead I mumbled something about a new canal having just opened.

That's when he dropped his bombshell. At first I thought it was a wind-up. 'This Huddersfield,' he asked. 'It's in the North, isn't it?'

No, you lamebrain, I wanted to scream. Whatever gave you that idiotic notion? Is it the fact that Huddersfield is forever associated with that paradigm of northern man, Prime Minister Harold Wilson, who was born in the place? Could it be because its name will always be linked to that iconic northern game of Rugby League, since the Rugby Football League was formed in the town? Or was it, you dipstick, possibly because I just told you, no more than just a couple of minutes ago, that I was travelling north, and that I was going to Huddersfield, a juxtaposition that should surely have given even you some general clue to its location?

But I said nothing. After all, no one loves a smart ass.

He took a long pull of his beer. Such matters were beyond his understanding. Mind you, most things in the world were – including, it would seem, how to swallow properly. He suddenly started coughing, great droplets of saliva spraying from his mouth. I tried to ignore him as best I could, but then he furrowed his brow and screwed up his eyes, as if the blazing sun itself was trying to burn through his eyelids.

Which, in a way, I guess it was.

He'd had an idea, you see. Probably the first idea he'd ever had in his whole life. He was remembering something, remembering two things, in fact. And painfully trying to put them together in a way that might make coherent sense. It was a performance agonising to behold, yet somehow compelling too. You could see all the activity was making his brain ache. You could almost hear the cogs turning. Almost see the steam coming out of his ears.

'The telly,' he mumbled, 'I saw something on the telly...'

'Really?' I replied, trying not to encourage him.

'The North,' he said.

'Yes. What? Coronation Street?'

'No, not Coronation Street. But the North.'

He dug the heel of his hands into his eyes, as if trying to push his eyeballs into the back of his head. Perhaps he was hoping this might stimulate his memory since it was evident he'd got no better strategy for getting his brain to work.

'Yes. The North!' he announced eventually. 'It *is* the North I'm thinking of isn't it? Didn't they have some sort of trouble up there? Didn't they have riots?'

I shrugged my shoulders noncommittally. He must have taken this as a request for advice, for he sat back, folded his arms and for some minutes gave the matter some serious thought.

Eventually he leaned in my direction as if he were about to impart some confidence of a critical nature. 'I tell you what I'd do if I was in your position,' he said. 'In your position I'd leave the boat here and drive to Huddersfield. You'd get there a lot quicker, and you could get away sharpish too if the need arose. You know, if it got nasty…'

I knew what he meant. Listening to him going on like this, I felt that way about Braunston.

I decided on an early night, the better to facilitate an early departure.

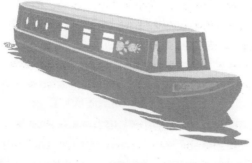

Six

On the way to Coventry the next day I passed a pair of old working boats steered by someone I first met years back when he had a Springer and moored next to Em and me at Bedworth. One day he announced he was going to live on the cut, and I came back the next week to find he'd bought himself an old coal-boat and reinvented himself as a 'traditional' boatman, complete with a moleskin waistcoat and a spotted red 'kerchief around his neck.

We all do that on the canal. Reinvent ourselves, I mean. In that sense, the waterways are a massive theatre, one of the greatest stages in the country. I know City traders who throw off their Armani suits at the weekend and never wash until they get back to London on Sunday nights. I know social workers who have jacked in the secure jobs they spent years training for in order to run a boatyard or captain a trip-boat. I know one of the country's top heart surgeons who lived on the cut for years until he got evicted by British Waterways as a dosser. But as I say, we all do it.

It's just the level at which we pitch our performance that makes us different.

'People are more genuine on the cut' – how many times have I heard that? But actually, no, they're not genuine at all. Or not genuine in the sense we mean genuine nowadays. Not genuine in the sense of 'what you see is what you get'. What you see is rarely what you get on the cut. Every weekend, all over the country, thousands of us flock to our boats, and no sooner do we feel the water under our feet than we turn into totally different creatures. Urban men who wouldn't have a good word to say to a neighbour during the week suddenly go all social and walk along the towpath with an inane smile on their face passing the time of day with anyone and anything. They nod at locals; they nod at other boat-owners. They even nod at telegraph poles. They're like that aggravating bulldog with the Yorkshire accent nodding away in the insurance ads. (Don't you want to shoot it? Oh, yes, yes, yes.)

Blokes whose weekday job is pushing around bits of paper and who don't know a spanner from a screwdriver suddenly contrive to get their faces covered in grease and start talking about valve clearances and piston-head rings like time-served mechanics. The women are no better. At home they may be delicate wallflowers, never out of pastels, but put them on a canal-boat they start wearing dungarees and smoking roll-ups. Or they take to making pies out of every diseased bit of wild fruit they can scavenge, whereas at home they wouldn't nibble on a sliver of Madeira cake if they suspected it was a day past its sell-by date.

I love it. I love this idea that people don't have to be anything except what they decide to be at the time they decide to be it.

I love it especially that people don't have to be limited by what they've decided to be in one part of their life. We're different people all the time anyhow, aren't we? We're brothers as well as sons, mothers as well as wives. That Master of the Universe who's cutting a deal in the boardroom, high-fiveing it with his mates at the success of some key contract, is the same guy who will be holding back his tears at home after one of those same mates has got a promotion he thought was his.

And that glamorous sophisticate, made up to the nines and walking to her restaurant table as if she were sashaying down a catwalk, is the same woman who two hours before was wrestling with a couple of kids, one who'd just puked over her cardy and the other who was trying to kick her shins off.

Why shouldn't we be different people? Human beings are too complex to be pigeonholed. The canals free us up this way; they release us from the constraints life imposes on us. They let us be ourselves, yes; but they let us be our *other* selves too. When we're on our boats we can play different roles; we can indulge new dreams and fantasies. It's amazing what an old pair of jeans and a torn T-shirt can do for the human spirit. And amazing how different you can feel when you haven't had a proper wash for a week and don't really want one either.

I only wish it could do it for me like this.

At home, I'm a cantankerous old git. On the boat, after a week's cruising, I'm just a cantankerous old git with dirty hair.

As he passed, I said hello to the guy who used to moor next to us at Bedworth before he bought the coal-boat and crossed to another life. Let's call him Bill.

'Hi there, Bill,' I said. 'How're you keeping?'

He ignored me. Next time we meet he'll doubtless greet me like a long-lost brother. Or maybe he won't, depending on how he feels.

People on the cut can be funny like that. But people on the cut can be anything they want.

Justice got into her stride, a spume of prop-wash frothing from her stern and a couple of gentle feathers forming at her bow, rippling away to the bank in long fronds. I passed through Hillmorton Locks where I saw Jen and George who I'd first met a couple of years back near Stratford. Soon I was in Rugby where I stopped at the supermarket, and ran into Gerry at the bread counter. He shouldn't have been anywhere near there; I'd heard on the towpath telegraph that he was heading down the Severn this year. But he'd changed his plans, he told me. He was on his way to see his sister in Leamington. In Newbold, I stopped for a drink at one of the two pubs that used to be on the waterside until they built the tunnel and left them marooned either side of a small track that goes nowhere. In the bar, munching egg and chips, I met Jean and Mick, which was no surprise since Gerry had alerted me they were heading this way.

They say you get away from things on the cut, but sometimes you've more chance of solitude standing in a football crowd. Thirty years ago you could cruise for days along some routes without seeing a soul, but those times are long gone. Nowadays, there are more than 30,000 boats on the system – a population larger than a lot of the towns along the waterway. It's a linear community tied together by a single consuming interest. People

CHAPTER SIX

you meet in one part of the country crop up unexpectedly in another, and acquaintances become friends when you moor next to each other overnight, or travel together in the same direction for a day or two. For some people, this aspect of the waterways is as much their appeal as their prettiness, and I'd be lying if I said it didn't attract me too: the fact that in this linear world, which stretches from Wales to the North Sea, from Bristol almost to the Lake District, there are people all over that I know; people who know me.

Even so, I sometimes yearn for those days thirty years ago when setting off up the Leicester Section of the Grand Union was like an expedition up some secret South American river, the canal then so unkempt and untended that in places the trees on either side used to meet in the middle and you'd be cruising through a dark tunnel, isolated from the world. There were reed banks so thick they'd broken away, hanging in the water like impenetrable lost islands blocking your passage; and coots with their cry like a death scream, curdling your soul in the early evening when the shadows began to lengthen and the bats around lonely Saddington Tunnel kissed your hair with their wings.

Back at *Justice* I wanted to check a few things and I threw open the engine-room doors to let in the light. When I raised my head from the bowels of the machine it was to find a young boy standing above me on the towpath examining me intently. Behind him was a mongrel dog assaulting him with its snout, an activity from which both were evidently deriving much pleasure. The boy had a smile on him like a cat that's just got the cream, and the dog's tail was going thirteen to the dozen.

'What you doing then, Mister?' he asked. His voice was reassuringly Midlands. A main ingredient of downbeat Coventry spiced with the odd pinch of something Bromsgrove-way. I know I should be more sympathetic to young boys. After all, I used to be one myself. But I am sad to have to confess that nowadays, on the whole, I find them irksome creatures. Especially when they poke their heads through my engine-room doors, disturbing my peace and quiet when I'm trying to get a job done.

I thought I'd blind the nosey sod with science. Or fiction. Or science fiction.

'Shush!' I said. 'I'm retuning to Mach 4, it's a delicate job.'

The smile fell away from his face. Even the dog stopped its explorations. 'Mach 4?' he said. 'What's Mach 4?'

'It's the next timeband,' I said.

'The next timeband?'

I examined his face more closely. His brow had furrowed. He seemed confused, but intrigued. I had caught his flighty interest like a butterfly in a net. Served him right for not realising that on boats we have a right to privacy too.

'Yes,' I explained. 'It's for Omega 6 – so that we can warp to ten thousand plus on the solar crossovers.'

'Wow! You don't say,' he said.

'Actually, I do,' I said. 'But it has to be our secret. A lot of people don't know that narrowboats are not boats at all but powerful time machines capable of traversing centuries at the mere flick of a switch.'

'What? And your engine can do that?'

'All that,' I said, 'and more.'

'But it's a JP, innit?'

'What?'

'Your engine, isn't it a Lister JP? A three-cylinder job, 27hp, old one by the looks of it. You'd have trouble getting to the next lock. I don't know about time travel…'

'Piss off,' I said. 'You're a troublemaking oik.'

'And you, you're just plain crazy,' he said, 'Mach bloody 4… Omega 6… you sound like a margarine ad…' And with the dog following him, still attempting to get its nose in the back of his trousers, he walked off chuntering about old people going soft in the head.

Mind you, I guess I'd asked for it. This was the Midlands, after all. This was near Coventry, onetime centre of the British car industry, where the kids were weaned on engine oil and cut their teeth on Whitworth spanners. Why did I think anyone in that area wouldn't recognise a vintage engine?

But I was right. I might have been winding him up, but I was essentially right. Narrowboats are time machines. Or – to be more accurate – we make them into time machines. We get out of our cars, we open up our boats, and to all intents and purposes we step back two hundred and fifty years to play the part of itinerant Victorian labourers, a decorative background to the new canal age.

OK, I grant you, we have a few advantages over itinerant Victorian labourers. We have central heating in our boats for a start, we have running hot water, we have baths and showers and fridges and televisions. But what distinguishes us from them most are things we don't have which they did. Like fifty tons of coal up the front end, for instance. Like the need to get it somewhere before the end of the day. And the pressure to have to shovel it out by hand, and then take on another fifty tons to get somewhere else by the day after.

Even so, there is enough in contemporary modern boating to trigger some folk memory of what things used to be. Most people only see canals in the glorious sunshine, in the dog days of July and August at some pretty set of locks or some picturesque canalside village where the wharf's been converted to a pub and everyone's sitting outside clutching cold beer. Believe me, it's not like this all the time. This is England, after all. Most of the time in England, it's raining. It rains particularly in the summer, and invariably on Bank Holidays. Away from the pub and the twee lock-flights, the English countryside in the rain can be a dismal place. Steering a narrowboat it can be more dismal yet. Narrowboats weigh upwards of twenty tons, remember. They are heavy and cumbersome to handle, and they are not much fun when it's blowing up choppy, with waves biting the surface of the water and the rain seeping down your neck.

This is the moment when you know you will get something wrapped around your propeller. You know it with such certainty you are waiting for it to happen. In fact, such is the stress of the anticipation, that when it does happen it comes as something of a relief that it has. Even though you know it means lying in the bottom of the boat for an hour with your arms in freezing cold water up to your shoulders.

There's no alternative, though. A boat with something around its propeller is like a car with a bag of nails in its gearbox. Neither of them is going to go very far in that state. Like it or lump it, you've got to clear the obstruction.

CHAPTER SIX

Personally, I take a phlegmatic approach to clearing my prop. Which is to say I clear my throat of as much phlegm as possible before starting the job. This is because in delving underwater you never quite know what you will find, and a certain amount of what you will find is likely to make you gag in a way that makes the presence of phlegm (or, indeed, anything else which might impair the proper workings of the epiglottis) most unhelpful. In the countryside, you might, for example, plunge your arm unknowingly into the body cavity of some decomposing animal. This, take it from me, is not the most pleasant of rural experiences. It does not compare favourably with gambolling through a spring meadow, for instance. Or kicking up leaves on a bright autumn day.

Even so, I prefer it to other things you can get around your prop. A dead sheep may be putrid, but at least it's organic. And at least it's fairly easy to get off, whereas the sort of heavy-duty fertiliser bags the modern farmer throws around with much sensitivity to the environment cleave to the propeller like clingfilm. Eventually, with the friction of the engine, they weld themselves into a solid block around the shaft. Take my word for it: they are a devil to dislodge. You have to hack away at them for hours. I had to do it near Stafford once and I spent most of one afternoon with my arm submerged in the canal wielding a large kitchen knife which was the sharpest implement I had on the boat. I'd almost finished the job when I accidentally dropped the knife, and I grabbed at it without thinking about the consequences.

It fell blade upwards and I put my hand straight onto the point.

On the bright side, I did manage to retrieve the knife – even though it meant extracting it from my palm where it had skewered me like a chunk of meat on a barbecue.

I didn't have to wait too long at A and E either.

In towns it's worse. In Birmingham I once got a mattress around my propeller and had to cut my way by hand through every single bedspring. On another occasion in Leicester, opposite one of the few remaining canalside textile factories, it took me the best part of an hour to free myself from a bundle of rags which stopped me dead in my tracks. After I'd managed to unravel it and haul everything onto the towpath, it was like the leftovers from a jumble sale – such a mountainous pile that the factory which had dumped it in the first place became embarrassed, and sent out a bloke with a supermarket trolley to clear up the mess.

His heart wasn't really in the job though. Most of what I pulled out, he threw back. What was left he carted off in the supermarket trolley.

Then he threw that in too.

Mind you, I suppose I can understand it with the trolley. So many supermarket trolleys find their way into the cut that anyone could be forgiven for thinking that canals were their natural habitat, as much a part of the natural order of things as moorhens or water voles. Indeed, in some places there are so many of them you'd think they were a protected species. You can be cruising along, minding your own business, enjoying the day, when suddenly you'll hear a noise like fingernails on a blackboard, and your boat will rise up under you. Then there'll be a sickening crunch accompanied by scraping, and sometimes, if you're lucky, you'll catch sight of one you've just hit breaking the surface like a whale breaching. It's lucky if you see it because that means you've passed over it. It you don't see it, the chances are it's jammed under your boat bottom and that's the end of any idea of a pub lunch that day.

Supermarket trolleys, like plastic fertiliser bags, are one of the banes of a boater's life. But I guess they can't be a lot of fun for British Waterways either, trying to keep the canals clear of them when the major supermarkets seem so uninterested in what happens to them. I've never understood it. Don't they cost anything to make? Or is it that Tesco is running some community job creation scheme somewhere so that dumping them in the cut is a sort of social service for the unemployed?

Lost in musings, I find myself approaching the outskirts of Coventry, the point where the Oxford Canal ends and another canal begins. This one, somewhat unsurprisingly, not to say unimaginatively, is called the Coventry Canal. You can always tell when you are getting close to it. Suddenly the air seems to darken, and all around you appear the shadows of giants on great legs, their arms outstretched as if to encompass you in their steely grasp. They are only electricity pylons, for this is the site of the long-demolished Hawkesbury Power Station. But it is not a place I like. The towering pylons – thirty of them, forty, maybe more – make me feel insignificant as I thread between them, the hum of the current from the cables draped between them like a chilling dirge of the dead. Maybe it's the voices of the old power station workers, maybe the ghosts of the old boatmen who in the past used to deliver coal here. Maybe it's just my imagination.

One way or another, I cannot wait to get away from the place. I moor for the night at the junction close to the Greyhound. This is the very spot where thirty-odd years ago I pushed a boat out from the bank and finished up in the water for my trouble. There is a knack to pushing out a boat from the bank of a canal. The knack is not to push it so far that you either can't get onto the boat, or can't get back onto the bank. It wasn't a knack I had mastered at that stage in my life. But I was young then. I was also blind drunk. Anyhow, the closing-time crowds leaving the pub thought it was hilarious, the cabaret for the night.

Personally I couldn't see what there was to laugh about.

It was a quiet night in the Greyhound. The barman who'd seen me moor up in a place where we both knew I shouldn't asked me where I was heading. He seemed as confused at the concept of the North as the bloke in Braunston. Mind you, people from Coventry can be very insular. For many of them the concept of anywhere except Coventry is a difficult one to grasp.

I made another early start the next morning. It was raining.

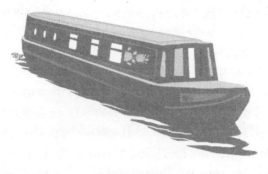

Seven

I'll tell you how crazy Atherstone is. Atherstone used to have a hat industry, that's how crazy it is. Think of the Mad Hatter in *Alice in Wonderland*. Think of the phrase 'as mad as a hatter'. You get my drift? Actually this is more than just a figure of speech. In the nineteenth century they made hats by washing animal fur in mercuric nitrate. It stiffened the hairs and turned them into felt. But the mercury made the workers mad. It gave them the shakes; it gave them holes in the brain. If that wasn't bad enough, it blackened their teeth, so destroying Atherstone's chances of ever featuring as the location for a toothpaste ad.

Atherstone was no place to be when it was a hat-making town. It was filled with aggressive gangs of young men with brains like a Gruyère cheese and teeth like broken gravestones. Mind you, it can still seem a bit this way nowadays on Saturday nights at closing time. But that's Atherstone for you. It's a place whose main claim to fame is that it *may* have been the site of two historically critical battles. One was when the Romans finally secured their hold on Britain by crushing the revolt led by Boudica. Or should that be Boudicca? Or Boadicea? (God, what was wrong with the woman? Couldn't she spell her own name properly?) The other was the Battle of Bosworth which ended the War of the Roses. Except I don't understand this. If the Battle of Bosworth had happened near Atherstone, as some recent research suggests, then it wouldn't have been called the Battle of Bosworth, would it? It would have been called the Battle of Atherstone.

Confusing? Well, yes. But at least Henry Tudor didn't spell his name half a dozen ways.

All this uncertainty as to whether Atherstone was the site of one battle, or two battles, or no battle at all, has had consequences for the place. Perhaps people living there think less of themselves because of it? Perhaps they feel their manhood impugned? One way or another – maybe as a way of compensating – they nowadays hold a sort of annual battle of their own every Shrove Tuesday. However, to ensure there should be no confusion over the question of its location, they hold it slap bang in the middle of the town where no one can claim it happens anywhere other than where it does. They call it the Atherstone Ball Game. Or at least that's what the traditionalists call it. Everyone else calls it a riot.

For anyone used to other games where the idea is to get the ball into a goal, or over a net, or into a hole or something, the Atherstone Ball Game is a very difficult to describe. Apart from working off the effects of too much beer, the main purpose of it is to get hold of the ball and... well, just keep hold of it. Making sure nobody else gets it so that eventually you can get back to the pub for more beer yet. I agree this doesn't make for much of a spectator sport. It hasn't got the subtlety of rugby, say. Or the excitement of football. In fact, being honest, the Atherstone Ball Game is, competitively, a rather dull affair consisting for the most part of a mêlée down the boarded-up high street involving several hundred scratching, kicking and punching participants.

Most of these are probably just local football supporters on a spring awayday. Occasionally though, a local fresh to the area and keen to impress his new neighbours chances his arm at the game before getting it ripped off by someone as a souvenir.

Now if I was to go to a small town anywhere in the country and suggest something like this as a Bank Holiday entertainment, the idea wouldn't get further than the first police consultative committee. It only happens in Atherstone because it's been happening for 800 years and no one can think of a credible way of stopping it happening. This means it has become a part of that rich cultural tapestry which we call English folklore, and as such it is sacrosanct. This is a great way of dealing with rioting. We should do it more often. We should do it in Brixton and Handsworth and Southall and Oldham. Every year we should let them all have a day's officially sanctioned mayhem and sell it like they do in Atherstone as a tourist experience.

The game ends when a klaxon sounds, and whoever is left with their hands on the ball wins some sort of prize. However, I'm not certain whether they have to have the rest of their body attached to their hands to claim it. Either way, once it's all over and the nurses at George Eliot Hospital have sewn everyone back together, Atherstone goes back to being the sort of sleepy, slightly run-down Warwickshire town that it is.

I'm actually rather fond of it. Somewhat improbably for a place that's defined itself so much by the physical, it's recently been attempting to turn itself into one of those intellectual book towns like Hay-on-Wye where it's difficult to buy a pint of milk for people wanting to flog you an existentialist novel or a new biography of Virginia Woolf. I hope the project succeeds. Atherstone has a lot going for it. It has some good pubs, some nice open spaces and a great butcher. I once shopped there for some lamb and in my snotty London way I made the mistake of asking about the provenance of the meat.

The butcher nodded towards a bloke standing next to me. 'You better ask him,' he said. 'He farms it.'

Most of all, Atherstone has got the canal, which skirts the town on a flight of attractive locks, many of them with side pounds which were built as a clever way of saving water. Today, they look like decorative ponds tucked away in the shade of overhanging trees, giving the place a certain rural charm. At the top is Rothen's Coal Wharf which, as landmarks go, sounds about as attractive as a sewerage farm, but which is actually surprisingly picturesque.

The main feature of the yard is a small, unassuming office which was restored not so long ago, so that what might have been no more than a bland and nondescript hut is a little classic of what we now, grandly, call 'vernacular architecture'. This is just a posh way of saying that it's a bog-standard building constructed in the local style using local materials. The office at the wharf is built of industrial red brick, edged with blue, and topped by a single plain chimney with a castellated stack; and it has a simple door set between two cast-iron, dome-shaped windows of a sort familiar from a thousand early Victorian factories.

But the most remarkable thing about Rothen's Coal Wharf is that in this era of oil and gas-fired central heating it's still a working coal wharf. A measure of the change there's been on the waterways, though, is that in the past narrowboats would have delivered coal to the wharf for local distribution. Now, boats pick up coal here to sell onto to the waterways community which still uses it for their stoves and fires.

Before tackling the locks I moored to make myself a quick sandwich for lunch, and it was while doing so that I first sensed the shadow of a figure on the towpath above me. Soon I became aware that I was being watched. There was a face pressed against my porthole, not a foot away from me. A tiny Japanese girl, with eyes as big as saucers and a smile to match.

When I went out to investigate I discovered there were actually two girls, both dressed like dolls in improbably short skirts, ankle socks and shoes with heels as high as kerbstones that still didn't manage to make them appear any taller. They looked about twelve years old, though knowing the tendencies of Japanese women to grow up like Peter Pan, they were probably both married with grandchildren. My hello was greeted with a volley of giggles and even wider smiles. One of them had a face which for some reason reminded me of a cat I once owned. She was carrying a camera and started taking photographs of me as soon as I made an appearance. The other one spoke English. Well, she spoke it after a fashion. The fashion of one who had learnt the language for all of ten minutes. Mind you, I shouldn't get on my high horse since it's ten minutes longer than I've learnt Japanese.

She said: 'Kono ojisan ni nosete moraou ka.'

Or at least that's what I think she said. What it meant, I had absolutely no idea. I just smiled and nodded. Which I guess she must have taken as a sign of assent, since before I knew what was happening, she'd jumped on board and was clutching me round the waist with Miss Kitty snapping away on her digital as if her life depended on it. A passing local walking his mangy Jack Russell was even conscripted into the operation, and while he struggled with the complexities of Miss Kitty's zoom lens, she hopped on board too and clutched me on the other side. I looked like a proud grandad with two lost kids from Osaka.

So I offered them tea. Well, 'offered' is probably the wrong word here. What I actually did was ask them how long they were visiting England and whether they had enjoyed their stay so far. At this they both darted inside the cabin, with so much ooing and aahing, and so much fresh giggling, that I felt no option but to provide refreshments. By now Miss Kitty had retrieved her camera and was happily snapping away at anything that took her fancy, from the boat radiators to the stove pipe. I was a particular target of her attentions. When I put on the kettle, she photographed me; when I washed a cup, she photographed me again. Even the half-prepared evidence of my lunchtime sandwich didn't escape scrutiny, Miss Kitty capturing it from every conceivable angle as if it had been some archaeological relic of key value to understanding Western civilisation.

Eventually, with some relief, I managed to get rid of them. Never mind the privacy question, my face was in rictus from smiling at them smiling at me. As they left the boat they thanked me with much bowing and renewed expressions of genial friendship. I thanked them in return. Then Miss Kitty took the opportunity of thanking me individually, and I reciprocated by thanking her. Then her friend thanked me, and I returned the honour, and afterwards Miss Kitty thanked her friend, and her friend thanked Miss Kitty. Eventually I finished up thanking myself. But at least, finally, I got them off the boat.

Imagine my surprise when two locks down, I met them again. Or at least I thought it was them. In fact, I could have sworn it was them. It actually turned out to be another couple of Japanese twelve-year-olds clutching cameras. An almost identical couple. Soon the same process of photographing me started again, except that this time I smiled less, and kept the boat doors well and truly shut to visitors. It was just as well. The two twelve-year-olds quickly became four, and then six, until eventually I had a school full of them on the towpath swarming about like paparazzi, pursuing me down the flight.

Every now and again, when I left the boat to open a paddle or close a gate, one of them would dart out impishly, grinning, and stand next to the boat for a second or two, resting her hand on it lightly, allowing the others to use up megabytes of memory recording the incident for posterity. Eventually I felt both and the boat and I had been photographed with half of Tokyo, and though I am always happy to do my bit for international peace and understanding, there's a limit to my patience. Ten minutes as an icon of quaint Englishness is about enough. Take it from me, after half an hour you begin to have an identity crisis.

What I couldn't understand is how they'd all got here. Obviously by plane, I know that. And almost certainly via Heathrow. But why here of all places? Why Atherstone? Had they actually wanted to come to Atherstone? Had they actually, sound in mind and spirit, gone to a travel agent and booked for a trip to Britain taking in London, Edinburgh, York, Bath and... and Atherstone? Or had some unscrupulous travel agent lured them to the place with promises of battle sites which might not even be battle sites? Maybe even with the Ball Game? Or even the canal? I can imagine the brochure.

Atherstone is a beautiful place on the glorious Coventry Canal. There you will find traditional English canal boats and their cheerful captains who will be happy to show you around their craft and pose with you for photos...

Later that afternoon, the locks behind me, I made a pit-stop at a passing pub in Polesworth and had a pint or two of Pedigree. Afterwards, of course, I had to have a pee.

Then I began the gentle journey that would take me into the Trent valley and from there towards Manchester. It's a funny old canal is the Coventry. Not by any stretch of the imagination can it be called pretty, but historically it was a key waterway in terms of linking parts of the system together – especially connecting the network to Birmingham where so many of the country's main canals converge.

Construction on it started in 1768 but three years later, having got no further than Atherstone, the company ran out of money and it was left half-finished for another nineteen years. Eventually a couple of other canal companies, who were counting on increased business when it linked up with them, lost patience and dug out most of the rest themselves. This means that today when you cruise up the Coventry Canal, what you're actually doing is cruising the Coventry Canal for a bit, and then cruising the Birmingham and Fazeley Canal – before going onto a section built by the Trent and Mersey company.

In practice this means… well, scarcely anything, actually. Except that the bridges on the Birmingham and Fazeley section have names in line with the custom and practice of that company, whereas those on either side have numbers, which is what the Coventry Canal did. Quirky historical facts like this are the sort of thing that get the heart of your average canal enthusiast beating fast enough for you to worry about their coronary health. But that's the way they are. They – we – get excited by these oddball facts that leave the rest of the population entirely unmoved. That is why we are so unhappy when people call our narrowboats 'barges'. Barges are broad boats, twice our width. They are an entirely different design of boat. They are like chalk to the narrowboat's cheese. Please do not call our narrowboats 'barges'. It makes us cross and we cannot be held accountable for our behaviour when we become cross. We stamp our feet. We launch petitions. We write to the editors of national newspapers, and to the Queen.

Perhaps the explanation for the intensity of our feelings about such minor matters (however gently we express them) is that when you cruise the watery highways and byways of England at the speed we do, you develop a sense of wonder at the detail of life. You begin to realise just how important detail is. At 4 mph you're not exactly haring along, but it's your top speed on a canal – the equivalent of 70 mph on the roads. And in the same way that if you travelled on the roads at 70 mph, you'd be going too fast most of the time, so on a boat if you're doing 4 mph you're probably going too fast as well. In many places you can't travel anything like that speed: canals are very shallow and the lack of water prevents it. But even on those waterways which are deep, canal people won't rush. We are life's potterers rather than its boy racers. On the whole we tend to go placidly amid the noise and the haste.

It is no coincidence that 4 mph is walking pace, and that walking pace is the speed at which the human brain can absorb and analyse the myriad of minute details around it. On a canal boat, wandering somewhat aimlessly around the countryside, you soon begin to realise that it's the sum of these details that compose the nature of the place you are in, and that the way they change is the difference between one place and another.

It might be a slight shift in the lie of the land, or an almost imperceptible variation in the field structure. It might be the way the variety of trees change or the way the composition of the hedges begins to alter subtly. Sometimes the difference isn't in the landscape at all, but is somewhere deep in your subconscious. Maybe it's in a part of your mind, more instinctive than rational, a part that can be triggered by a sensation as trivial as a breeze in your hair, or the faraway, sad sound of a train screeching between the hills. Whatever it is, wherever it resides, it hardly matters. Over an hour or two, or a day or two, you'll become aware, at first gradually but then quite suddenly, that things are changing, that they have already changed, and changed inexorably, so that the countryside through which you're travelling is now completely different to what it was before. You'll find yourself daydreaming and wake from your reverie to discover you've lost yourself, and you're not even in the countryside at all now, and that somewhere, somehow, you've left it behind and slipped almost unnoticed into a town.

It's the same process as life itself, when seconds become hours, and hours, unnoticed, turn into a lifetime. It's why, as you get older, you keep looking in the mirror and wondering where on earth the years have gone. You become part of history, I guess; your life one of those details that compose the whole.

Maybe that's why we enthusiasts get so incensed when the minor details of the waterways are destroyed with such scant regard to their value rather than just their price. Recently, for instance, the authorities have taken to selling off old lock cottages, using the proceeds – almost unbelievable, this – to invest in office development around Canary Wharf in London. They argue that the cottages are better off in private hands and that local planning authorities can be relied upon to maintain the integrity of the buildings through existing laws.

And sometimes they're right. Sometimes it works. Sometimes old cottages which were previously rented to tenants have been given a new lease of life in the hands of owner-occupiers willing to invest their own money in buildings which were often in dire need of some TLC.

But just as frequently it's ruined the buildings as owners have tacked on inappropriate extensions, or prettied them up, covering these basic workmanlike structures with so many pots of geraniums and window shutters painted with twee swags of canal roses that they look totally out of place, their functionality masked by absurd decoration, like an Irish navvy wearing a tutu. Sometimes – worse almost – the cottages have just disappeared. Well, you could have predicted as much if you'd have thought about it. Canal cottages were constructed for a purpose. They were the place where tolls were collected, or where the lock-keeper who kept an eye on things lived. They were built to see the canal, and to be seen from the canal. Which hardly accords with the fetish of privacy that characterises our modern age. The first chance they get, these new owners surround their properties with high fences; or if they can't do that, with hedges and fast-growing trees. Believe me, there are some places where you can pass within feet of a canal cottage without knowing it's there, hidden as it is behind its green screen.

Mind you, why should I be so worried? There are times I'm at the tiller when I'm so lost in my own fanciful musings that I could pass through a city the size of Leeds without even knowing it was there. On such occasions when the hypnotic sound of the engine has lulled me into a trance, it's as if I'm in a different world, a world where the present merges into the past, and where different pasts themselves merge into a single dreamscape. It's a place of barely remembered kings, and battles whose names are forgotten, a place of ploughmen, engineers and navvies, of a thousand boatmen and a hundred thousand journeys, each of them strange and different, but each of them familiar too.

Narrowboat dreams, narrowboat dreaming. The tiller trembling under my touch at the flow of the water across the rudder.

And of course, my own past is locked away here too, a part of all this, every twist and turn of this meandering ditch linked with some friend or passing stranger, a part of some personal recollection or another. Was it at this bridge I met that odd bloke that time? The one with ferrets on leads? And was it here that my dad was with me the year before he died? Or was that somewhere else? Was that another trip the year before? Or ten years before that? Or even thirty? The inhospitality of memory teases me with vague recollections.

The rain had finally cleared up, and in that last hour or so before darkness fell, an agonising sunset, like a flesh wound across the horizon, scoured the world. Long shadows of trees fractured the fields and mists rose above the meadows. At Fradley Junction, outside the Swan, the Coventry Canal becomes the Trent and Mersey, and soon afterwards is the Staffordshire town of Rugeley where on my first-ever trip on a canal boat, my mate Dave and I couldn't even find a towpath mooring close enough to get off, so that we finished up having to tie up on the other side under a steep bank of stinging nettles which we had to hack our way through to get to the pub.

My namesake village of Great Haywood is next, close to Shugborough Hall, the home of the Queen's late cousin, the photographer Patrick Lichfield. Then come the unmistakable brick bottle kilns of Stoke, and the mouth of the fearsome Harecastle tunnel.

It's a journey of three or four days. Sometimes, dreaming, it can seem to pass in an hour.

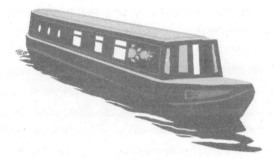

Eight

The Harecastle tunnel terrifies a lot of people. Some won't go through it on a boat for love or money. Mary was like that. She was a friend from years ago, and she used to get off and walk over the top. Mind you, she was claustrophobic and used to walk across the top of every tunnel. Thinking about it, there were bridges she wouldn't go under too.

Despite its reputation, it's not the longest tunnel on the system. At about 3,000 yards (2.7 kilometres: almost one and three-quarter miles), it's only half as long as the Standedge tunnel which lay ahead of me on my way to Huddersfield. It's not the most constricted tunnel – there's one at the top of the Caldon Canal which is so low that most boats are too high to get through it. It isn't even the wettest tunnel either: there are tunnels on the Grand Union near Leicester which leak so badly that going through them is like being caught in a rainstorm.

But, all in all, given that the Harecastle *is* long and it *is* low and it *is* wet, it probably *is* the most unpleasant tunnel on the system. I can quite understand Mary refusing to go through it. In fact, I've often thought about refusing to go through it myself, but there's not much of an alternative except a long detour through Shropshire.

It only takes about forty minutes to get from one end to the other, and nowadays there's a ventilation system in operation so that at least you can breathe inside. When Em and I first went through years ago, it was like cruising in an exhaust pipe. Diesel fumes hung in the black gloom: a thick, poisonous miasma so caustic that your chest began to tighten as soon as you got under the portal. The tunnel wasn't used much then – unlike today – and you could always tell from how you reacted to the polluted air if any boats had recently been through. If all it did was make you feel wheezy and a bit sick, then you knew the tunnel hadn't been used in weeks. If you were coughing up blood then you knew something had gone through in the previous twenty-four hours.

The tunnel is only wide enough for one boat so there's always been a system of deciding craft priority to avoid subterranean stand-offs. In the old days you could only go in one direction in the morning and the other in the afternoon – the way it sometimes seems to be at some of London's slower traffic lights. As a result you'd sometimes have to go through the tunnel with other boats – which was the way the authorities had of hinting they'd rather you didn't go through at all.

If you were leading the convoy, then it wasn't so bad. You could just about manage to gasp your way through with the fresh air seeping from the other side. But if you were behind – or worst of all, last in a queue – not only could you not breathe because of the exhaust fumes belching out from the boats in front, but you couldn't see either because it was stinging your eyes. Steering in those conditions became a bit hit and miss. Much more hit than miss, actually. Once, after ricocheting the whole length of the tunnel, I emerged into the daylight with a chunk of genuine Thomas Telford, Grade One listed heritage brickwork sitting on my deck. I kept it as a souvenir and moved it onto *Justice* when Em and I had her built. It is still there today. I use it as a bookend. It supports my copy of *1001 Reasons I Hate the Harecastle*.

Telford completed the tunnel in 1827 to supplement an earlier one constructed by the engineer James Brindley fifty years before; and because of improvements in engineering technology which had taken place in the interim, he finished it in three years, rather than the eleven Brindley took. The two tunnel entrances were built adjacent to one other, and for a while they were used in tandem, until subsidence from local mining affected the original and it had to be closed. The same problem has plagued the more recent tunnel too. It was built with a towpath which has long since fallen into disrepair and been removed, and in places the roof has sunk alarmingly low. Indeed, in the early 1980s it collapsed completely and the tunnel was closed for more than a year for repairs – which makes me realise it couldn't have been all that stable those times Em and I blithely boated through it in our youth.

Even now I'm never confident that it's safe and I have these nightmares of being stuck inside after a roof fall. Even close to the portals, the Harecastle is cramped and constricted, like a dank sewer; but as you get further in, it gets worse. The vaulted roof is uneven and gets lower and lower until eventually it seems to be caressing the top of your head, with the full weight of Harecastle Hill above bearing down on you. There are sudden tight spots too and at times it veers unexpectedly in different directions when it should be straight.

Of course, nowadays the heath and safety police count you as you go in, and count you as you come out; but there's still a whole list of rules and regulations of things you can and can't do posted at the entrance like the Ten Commandments. *Thou Shalt Keep Within the Profile of the Boat. Thou Shalt Not Have Naked Lights Burning. Thou Shalt Believe that Life is Riskless and that in Passing through this Vaporous Damp Hole in the Ground Thou art taking no More Chance than Thy would Crossing the Road at Home.*

Years ago, when engines were less reliable, and there were a lot of rickety old wooden working boats cruising the system, there always seemed to be craft breaking down and people getting stuck inside. My friend Phil was on one of them. The decrepit old coal boat he was on with some friends had warped over the years and it got jammed. After an hour waiting for someone to register that they were still inside and send help, it dawned on them that they were on their own and that they had to roll up their sleeves and rescue themselves. It was the early hours before they got out, and only then after one of them had jumped in the water and planed the sides of the boat until they could squeeze it around the obstruction.

Me, I'd have to be given a great deal of money to tempt me to jump into the Trent and Mersey at any point – least of all in the middle of the Harecastle tunnel where the murky water, rust-red from all the iron oxide in the soil, seems to turn black in the gloom, like molten lead. I've accidentally fallen into the canal a couple of times, and once I jumped into the Grand

Union to retrieve a propeller that had fallen off a boat I was steering. This, believe me, is more than enough for one man in one lifetime. I was nervous about negotiating the tunnel this time. I'd done it many times before, but this was my first time on my own. My first time without help or company. I was convinced it was going to be a disaster. That I'd never get out alive.

I have an over-fertile imagination, you see. Most of us do where self-preservation is concerned. I had this mental picture of accidentally stumbling off the boat leaving it to bounce through the tunnel without me. I visualised clinging to the wall for dear life, getting increasingly weaker until finally, exhausted, my fingers lost feeling and I slipped beneath the surface, cold and lifeless…

This was not exactly my idea of fun. It wouldn't be anyone's idea of fun. So I rang Em.

I said, 'Are you doing anything this weekend?'

'This weekend?' she said. 'It's Friday already, Steve. It *is* the weekend.'

'That's what I mean. Are you doing anything? Have you got any plans?'

'What? Plans apart from shopping, you mean? Apart from doing the washing and ironing, visiting my mother and catching up on work from last week? Hey, but yes – now you mention it I have got plans for the couple of free hours I have available. I was actually planning to sleep if that's OK with you.'

'I'm at the Harecastle tunnel,' I said. 'I was wondering if you fancied, you know, coming up tomorrow for a trip?'

'A trip? You make it sound like a jaunt in the country. What you mean is six hours motorway driving and forty minutes in a drain.'

'I'm worried,' I admitted, 'I am not a brave man. What if I fall in and drown? What if I'm lost overboard and never found again?'

'Well, it was your stupid idea to do this journey,' she said. 'Besides, it's not as if you're rounding Cape Horn, is it? Go through with another boat. They can fish you out if you fall in.'

'But what if there isn't another boat.'

'Then wait for one,' she said. 'Or tie yourself to the tiller. Or wear a lifejacket. For heaven's sake, Steve, show some initiative...'

So I did what she suggested. Waited for another boat, I mean. Tying myself to the tiller would have been a bit excessive even by my standards, and lifejackets on canals are still considered a bit wussy, like wearing hiking boots on the towpath. I waited for an hour. I waited for two hours, three. Unfortunately no boat came, and so eventually I screwed my courage to sticking point and went through on my own. I had no choice really. It was the last passage of the day for northbound traffic, and if I hadn't gone then I'd have been stuck till the next morning.

You'd have thought after all this I'd at least have been prepared, wouldn't you? And in some respects I was. I'd made myself a cup of coffee for the trip, I'd put on a coat and a hat for when it got wet, I'd even put a waterproof torch on the back for emergencies.

Unfortunately what I forgot to do was the most obvious thing of all. I forgot to turn on the boat headlight.

I realised as soon as I'd got far enough inside for my eyes to attune to the gloom. By this time it was too late. I was a hundred yards in and the doors which are part of the new ventilation system closed behind leaving me in the pitch dark.

On any other vessel this would be a minor setback, so insignificant as to be hardly worth mentioning. It would simply be a matter of turning on the light by throwing a switch on the instrument panel. Not so on *Justice*. *Justice* is built to a cussed design and the instrument panel is in the engine room: the engine room which I had locked from the inside This meant I could only get into it by walking along the gunnels – the narrow ledge which runs along the outside of the boat. From there, it was just about possible for me to prise open the side hatches enough to squeeze in.

Walking along the gunnels in a tunnel wasn't exactly an enticing prospect, but at least I had the torch. Yes, the torch. I'd gone to the trouble of ensuring the torch was available for this sort of emergency.

Sadly, I hadn't actually checked the torch was working. When I switched it on, the batteries were flat – the way batteries in torches always *are* flat when you need them. The upshot of all this was that I had no choice but to manoeuvre my way along the gunnels in darkness. At the best of times this would have been a precarious exercise. Late in the day, with me tired and the gunnels greasy from the dripping tunnel roof, it was folly verging on recklessness.

I began feeling my way along blindly, step by step, as if I was walking along a tightrope.

The tunnel keeper shouted from the near portal, disturbing my concentration just at the time I needed it most.

'You all right?' he said. Despite the echo in his disembodied voice I could sense his irritation.

'Yes, no problem. Just a few, er, minor difficulties…'

'You best be getting along then, we're wanting to get home.'

When I finally succeeded in getting into the engine room and switching on the headlight, I felt like some swashbuckling hero from Hornblower.

But my problems weren't over. I soon realised the light was out of position. I'd probably knocked it, caught it with my arm sometime. It was now pointing uselessly at the roof of the tunnel. This would have been OK if I'd have wanted to see the roof of the tunnel. If I'd been researching Victorian brickwork or fat hairy spiders, for example. It wasn't a lot of help steering though. There was nothing for it. Once again I had to shuffle up the gunnel, groping about this time, not because of the lack of light, but because I was blinded by too much of it.

'You *sure* you're OK?' the tunnel keeper shouted. 'Do you want any help?'

When, at last, I managed to get the boat through the tunnel and out the other side, I was elated. I had found the source of an African river. I had battled my way to some lost city of the Amazon. I had hacked my way through unexplored jungle.

The tunnel keeper didn't quite see things the same way. He was half an hour past knocking-off time and he wanted to get home. He wasn't particularly sympathetic to what I'd been through. Or particularly interested either. His customer relations training obviously prevented him from saying so directly, but it was obvious he thought I was a lamebrain getting myself into the difficulties I had in the first place. He certainly wasn't going to congratulate me for surmounting them.

Instead, he asked, 'Do you know yet if you're coming back this way?'

'No. Why?'

He looked at me acidly. 'Just so I can arrange to have a day off,' he said.

There's a canal tunnel in Foulridge near to Colne in Lancashire celebrated for the fact that in 1912 a cow called Buttercup (what else?) fell in at one end and swam a mile to the other. This was before anyone knew about bovine spongiform encephalopathy or else people might not have thought so much of the stupid creature. As it was they revived it with brandy and promoted it to the status of a local icon.

At least they didn't name a pub after it though.

At the northern side of the Harecastle is a pub called the Romping Donkey, though I've never been able to discover what the donkey did that the cow didn't. Was it another swimming feat? Perhaps the donkey swam through Harecastle? Twice? Maybe it did it backstroke? Who knows? Perhaps it was in a competition against the cow for the Allcomers Quadruped Cup?

I moored just down from the pub that night and while I was making dinner a procession of owners from a nearby estate brought their dogs for their evening constitutional. Each one of them persisted in doing its business directly in front of my window. This is another bane of the boater's life: dogs crapping on towpaths. They were all at it with a vengeance that night, from the smallest poodle to the largest of banned breeds. The Jack Russells seemed to do it with more enthusiasm than most. Or maybe it's just their size that makes it seem that way. In any event, I just can't understand how something that small produces something that large. Eventually I went off the idea of food and went up to the pub.

When I came back there was even more of the stuff outside.

It was piled up in great mounds, massive steaming mountains of the stuff. I wondered if it was sport in these parts, like the boat shining in Braunston. Competitive dog crapping. Who knows, contemporary taste being what it is, it might catch on? Endemol, who make *Big Brother*, might even develop it as a television programme.

They could call it *New Faeces*, perhaps?

To complement the rest of the faeces they make.

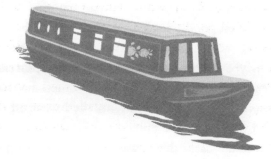

Nine

I was in Manchester. How I'd got to Manchester, I wasn't entirely sure. It was strange. I guess I must have gone into a trance or something, somewhere after the Harecastle. Somewhere around Rode Heath perhaps? There used to be this beautiful Victorian warehouse at Rode Heath, built of red brick and as high as a five-storey house. It had an elegant loading bay that overhung the canal and when the sun shone in the right direction it used to glow blood-red like polished granite. But for some reason they knocked it down. One year, without so much as a by-your-leave, it just disappeared. As I was cruising past the site where it used to be, I remember thinking how sad it was that it wasn't there any more. But then – it was very odd, this – I happened to glance upwards and in that instant I could have sworn I saw it again. As it used to be. As if it hadn't been demolished at all.

I must have been away with the fairies. Too late in the day and me too tired, too long cruising on my own. Being on a narrowboat does this to you. It gives you too much time to think about things, that's what it is. You go soft in the head. The same thing happened when I passed Thurlwood. At Thurlwood there used to be a remarkable steel lock built like a loading gantry to strengthen it against the subsidence from the salt workings in these parts. They left it to become derelict, and then moved in one day and demolished it before anyone noticed except the people living opposite who were pleased to see the back of it because by then it had become an eyesore.

Yet as I was manoeuvring the boat into the lock, my attention focused on steering, I felt the shadow of the old gantry pass over me, and for an instant I could have sworn I was going into that old lock. Of course, it was just a trick of the light, sunspots on my eyes from the reflections in the water. On this section of the canal the locks were built in pairs to make it quicker for the working boats. Now at Thurlwood, where the old lock was, there's a great gap, like the space in a mouth where a tooth used to be.

Amazing, though, how your mind can play tricks with you, isn't it? Amazing how it can take us into other worlds while we're still in this one. How it can take us into the past when we're so rooted in the present. I must have drifted off somewhere along the way, lost in dreams, intoxicated by my journey. I was suddenly in Cheshire, passing the salt towns of Sandbach and Middlewich where the canal is wide and deep, and where *Justice* seemed to stretch herself and fly like Pegasus, the feathering water from her bow like powerful beating wings carrying her along.

At length I passed the salt flats further north where the banks have collapsed into the fields forming narrow lakes like water meadows. Here sometimes, in the evening, the wind lashes the surface of the still canal, fracturing it into wavelets which lull you to sleep with gentle lapping against your hull.

Was that where I stayed that night? Was that where I moored? Even now, with a map open in front of me, and my logbook to hand, I can't be entirely certain. Your recollections get skewed when you get pensive like this. Everything becomes vague. It was like this for me, as if I was in a coma that I only emerged from at the tunnel at Preston Brook where the Trent and Mersey joins the Bridgewater Canal. I'd been through this tunnel often enough without ever being delayed, but this time I got held up at the entrance waiting for oncoming traffic and I got chatting to some bloke there walking along the towpath. He'd got a thick Scouse accent and his face was the texture of crumpled brown paper.

He asked me where I was going, and when I told him I was heading to the North he looked at me as if I was some sort of weirdo who'd lost it completely. Because I was in the North now, wasn't I? Because somewhere along the way it had happened, and I'd arrived in this strange and different country without so much as a murmur, let alone a border-crossing, or customs, or passport control.

He said, apropos of nothing at all, that he grew Vivaldis. Potatoes, he explained. On my allotment, he added, lighting a fag. They haven't got as much starch in them as other spuds, did you know that? They're slimming potatoes, he concluded with a self-satisfied smirk. He was as thin as a rake, you see. He had less meat on him than a butcher's pencil whereas I have a pot that wouldn't look out of place in a maternity smock. I thought at the time he was having a go at me. Now I think

I was being oversensitive. I'd been on my own too long, you see. I was starting to get introspective.

I called Em that lunchtime. She was at work and not inclined to be sympathetic.

'It worries me,' I said. 'This seeing things all over the place.'

'I'd be worried if you weren't seeing things all over the place. You'd be blind then, wouldn't you?'

'But I keep, you know, imagining stuff – as it used to be.'

'I'm not coming up to help you through the Harecastle, if that's what you mean,' she said. 'Even if you start manifesting religious visions.'

'I'm through the Harecastle now,' I said. 'I even went through Preston Brook. I'm in the North now.'

'The North? Can you be sure? You're not just imagining it, are you?'

'You're not taking me seriously,' I said.

'I always take you seriously, Steve.'

'Then tell me – seriously,' I asked, 'do you think I'm too fat?'

I moored at Lymm that night. I think I may have stayed there the next night too, maybe even the night after that – though in the abstracted state I was I couldn't be sure what I was doing and would often revert to a dreamy reverie watching the world go by through my portholes, or from the deck, losing all track of time. An hour or two would pass in the blink of an eye. A day would go by and I wouldn't notice.

Lymm was a perfect place for the mood I was in. It's a magical place, an Aquarius of the North, a town of still pools and seeping waterfalls; a damp, sopping, saturated town of red sandstone and great, broad-leafed plants that seem almost tropical, dripping as they are with a Pennine drizzle that could just as easily be the heady condensation of a rainforest.

The Bridgewater Canal cut the place in half when it was completed. Fifty years later came more construction work when they built a dam across a local stream to accommodate the turnpike which they didn't want passing through the village centre. Though some say it wasn't the road but the need for water which made them build the dam. One way or another, the result was to create a lake, but a much wider lake than those on the salt flats; a real lake, a lake which glistens when it catches the sun, a lake surrounded by oaks and beeches, where wood sorrel and red campion grow and where mallards nest along the banks.

At one time Lymm was a centre of fustian cutting, I discovered. I made a note to this effect at the time, though I had no idea of what fustian was, or why on earth you'd want to cut it. I think I only wrote it down because I liked the sound of the word fustian. Because it made me think of damp old libraries and the musty smell of leather-bound books which for some reason I found strangely reassuring. It was only later, back at home in London, Googling on the computer with Em downstairs watching *X Factor* or something, that I discovered that fustian was a sort of cotton fabric and cutting was part of the process by which it was manufactured. It was woven in such a way that you had to cut it to separate one side of the fabric from the other. This created a pile or nap in the middle, and it was this that characterised the material and made it both warm and resilient.

CHAPTER NINE

A lot of people were employed in Lymm as fustian cutters. But it wasn't just in Lymm. In the nineteenth century fustian cutting was a major occupation right across the North West and thousands of people in the cotton towns were employed at it. Sometimes the work was done at tables but more often than not the cloth was stretched across rollers and they'd walk up and down all day, slicing through the threads of the weave row by row, using tiny blades fashioned from watch springs and honed until they were as sharp as razorblades. Cutting even a basic fustian, they could walk ten or eleven miles over the length of a shift. With more sophisticated fustians – fabrics like velveteen, for instance – you had to walk further, much further. Velveteen was a sort of velvet made from cotton rather than silk. It was woven as a series of loops, each of which had to be cut to produce the characteristic nap of the cloth. You had to make as many as five lengthways cuts an inch to achieve it on some of the finer velveteens. That could mean a walk of more than seventy miles to finish a bolt of cloth.

It's like another world, isn't it? Walking up and down a mill floor, hour after hour, day after day, bored out of your head for the ten or twelve pence a week, or whatever pittance you got paid. And that was just fustian cutters. Just one of hundreds of lost occupations in the textile industry, one of thousands of our industrial past. What about tacklers? Fullers and fetlers? Doffers and tuckers? Jobbers? Even without Googling you know, don't you, that these jobs were hardly fulfilling careers for the men and women who did them? Hardly the sort of thing to have you bouncing out of bed on a wet Monday morning, full of the joys of life.

You can certainly see why boatmen gravitated towards the waterways, and why they seemed to love their job. It might have been hard graft, lumping and hauling and loading and shovelling. But at least on the waterways you were outside in the fresh air, moving about, not constantly deafened by machinery and deadened by the repetition of the work. At least when you'd cast off you were your own boss with no one breathing down your neck every five minutes telling you what to do and how to do it.

The Bridgewater Canal provided the necessary transport for uncut fustian to be brought to Lymm and the cut cloth taken away. In this sense it created fustian cutting as an industry. But the same might be said of the canal's effect on other Manchester industries too. In fact, it's not exaggerating to say that without the Bridgewater Canal, there wouldn't be a Manchester. Or certainly not the sort of city we know today. When Francis Egerton, the Third Duke of Bridgewater, started building his waterway in the 1760s the only way of transporting goods of any type was by loading them onto packhorses and carrying them across what poorly built, ill-kept roads there were. Egerton could see that he'd make a fortune if he could get coal from his mines to the markets of growing Manchester quickly and reliably. The place then was a small town of some 20,000 people. After the canal was built the immediate effect was that coal prices dropped by about half. Suddenly there was cheap fuel available, not just for domestic use, but to power the mills that were springing up all over the place, as industrialists began to be import cotton from the new empire.

By 1801, 90,000 people lived in Manchester. A hundred years after the coming of the canal there were 225,000 – a rate of growth comparable to anything happening in China or India at the moment.

Today, the Bridgewater Canal is a shadow of its former self, like a shabby Victorian stately home which has fallen into disrepair. It's an uncharacteristically wide waterway and in places an unusually straight one too: unprepossessing, sometimes rubbish-strewn with buildings lining the towpath often covered in graffiti. Yet the Bridgewater was once the cord along which the pearls of the city's industry were threaded. Here, backing onto the water where now are unsightly residential suburbs, used to be the industries that serviced King Cotton: the iron foundings, the precision engineering plants, the chemical shops.

Most of this disappeared long ago of course, swept away even before Thatcherism reduced great swathes of our industrial landscape to arid wasteland. But today any wasteland – especially close to water – is a development opportunity. And all along the Bridgewater more and more building is taking place, much of it blocks of studio apartments built to accommodate Manchester's trendy young. You may not always like the architecture, but you can't help but admire the energy of these places. They have a real confidence about them. A sort of brashness that speaks of the future more than the past, of hope more than despair.

But Manchester's always been like this. That's why the Bridgewater was built in the first place. In its day it was cutting-edge technology, state-of-the-art engineering. It was a signpost to the future, as much as any of these modern buildings are now.

I lived in Manchester in the dark days of the 1980s, and even then you felt the vitality of the place. You couldn't help but be caught up by it. It was a time when Tony Wilson's Factory Records was beginning to redefine contemporary music, and when his Hacienda club seemed to be the centre of the world. I was working in the TV newsroom for the BBC at the time. We were a sociable group and some nights after work the whole department used to pile in there for some R&R. And some nights we used to pile straight out again since the place was so cold it could freeze you to the floor if you stood still for too long.

We used to have office outings to Bernard Manning's club too, but that wasn't anything like as hip.

It had heating for a start.

Mentioning this dates me terribly. It all seems so long ago, another world. Especially since Tony Wilson and Bernard Manning are both dead. Manchester, though – the city that generated them, the city whose character they helped define whether by new wave music or sod-off political incorrectness – goes from strength to strength. You see it most from the canal at Old Trafford where Manchester United Football Club looms above you, the intricate tubular scaffolding of its stands a steel filigree against the sky. Old Trafford from that angle looks like what it is: less a football club, more the HQ of an international marketing conglomerate whose brand identity is known from Singapore to Senegal. Less a theatre of dreams than a centre of moneymaking.

Unless you want a stadium tour – and that'll cost you the best part of a tenner – it's not a place you can get into very easily. Casual match tickets are virtually unobtainable through official channels and if you are lucky enough to get hold of one it'll be so expensive it will make your eyes water. Season tickets are even harder to come by. They become family heirlooms, the waiting list to get one years.

But it wasn't always like this.

In 1969 I had a football-loving girlfriend in Manchester and when I made the trek from the Midlands to see her, she'd often as not suggest going along to a match if United were playing at home. In the days before the Premiership and the influx of television money changed the game beyond recognition, Old Trafford was like most football grounds: just a four-sided cowshed surrounded by terraced streets. We'd stand in the Stretford End which was later to become notorious as a magnet for every machete-wielding head-case in the city but which was then just the place where the hardcore fans went to sing about the referee's parentage.

This was the year after Manchester United won the European Cup. It was the famous Busby team of Denis Law, Bobby Charlton and George Best. Yet still we could leave the decision as to whether we went to a match until after lunch – which, being the good working-class kids we were, we still called dinner. We'd pay on the gate and they'd cram as many of us in onto the terraces as they could, though I don't remember it ever feeling unsafe. Or ever feeling full either – even when we went to see the north-western haka, which is the local derby against Manchester City.

It couldn't have cost much either. We didn't have much money in those days. We wouldn't have been able to afford it if it had.

Football then didn't have the same all-embracing appeal it does now. Like canals, in fact. Both have undergone a social revolution; both now attract the attention of people with more disposable income than in the past. The middle classes, you'd have called them once, except this is a cumbersome definition nowadays when everything is judged on money, not social background. Spending power is what it's all about today; and the newcomers have forced up prices by their willingness to pay. Nowadays if you want to watch football, or go canal-boating, you're going to have to fork out far more than you once would.

At least on the Bridgewater it isn't as expensive as other places. The licence is cheaper for a start because the canal is one of the few still in private hands, owned by the same company that owns the Manchester Ship Canal. This means that when you buy a Bridgewater licence, the Bridgewater Canal is all you can cruise. And the price reflects it. The moorings are cheaper too, which means that the canal attracts a different sort of boater. It's like going back thirty years because there's something undeveloped about it which isn't true of the twee Midlands waterways. These get more and more like long parks with every year that passes.

On the Bridgewater things are generally a lot shabbier, a lot less polished. But it's the better for it. It's the difference between visiting a show home where everything's for display and a working home where the dirty dishes are piled in the sink and the kids are screaming happily in the back room. The Bridgewater feels less like a series of picture postcards, and more like a proper canal. The sort of canal that's used by ordinary people who aren't going to be able to invest £100K or more in a boat – which is what a many better-off newcomers are being persuaded to part with nowadays.

There are a great many low-cost PVC cruisers on the Bridgewater – as there used to be on all canals in the 1970s. And there are more smaller boats too, and boats of different shapes and designs – not just the standard sixty-foot narrowboat which has almost become the industry norm in the South. The craft on the Bridgewater, like the canal itself, are more idiosyncratic and more individualistic. Even a standard narrowboat on the Bridgewater is likely to have been customised, many of them sporting homemade canopies over the back deck to protect their owners from the inclement northern weather. These strange constructions have been christened 'Bridgewater bivouacs'.

As canal practice goes, this is about as traditional as painting your boat tartan, and it's guaranteed to upset the purists like me who feel that in order to guarantee the full canal cruising experience you need to have rainwater running down the back of your neck.

All in all the Bridgewater felt very different to other canals. It had a different atmosphere, a different ambience. At first I couldn't understand it, but then the penny dropped. I was in the North, wasn't I? I was in Manchester. This was a distinctive Manchester canal. It was as characteristic of Manchester as a pint of Boddingtons and a plate of fish and chips. As emblematic as a Lowry painting. As in your face as Noel Gallagher.

Which brought me back to the central question: if I had arrived in the North, where precisely had it happened? Had there been something at Rode Heath? Not something that I'd seen which wasn't there, but something that had been there which I'd missed. Or was it at Thurlwood? Or Lymm? Had the North just happened in the tunnel at Preston Brook, or maybe even earlier, in the inhospitable darkness of the Harecastle itself?

I moored that night at Castlefield, near the studios where Granada TV makes *Coronation Street*. It's a mile or so from the centre of town, a buzzy, voguish development of fashionable shops and chichi restaurants. No sooner had I showered and settled for the night than I heard the riotous noise of a crowd outside. Soon afterwards there was a knock on the top of the boat. When I stared out of the porthole to see what all the commotion was about, I was confronted with an enormous assemblage of towering female legs, every one of them teetering uncertainly on a heel of precipitous height. There was a veritable forest of them, an impenetrable tangle, each clad in tights that were glossier or sheerer or more spangled than the next; each improbably long, stretching onwards and upwards until they disappeared into the recesses of tiny skirts no bigger than belts.

They belonged to a party of young women – twenty or so of them, maybe more – who were shrieking outside, constantly doubling up into paroxysms of laughter at what one or other of them said. On their dresses or tops (none of them wore a coat) they all sported badges made out of paper plates and scrawled with a felt tip pen. One of them said 'Horny Bridesmaid'. Another proclaimed 'Gusset in Chief', a pun on the word guest, I guessed. Without exception they were all smoking, and with it being such a still evening, a great cloud of cigarette smoke hung above their heads as caustic as the discharge from a chemical plant.

I went outside and was hit in the face with a blast of cheap perfume and profanity.

Dispensing with formal introductions, one of them asked, 'You don't f***ing live on this, do you?'

'No, but I play on it,' I replied – which was probably not the wisest thing to admit since it had the effect of detonating another explosion of squawking.

'By yourself?' another screamed, releasing a new torrent of high-pitched hilarity from the group.

'It's f***ing big enough,' someone else shouted. More hysterical laughter.

'Yeah, but size isn't everything,' someone else announced. More laughter yet. Gales of it. Storms of it. Veritable weather systems of it.

Eventually one of them stepped forward confidently. 'Can I come inside?' she asked. And then she stopped dead in her tracks as the full import of what she had said dawned on her. The rest of them were a lot quicker on the uptake. Even before the question was completed they were howling with delight.

God knows how she succeeded in doing it but in the middle of all this one of them managed to scream above the others loud enough to make herself heard.

'No, that's his job,' she yelled.

For a moment everything went quiet and then there was a chorus of recrimination.

'Chelle, you always go too far.' 'Oh, you are so coarse, Chelle.' 'That's terrible Chelle, how can you say things like that?'

They began to drift off.

One of them came over to me, more remorseful than I could have imagined. She had wide, grey eyes and a pale, perfect face camouflaged by make-up. She couldn't have been more than fifteen, sixteen at most. 'Sorry about that,' she said. 'Chelle always goes a bit over the top. It's the tequila…'

'The tequila?'

'Yeah, you know, that Mexican stuff. That drink. It sends her lairy. I hope she didn't embarrass you.'

I shook my head. By now the others had disappeared round the quay. I could hear their voices echoing over the water.

'Anyway, I'm sorry, please accept my apologies,' she said. Separated from her friends, she'd reverted to the polite convent schoolgirl from Didsbury that she probably was. That they all probably were. 'Anyway, we won't disturb you again.' She smiled before finally disappearing into a night that I guessed wouldn't end for them until the early hours.

I went off to bed. I needed to get a night's sleep. It was going to be another early start.

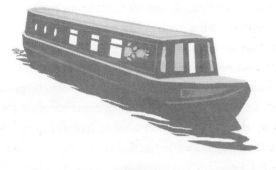

Ten

More often than not the road sign at the top of Manchester's Canal Street is vandalised. People obliterate the first letters of the words. Even if you hadn't seen the cult Channel 4 series *Queer as Folk* which immortalised it a few years back, this would give you a clue as to the sort of area it is. It's actually one of the liveliest parts of Manchester, packed with people of every age and persuasion, a chaotic melting pot of contemporary metrosexuality.

Well, normally it is. At night, I mean. At five in the morning it's as dead as a cathedral graveyard. Eerily so when you're going through it in what is an enclosed, echoing gully, almost like a long tomb.

I slipped moorings at first light and as I turned the bend to the start of the flight of locks that take you out of the city, the place was unnaturally silent. In the chasm created by the streets and the walls of the converted warehouses opposite, my engine sounded surrealistically loud. The clubs and bars characteristic of this part of town were dark and empty, lit

– if they were lit at all – by just one or two dim lamps left on for security. Outside, the street lamps reflected on the damp tarmac, vestiges of a night that was ending and a day that didn't yet seem to realise it had begun.

I seemed to be the only person up and about. There wasn't even a lone car audible above the city's silence, not even an early bus or tram to fracture the stillness. It was if I'd arrived at a party that was over. One that had finished before I'd even arrived. Here and there were odd items to remind me of what I'd missed. Curious objects standing like installations in a gallery. On one wall were two wine glasses, one of them full, the other standing upside down as if celebrating in that position its functional uselessness. Further up was a discarded sweater tossed casually over the palings of an iron fence. Stale remnants of some crazy moment; a silent, ghostlike testimony to transitory pleasure.

The first lock barely delayed me but the second created problems which I hadn't anticipated. I was on the Rochdale Canal now, you see, travelling uphill. Every gallon of water on this canal washes down from the Pennines. On normal canals if it's washing down too much and gets to a lock, the overflow is diverted to run round the sides in what are called by-weirs. But the by-weirs on the Rochdale were built over years ago. Now when the water hit the locks it floods straight over them in great cascading waterfalls.

This makes boating single-handed a bit tricky. You might think a tumultuous ferment like this would push a boat away from it, but what it actually does is act like a plughole, drawing a boat into the perilous core of the turbulence. If it ever got caught in it, a boat like *Justice* with an open deck would sink in seconds. Mooring before a lock, you can stay well back from the lock waterfall, keeping relatively safe. But going into a lock chamber is a different matter altogether. Now the waterfall is crashing over the top gates and you have to steer the bow to within a few inches of where it is landing. Nervewracking hardly describes it. At every lock you're dicing with the survival of the boat. With your own survival too. My stomach was in knots. I felt physically sick with the worry of it.

Perhaps I should have waited for another crew to travel with. Perhaps I should have hung around until more people arrived who I could have conscripted to help? Maybe. There are lots of sensible things we should do in life, yet somehow don't. I decided to press on regardless.

The ascent up the flight was exhausting, requiring intense concentration. And it was agonisingly slow. It meant taking the boat into the lock chambers at the lowest possible speed I could manage while still retaining steerage. Then once inside – but not too far inside – I had to clamber onto the roof and leap off onto the lockside, taking a rope with me. This way I could pull the boat back before it was sucked into the churning water which avalanched over the locks in a solid, seething wall.

A couple of times I misjudged the manoeuvre and had to reverse the boat out and start again. Once, more alarmingly, I misjudged it entirely and the bow kissed the edge of the overflow despite me frantically hauling on the rope to prevent it happening. It touched for just an instant – but in that fraction of a second the boat lurched and pitched and the front well-deck flooded. My heart was in my mouth; my mouth was so dry I couldn't swallow.

The hours flew by. It was six o'clock before I knew it, then seven, then eight. At last the canal disappeared under Piccadilly where so many buildings have been constructed overhead that their massive concrete supports form a wide cavern of intimidating dimension, curtained with spider webs the size of fishing nets.

The canal towpath was flooded at this point and to operate the lock which is there I had to roll up my jeans and go paddling. Above me, the railway lines bore down on my head and I went into a low tunnel, black and dank. There was a dosser sleeping there on a wooden pallet in the recess of a graffiti-covered wall. His stench hit me before I saw him. He was wrapped in a filthy blanket, a can of Special Brew at his elbow. As I passed he grunted and shifted position as though to defend it. As if he suspected I might suddenly dart off the boat and steal it from him.

Frankly I'd have rather drunk the canal water.

Above me Manchester was stirring. I could hear the rumble of trains over my head. I could hear commuters spilling out onto the platforms. I could almost smell the coffee from the cappuccino kiosks on the concourse.

There was only one more lock to go, thank God, after which I planned to stop for a break before heading north-east over the Pennines to Huddersfield. The water at this point was thick with the accumulated litter of the city – discarded cans, polystyrene cups, and bottles hovering half submerged in the grey scum. As *Justice* edged through the squalid mess, sweeping a path for herself, her bow seemed higher than normal, as if she was wrinkling her nose with distaste at what she being asked to do.

Not that I cared. The canal at this point may have been squalid, but at least I was leaving it. It couldn't have been more delightful if had been a clear mountain stream running through a glacial valley.

The whole purpose of starting out so early was to get through central Manchester in the morning as boaters are advised to do. This is to avoid afternoons in the suburbs of Droylsden which, along with nearby Failsworth on the Ashton Canal, have been mythologised in waterways folklore. 'Here be Dragons' was what they once put on maps to indicate that a region was unexplored and dangerous; and it could just as easily apply today to some of these outlying areas of Manchester which are visited so infrequently by the boating community of the South that to all intents and purposes they remain undiscovered. No wonder people are terrified of them. No wonder it's generally believed that the undesirables have taken them over and that a sort of towpath anarchy rules. There are stories of marauding gangs of kids steaming through boats, stealing what they can as they go. Stories of boats being held up at gunpoint. Stories of craft being vandalised by drunks and stoned by drug addicts...

Though maybe I got that last bit wrong. Maybe it's the drug addicts who are stoned.

Cruising in the morning is supposed to avoid most of this, though I'm not sure I know why. Kids might sleep late, I guess. But what about drunks and drug addicts? It's not called the crack of dawn for nothing, is it? Surely they'd be up at first light looking for their first fix of the day. And what about the thieves? On the whole they are not the greatest of intellects, but surely if they went out to rob boats and there weren't any around even they'd notice eventually? Surely it would dawn on them that they needed a bit of the spirit of the early bird to make a living, even a dishonest one?

After all, even a life of crime requires a basic application to the job.

Of course, the idea that you're safer travelling in the morning is a fallacy. The truth is it's not dangerous travelling on a canal at any time. But try telling that to some of this new generation of contemporary boaters who are prosperous people living in prosperous areas who just don't understand the inner city. It frightens them. They catch sight of a couple of kids messing around on the towpath – as kids have always done – as me and my mates used to do – and what they see in their mind's eye is a gang of thugs out to attack them. Everyone walking up the towpath is a potential assailant. Everyone with a drink in their hands is a wino. Even a can of Coke.

To some extent I can understand it. Part of me shares their unease. On a boat you can hardly tuck yourself away discreetly. Not when you're sixty feet long and painted in primary colours. You feel vulnerable; you can't help it, and in that state your imagination runs riot. What if someone starts throwing bricks at you? What if they start shooting at you? What if they target you with ground-to-ground missiles?

Many nervous boaters nowadays pre-programme the telephone number of local police stations into their mobile phones in case of trouble. More and more of them carry cameras too in the hope that taking pictures of troublemakers might deter them. That's not a particularly good idea either if you ask me. Kids nowadays are too savvy. Nowadays they start posing when you take a camera out. Or they start reminding you of the copyright law regarding the reproduction of personal images.

The Ashton Canal starts soon after the flight of nine Rochdale Canal locks end. There's a very sharp junction which doubles back on itself. Almost immediately the canal passes through the tidy but soulless new development of Piccadilly Village where the architects came up with this novel idea of designing red-brick blocks of flats to look like traditional waterside warehouses. This would have been a great idea if it hadn't already been done by every other waterways architect in the country so that now there's a sort of tedious uniformity to it which is contrary to the spirit of canal building which was originally done by local craftsmen in local styles.

But hey, you don't expect architects to be creative, do you? That's a very old-fashioned idea.

At Ancoats I came across the first of a series of towering mill buildings that line the canal at this point. I had a hunch they wouldn't be lining the canal for long. All around were signs for New Islington. Placards for New Islington were plastered across the mill frontages, canvasses emblazoned with the name New Islington hung on corrugated iron fences. There were flags for New Islington flying from isolated poles in the middle of nowhere. Walls were painted with the name New Islington. Fly posters for New Islington were plastered about wherever I looked.

From all this, I guessed there was a major new development afoot. Probably on the evidence, one called New Islington.

I didn't get too excited about this after all the other new development I'd seen in Manchester. For a start, the name New Islington was too redolent of old Islington for my liking and I'm no enthusiast for what that trendy, overblown borough represents even in London, let alone the rest of the country. Too many shades of New Labour for a start. Or New Conservative, for that matter. Or indeed any variation of the equation whereby the word 'New' + noun = a rebranded concept of questionable integrity and little substance. I wasn't too hopeful of the development architecturally either. I assumed it would be another version of Piccadilly Village: homes for affluent urbanites – inoffensive, unimaginative and sterile. A sort of bricks and mortar version of Phil Collins.

On all counts I was totally wrong. New Islington, I learnt subsequently, wasn't a poncey homage to the ciabatta-eating world of the capital's metropolitan chic but what the area's been called since the nineteenth century when it became home to Manchester's Italian immigrant population. And the development isn't exactly what you'd expect from your average urban regeneration scheme either. It's more a concept than a development – a partnership between Manchester Council, a developer with a snazzy name and a flash website, and English Partnerships, the government's national redevelopment agency. Together they've come up with a plan for the area which incorporates homes for people of different incomes and which promises some really innovative architecture including one canalside street of self-build houses, each one constructed to a different design. It's an idea they admit they nicked from Amsterdam. Which is no bad thing since what the Dutch don't know about canals isn't worth knowing.

What's more, it was the only case of thieving I came across as I went up the canal.

It was only when I got beyond Ancoats, past the new stadium that not long before had hosted the Commonwealth Games, and which is now home to Manchester City FC, the blue bit of the city, that I began to feel any real apprehension about the journey. Part of it was creeping tiredness after my early start. But it was no help that the canal had suddenly become very shallow. Every now and again I felt the bottom of the boat scrape against something metallic and then skew wildly to one side as if it was being thrown off a ledge. I went through a flight of locks at Clayton and one of the pounds there was low enough for me to see what I was dealing with. On the bottom, sunk in a beach of mud, was an unbroken layer of oil drums, old prams and abandoned pushbikes. At this stage I couldn't help but notice that there seemed to be rather a lot of blokes around clutching bottles in a way which made me suspect they weren't taking a lot of notice of the government's guidelines for safe drinking.

Or, putting it another way, they were out of their heads, stinking like a brewery tap. I'd have ignored them except that as I ascended the flight, I was meeting them at every lock. Some of them sat around on the scrubby grass but others seemed to be involved in their version of an eighteenth-century salon and were splayed over the lock-beams as if they were chaises longues. It meant I had to disturb them to make progress, interrupting their discussions which for the most part seemed to consist of aggressive grunting punctuated by bursts of profanity. This did not make me popular with them.

Eventually one of them floundered towards me, his breath so heavy with meths that as a final defence I could have lit it and launched him into space.

In fact, he only wanted to help. As I left the lock, he closed the gate afterwards, so avoiding the need for me to moor the boat to do it myself. I was genuinely obliged, so much so that I think I may have overdone it a bit on the gratitude front which may have led him to believe he'd made a new friend. He followed me up to the next lock, and the lock after that, where he did the same thing again. Mind you, I was no mug. I could see where all this was leading. No doubt he'd hit me for a contribution to his Staying Pissed Fund. Or maybe he wanted a bed for the night and was eyeing up my spare cabin. Maybe – worse – he fancied me and lusted after my body.

Actually, as he explained, he'd been going in my direction and he needed the exercise. Now he was sorry but he had to go even though it meant leaving me on my own. I'd better mind how I went though, he warned. I should especially watch out for the kids since the little bastards would chuck stones at me and do anything they could to make my life a misery, and he knew because there were stories he could tell me about them which would make my hair curl.

All this didn't do much for morale. But all of it – like so much of the blather traded as fact on the towpath telegraph – was actually nonsense. The kids weren't like that at all. Most of them seemed more frightened of me than I was of them. Mind you, I don't blame them. I'd been cruising for a while now and I frightened myself. My hair needed cutting. I needed a change of clothes. And I'd taken to unaccountable fits of Tourette's-like cursing at myself whenever anything wasn't going my way. Since a lot wasn't going my way boating up the Ashton where the paddles were stiff and the locks heavy, I was swearing at myself a lot. I even tried to pick a fight with myself at one point. Don't laugh. It almost came to blows.

Not surprisingly, the kids kept out of my way, though one snotty-nosed tyke was braver than the rest. He was only about seven or eight, too young to be out on his own really. But there was a world weariness about him that I found charming. His ambition was to get a ride on a boat, but he was canny enough to know he'd only get refused if he asked outright.

He said, 'I know you can't give me a ride. Insurance, innit?'

'I'm sorry, it's just too much of a risk,' I said, wheeling out the same excuse he must have heard from boaters a hundred times.

'I won't rob you,' he said. 'I won't nick stuff. Promise.'

'No, I didn't say you would. It's just this passenger liability clause…'

The kid nodded knowledgeably as if he knew what I was talking about. 'Yeah, and you don't know what would my mum would say if I got hurt.'

He followed me up to the next lock. 'It's the cover, innit?' he said. 'I ain't got enough cover.'

'That's about the size of it,' I said.

'If I got myself some covers, you'd give me a ride then, wouldn't you? Where do I get covers, do you know? Have you got any I can have?'

Of course, I knew it was wrong. I knew that it would only encourage him to pester other boaters, or that he'd have an accident, or that I'd get arrested as a paedophile. I knew all that. But sometimes you can't play by the rules. Sometimes you've got to take a risk, haven't you? And there are worse risks in life worse than giving a kid a ride up the Ashton on your boat.

'Hop on,' I said. 'But only as far as the next lock. And don't you dare touch anything or you're straight off.'

In the event it wasn't the kids that caused me trouble, but another boat. I was in Fairfield, not far from the factory where they make Robertson's Jam, and not that far from where I planned to moor for the night. There are a couple of locks there near the junction with the disused Hollinwood Canal which used to bring coal into Manchester from the pits at Oldham. As I approached the first of them, I could see through the open gates that there was another boat inside, a small PVC cruiser travelling the same direction as me. It was the first craft I'd seen all day in either direction and I slowed down to let it move through – though after a while it became apparent that it wasn't going anywhere. Mainly because it didn't seem to have any crew. It seemed to have been totally abandoned, like an inland waterways *Marie Celeste*.

I moored to investigate and climbed down into the lock to take a closer look. There I found a middle-aged couple cowering inside. Their terrified faces peered out at me from behind their curtains as I stepped on board. It transpired they were from Cheshire and had been coming down the canal from the opposite direction when they'd had problems with the kids. A group of them had kicked their football into the water. They had become unhappy at not being allowed to use the cruiser to retrieve it and things had got out of hand. Harsh words had been exchanged, stones thrown in anger.

CHAPTER TEN

The couple had attempted to get away, but they felt so uneasy they eventually decided to turn their boat around as fast as they could and go back to where they'd come from where they felt safe. But inevitably – because if you ever try to do anything fast on the canal, things go wrong – the lock developed a fault. The paddle gear started slipping and they'd had to call out British Waterways to repair it. They were waiting now, scared stiff the kids would come back and find them. Coming across another boater was a great relief, they told me. There was safety in numbers.

As it happened, the fault with the lock was just a minor one. The paddle gear had worked loose from its fixing and it was the job of a minute or two to tighten up the bolts securing it – the sort of routine job you did all the time thirty years ago when the canals weren't anything like as well maintained as they are now. Soon we were all on our way and in no time at all we were moored at Portland Basin in Ashton-under- Lyne, where a magnificent replica of a Georgian warehouse, built to replace the original which burnt down in 1972, marks the point where I would seriously start my assault of the Pennines.

Later, I went to see if the couple had settled. They had stuck to me like limpets since Fairfield and they were now moored next to me, so close that to have got any closer they'd have been sharing my bed. But they were still anxious about their safety. They kept asking me if I was sure – completely sure – that they'd be OK. After all, there was nothing to stop the kids from Fairfield walking up the canal, was there? It wasn't *that* far away, was it? And then there were the kids in Ashton, they'd heard they were even worse…

I reassured them as best I could, but eventually I lost patience with them. You can't convince people there's nothing to worry about when their fears are completely irrational. Nowhere is 100 per cent secure. Nowhere ever can be. But telling them that was no help at all. In their state, they were bound to see the downside of anything I said. Anyway, when I looked an hour or two later, I noticed that they'd gone.

They're probably still cruising about even now looking for that completely safe mooring. Like the *Flying Dutchman*, condemned never to find peace.

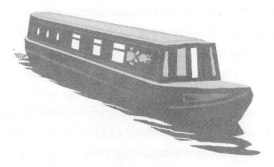

Eleven

So why do it? Why cruise into the centre of cities through some of their worst areas? Why risk the crime and the vandalism, even if your chances of experiencing it are low? What sort of narrowboat dream is that? What sort of dream of any sort is it?

I was in a pub with a bloke once. Regular kind of guy, I remember. Worked for some food company in Hounslow or somewhere like that in their distribution depot, I seem to recall. He couldn't understand it. As far as he was concerned, if he was spending a shedful of money on a boat, then he'd want it in the middle of the Cotswolds or the Yorkshire Dales. Somewhere where the sky was blue and the grass was green and the sun shone all the time.

He wanted Teletubbyland, that's what he wanted. He wanted a world of big hugs and wide smiles where the birds sang constantly and the lambs gambolled in the fields and never grew up to be Sunday dinner. But canals aren't like that – they never were. They were built as industrial arteries to carry goods from one place to another. They were a key part of a national economy based on manufacturing. It's us – now – today – who've idealised them and made them into Disneyworld UK. We've done a lot of this sort of thing recently with our past, taking our history and making heritage of it, reducing it to a series of folk tales and emasculated adventure stories. Fine, as far as it goes. It sells to the tourists better this way, that's for sure. But we shouldn't lose touch with the way it really was. Sanitising the past for others, we run the risk of deceiving ourselves.

Besides, it's better with a bit of contrast, isn't it? A dusting of bitter chocolate on the sugared cream. A squeeze of lemon on the strawberries. Are we frightened of reality, for God's sake?

Canals in towns give you a unique glimpse of a vanished world. They wind through desolate industrial suburbs and plough across bleak urban wastelands blown by litter, the last remnant of that world of manufacturing which was so familiar to our grandparents and to their grandparents before them. Just outside Stoke, the Trent and Mersey Canal used to pass through a steelworks – through the very middle of it. If you were on a boat late in the evening as Em and I were once, you were so close to the process you could feel the heat from the rolling mills, and see the sparks shooting off like fireworks, and feel the din echoing through your head. It was like something out of Dante's *Inferno*. In those days, in any town in the country worth its name, there'd be a row of busy factories adjoining the canal and as you passed you'd hear a cacophony of sounds from the different machines inside. Gradually though, the machines became silent and one by one the factories disappeared. Once, passing through Birmingham with my brother, we were held up while a demolition gang blew one of them up in front of our very eyes, bricks literally showering around us in the explosion, peppering the water. The last thing they expected was a boat to come along. It was so rare they hadn't made any allowances for it.

Somehow – and quite why I'm not certain, seeing that there seems to be so little concrete evidence of it remaining – canals even now manage to retain some essence of this past, something redolent of terraced streets and wet cobblestones, of mill workers in their clogs clattering home in the gloom of a winter's evening thick with the smoke of coal fires. Travelling along them, especially on one of those rainy autumn days when there's no one else around and clouds lie like a pall on the world, you experience something unique, as if you've gone back in time to another world, one abandoned by the present. It is – still – just – a secret world, a hidden world, a sanctuary from the city in the very heart of the city itself. Yes, they may sometimes be bleak and intimidating, and in places vaguely menacing, but urban canals draw you to them in an odd and compelling way, as you might be attracted to a derelict house, or an overgrown wood. Exploring them is like turning over the stones of hidden history. You can never be certain what you might find. You can never quite know what you might stumble across.

Though if you stumble across anything on the towpath of an urban canal these days, it's most likely to be one of the many signs for a heritage trail which local councils are putting up all over the place as a way of opening up city canals up for walkers and cyclists. Don't get me wrong, I have nothing against this more democratic use of public space. Nowadays canals in cities are more like linear parks where you can take the dog for a walk or go for an afternoon stroll. They're being promoted as corridors for wildlife too so that in some places you're as likely as in the countryside to see a heron standing sentinel on the bank, feeding in the early evening; or a kingfisher exploding in a burst of sapphire and orange as it flashes through the reeds.

But this has meant they've begun to lose their special appeal to old farts like me for whom they're an intrinsic part of childhood memory. They're becoming prettified, the towpath not just lined with new developments, but itself spruced up with posh paving, new banking and street lights to improve security. In Birmingham, around Brindley Place, it's peppered with clubs, bars and restaurants, a sort of a canalside theme park for the prosperous young. In Camden, north London, the towpath's become an adjunct to the bustling market there, so busy as a thoroughfare that they've had to lay down rumble strips and paint road markings to control the number of cyclists using it as an alternative to the city's treacherous roads. It makes life difficult for pedestrians, let alone boaters; and because London cyclists are merely two-wheeled versions of their aggressive four-wheeled cousins, it can only be a matter of time before some poor unfortunate finds himself unceremoniously bundled into the canal, or worse, splayed out across a set of racing handlebars going backwards very fast.

New Islington isn't the shape of things to come: it's a reflection of the way things already are all over the country. From Liverpool to Leeds, Bristol to Glasgow. Wherever you go it's the same. Everywhere is change. Everywhere

CHAPTER ELEVEN

the marketing of the waterside as a new Eden. Canals have become flavour of the month, the backdrop of choice for the iPod generation. Now everyone who's affluent aspires to loft-living, a waterside view the height of urban chic. The apartment blocks rise inexorably like so many phoenixes from the rubble of our industrial past. Apartments, you'll notice, not flats. A new transatlanguage for a new future.

Of course, it had to happen and in many ways I'm pleased it has. But all the same, I can't help missing the old days. I can't help missing the pang of apprehension I used to feel in towns and cities as I penetrated their dark hearts. Now, despite what the namby-pambys say about the Ashton, most urban canals are disappointingly tame, their reputation based more on what they used to be than what they are now, like an ageing rocker with arthritis fondly recalling some Bank Holiday dust-up on Brighton beach.

If you look at a map of the Huddersfield Narrow Canal you see that it doesn't really get into the proper countryside until it passes beyond Mossley, and even then it's not truly rural until it hits Yorkshire. Instead, it winds through the hills, threading around Wild Bank, Harridge Pike, Buckton Castle, Alphin Pike and Saddleworth Moor. In places it's actually a rather suburban canal, passing through places like Ashton-under-Lyne and Stalybridge which nestle in the valleys below.

But it doesn't *feel* like a suburban canal.

For anyone used to cruising the flat Midlands plains, this is a very different sort of waterway. From the moment you pass under the unprepossessing portal of Whitelands Bridge and go through Whitelands 'tunnel' (which is a misnomer if ever there was one since the top's been taken off it and it's more like a shallow gully) you're treated to regular tantalising glimpses of hills rising in the countryside ahead. It's this that makes it so different. Even in Ashton, where the town crowds the canal, you feel an unusual sense of space and scale. The hills suddenly appear between old mill buildings, which makes make you feel insignificant; and the canal climbing doggedly upwards seems determined to fly off into the Pennines like a bird taking wing. It lifted my spirits. After the disheartening ascent up the Ashton Canal, I felt invigorated, ready for a new sort of challenge.

It was just as well I did since, like it or lump it, a challenge was what I was going to get. The year was 2002. After a closure of nearly sixty years the canal had only reopened the previous year after a long and costly restoration. There were bound to be teething troubles. Already I'd heard on the towpath telegraph that water supplies were proving to be problematic and that this was having a severe effect on depth. For *Justice* this would make the going difficult. She has a draft of three foot and even on some of the main cruising routes in the South progress can be arduous. On the Huddersfield Narrow Canal I expected to be dredging the bottom most of the time.

But it was no use belly-aching; I knew what I was in for. Getting the canal open at all had been the priority of the restoration, not digging it out for boats like mine which are ballasted to make them look pretty rather than for any practical purpose. I knew getting across was going to be a struggle. Getting across on my own would make it doubly hard. But I was ready for that.

What I wasn't ready for – what hadn't really struck me until my first morning on it – was the nature of the canal itself. The canal? That's another misnomer like the Whitelands 'tunnel'. The HNC isn't so much a canal as two lock-flights separated in the middle by this pig of a tunnel. Two very long lock-flights actually – each of them stretching about ten miles, one going up and the other down. No sooner do you get through one lock than there's another to be negotiated. And then another. And another after that until after a couple of hours every muscle in your body is screaming in protest at the effort of it. That first morning was relatively easy in the sense that I only had to negotiate half a dozen or so in the mile to Stalybridge. But each of them was a challenge. On each, the paddle gear – the mechanism which allows you to release the water, and open and close the locks gates – was jammed solid. Getting them to work was like trying to jemmy open a rusty safe. It took me into hernia territory.

The new locks where the paddle gear was pristine, still painted in red oxide from the foundry, were the worst. At least with the older gear I knew – theoretically – that it was capable of working simply because it had worked in the past. This brand new equipment really hadn't been tested and I didn't have much confidence in it. Some of it I could only move by clouting it with a lump hammer. The new gates were no better. They seemed to have been concreted into the canal bed.

The only easy section of cruising the whole morning was a stretch on the approach to Stalybridge itself where the canal crosses over the River Tame on a short cast-iron aqueduct. This was the earliest of this sort of aqueduct built on the canals, and it replaced an original stone structure damaged by floods in 1800. Crossing it proved too much for *Justice*.

Halfway across she just stopped dead, her engine giving out without warning, a pathetic wisp of black smoke rising from her exhaust stack the only sign that something was amiss, like the silent last breath of a dying man.

I knew immediately what the problem was. Coming up the pound she'd been dragging the bottom and I'd had to use more and more power to make any headway at all. When the engine finally decided to give up the ghost, it was screaming like a jet plane, a classic sign of a fouled propeller. Though I knew I was blocking the canal I hadn't seen another boat all day, so I didn't think I'd be much of an obstruction to anyone. I disappeared into the weed hatch without giving the prospect a second thought.

It was sod's law that just a few minutes later a small rowing boat should appear from out of nowhere, followed soon afterwards by three canoeists travelling in the opposite direction. I extracted myself from the weed hatch somewhat sheepishly – though everyone was very good-natured about my predicament and mucked in to help me move the boat out of the way. But we couldn't shift her. Not an inch. She had somehow got jammed in the trough of the aqueduct and it was clear that however much we hauled on the ropes, there'd be no budging her without engine power. Once again I climbed down into the weed hatch.

Meanwhile, a small crowd gathered on the towpath. The first to arrive was a teenager with a pair of hissing earphones round his neck and a couple of impatient mongrels snapping at his heels. Soon he was joined by three old blokes who could have been understudies for *Last of the Summer Wine*; and after that by a couple of fishermen wheeling their kit up the towpath in a shopping trolley. They all watched intrigued as I emerged some minutes later with a twisted rope of old clothes which had wound itself around my propeller and which I deposited in a heap at their feet.

By now I'd identified the root cause of the problem: a sheet of builders' plastic that had wound itself around the hull like clingfilm. I delved around the waterline and managed to find the end of it, after which I enlisted everyone to help pull it off, a job that must have taken us a full half an hour to complete. Afterwards the canoeists and the man in the rowing boat set off up the canal again and the fishermen wandered up the towpath, chatting as they went with the three old blokes who had started grumbling about something or another, probably me. Eventually just the lad with the dogs remained. He stood, sound still sibilating uselessly from his earphones, surveying with some satisfaction the billowing mound of plastic we'd extracted from the water.

Then, half-turning, he looked me in the eye and pointed both his forefingers at me as if he were aiming a pair of imaginary pistols at my heart. 'Twenty-four carat,' he said cheerfully. 'What do you reckon? Textbook, eh?'

'Textbook?' I said. 'What textbook?'

'Not any particular textbook,' he replied. 'Just textbook generally – the job – you know? Pulling all this crap out the water. Where have you come from anyway?' he asked.

I told him.

'Back of the net,' he exclaimed. 'And where you going?'

I told him that too.

'Bumper,' he announced, 'Staying in Stalybridge tonight?'

'Maybe.'

'Annual edition,' he proclaimed. 'Opposite Tesco?'

'Possibly.'

'Grade One listed,' he declared, giving me the two-finger pistol treatment once more.

His dogs started whimpering in frustration. I could see their point. I felt like screaming for the same reason. This was life, Jim, but not as we know it.

'Tesco's is Grade One listed?' I asked.

'No, the moorings opposite.'

'*They're* Grade One listed?'

'No, not Grade One listed,' he explained patiently, 'Not literally Grade One listed. Just – you know – just Grade One listed.'

I started the engine again. Thank God it fired first time. 'Thanks for all your help,' I said.

'Catch you later,' he replied

And that should have been the end of that, except that without me being able to stop myself, and without me really knowing why I was doing it, I suddenly found myself giving him the same two-fingered shooting salute he'd been giving me. I could have curled up in embarrassment at myself. I wanted the towpath to open and swallow me up. Yet that wasn't the end of it. As the boat moved off I discovered myself shouting something to him. Again, I've no idea what compelled me to do it.

'Top of the class,' I said.

For an instant or two he seemed taken aback, as if he couldn't make up his mind what I was getting at. Then he smiled and did the pointing/shooting thing again.

'Now you're talking,' he said.

Which I suppose I had been.
Well, sort of.

There are a few things you need to know about the Huddersfield Narrow Canal:

1. It was completed in 1811 after taking seventeen years to build.
2. It was a mad project. Constructing it meant building seventy-four locks; untold numbers of bridges, aqueducts and culverts; and two tunnels, one of which was the longest, deepest and highest ever built in Britain.
3. It was abandoned in 1944. This was nuts too. We were on the verge of winning the war, on the threshold of a new leisure age in which people would value canals for the recreation they afforded.

There's one other thing you should know:

In 1972 a group of people came together to form a society with the intention of restoring the canal. They were bonkers too, every last one of them. The idea of restoring this waterway, which was by now totally derelict and partly built over, was more irrational than building the canal in the first place and more irrational than closing it. At least those decisions were justified on their own economic grounds. The idea of reopening it again was just naive optimism. It was crazy.

You want to know how crazy? Then consider this:

Two years after its inauguration, and with just £40 in its coffers, the Huddersfield Canal Society concluded the restoration would cost £19 million. It was a colossal job. It involved rehabilitating every single lock on the canal, including hacking out many of them which had been filled with concrete. It meant digging out and restoring the overgrown channel, and reinstating mile upon mile of derelict towpath. It entailed somehow getting into Huddersfield, where factories had been built over the course of the canal, and somehow getting through Slaithwaite and Stalybridge, where it had all but disappeared...

If that doesn't count as crazy, then I don't know what does.

The Stalybridge problem was almost intractable. Pictures of the town taken before the restoration show the scale of what had to be done. There was barely any sign that there'd ever been a canal through the place. Most of its original course was now a car park, and further along, a sports centre and a couple of factories had been built on top of where it had been.

And yet, here I was thirty years later navigating a boat into Armentières Square, the very centre of the town, through locks that had been specially built, and along a completely new channel which had been expressly constructed for the purpose. It was incredible. Incredible that I was doing it, yes. But more incredible was that such a small group of crackpots could succeed in bringing this sort of project to completion. Just thinking about it made me proud to be British. The restoration was a testament to our pig-headed determination which is a national characteristic and should be lauded the world over. Especially the determination of canal restoration enthusiasts who sometimes seems a different breed to us ordinary mortals.

I pulled up at the Grade One moorings opposite Tesco. It was a blustery August day but a bit of breeze isn't the sort of thing that deters folk in these parts from getting out and about. The town was bustling with people, shopping and talking or having a pint or a cup of tea in the cafés and bars which now surround the square – a place where the canal has become a new focus. With the canal so recently opened, the passage of any boat was still unusual enough to attract attention, but the passage of one proclaiming on its livery that it was from a place so far away – and so exotic – as Banbury excited particular attention; and I found myself surrounded by curious onlookers who bombarded me with questions about my journey. This was typical of the HNC. Everywhere I went I'd find this same inquisitiveness about the canal which, when you probed it, was a form of possessiveness, a fierce and partisan pride in what I think was just beginning to dawn on local people was an astonishing achievement.

How did I feel about the restoration, people wanted to know? Had I come here specially to see it? What route had I followed? People could scarcely believe you could get from Banbury to Stalybridge entirely by canal. One whale of a woman, in a dress like a circus tent, was convinced I must have craned the boat out at one stage; and when I continued to insist that I'd travelled every mile by water, she tossed her head dismissively and harrumphed off with the same scepticism she'd have displayed if I'd told her that I'd flown in that morning from the moon.

There was, however, some confusion about where precisely Banbury actually was, and I found this intriguing. 'Banbury? Isn't that near Bristol?' someone asked me. 'No, don't be stupid,' her friend said. 'It's near Gloucester.' This wasn't an unusual response and I'm sure I'd have got something similar from folk in Banbury if I'd have asked them about Stalybridge. But it was a measure of how far I'd come. A small but significant indication of the divide that exists between the two worlds of the North and South.

That night I decided to stay out of town. It was a mistake. On the far side of Stalybridge the canal got increasingly shallow and the going got slower and slower as a result. Eventually, as dusk descended I realised I was on a hiding to nothing and I attempted to moor. But I couldn't get close to the bank and was forced to go on looking for somewhere – anywhere! – that I could stop. At length it got dark. The maps told me I was only a mile or so from a pub where I was hoping there'd be a deep wharf, so I limped on through the sombre nightfall, leaving *Justice* to find her own path through whatever water she could find, barely touching the tiller for fear I'd steer her onto a mudbank. Finally, with the sound of gravel grating on her bottom plate, she ground to a halt in the middle of the channel.

Exhausted by her efforts, she could go no further. There was no more water. She was grounded, completely stuck.

How it was going to be possible to proceed the next morning, I didn't know. But by this stage I didn't care either. It was after midnight and I was dog-tired. I'd had it up to here with the day. The problems could wait. I turned off the engine and dropped into bed.

But it was a restless night. I kept dreaming of boats appearing from out of nowhere to find me blocking their way and of endless coils of plastic spewing from the canal, wrapping around me like a cocoon until I couldn't breathe.

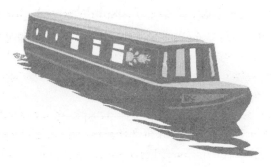

Twelve

E m rang the next morning from the train on her way to work. She was worried she hadn't heard from me.

'Whereabouts are you?' she asked.

Until she'd called I'd been sound asleep. I rubbed my eyes blearily and wiped the condensation from the bedroom porthole.

What I saw was puzzling.

'I, erm… I seem to be moored in the middle of the canal,' I said.

'In the middle of the canal? That's novel. Did you just get bored with the sides or something?'

'How very amusing you can be sometimes,' I said. Consciousness was beginning to dawn, and with it a fractured memory of events of the previous evening which I was starting to piece together. I'd finally remembered why I was in this predicament.

'I got stuck,' I explained. 'There was no water. I couldn't go on.'

This information didn't seem to interest Em much. She seemed distracted. Mind you, she was distracted a lot around this time. It was probably something to do with me spending the summer away cruising through attractive parts of Britain while she was left going into work every morning. I'd be distracted in her position; anyone would.

My way of dealing with it was to talk about what I was doing as if it was an onerous task that no one in his right mind would undertake willingly. I started to do that now. I became negative about the journey and described my trip from Ashton in harrowing terms, injecting into my story accounts of such a martyrish struggle against the odds that she could have been forgiven for thinking I was Humphrey Bogart and *Justice* the *African Queen*.

But the problem was, as we both knew, I'd written Katharine Hepburn out of the script.

'I don't know what I'm going to do now,' I said finally, playing the sympathy card for all it was worth. 'The way things are, I can't see myself getting to Huddersfield this year, let alone this week.'

The silence before she replied was the first hint I had that I'd hit the wrong note. But Em always delivers her best lines quietly. Not for her the histrionics of the over-emotional; not for her the rantings of the impassioned.

She said simply, 'I'm going to have to go now. I'll call you again later. I think something might be happening.'

'Happening? What do you mean happening?'

'Well, I'm a bit stuck myself,' she explained with eloquent understatement. 'The train broke down, you see. I've been outside London Bridge for almost two hours now. Jammed into a filthy carriage covered in graffiti. With a rather large number of obese men with BO attempting to grope me whenever they get bored with their newspapers.'

'Poor Em,' I said. 'It sounds dreadful.'

'Yes, it is. Particularly as there doesn't seem to be very much in the papers today. Anyhow,' she said, brightening up, 'someone's coming to rescue us now. We should all be out of here soon...'

I could see the point she was making – who wouldn't? I might be in a bit of a pickle myself, but I was at least in rural Lancashire heading into the deepest Pennines. Around me it was a rural idyll, the canal lined by pale pink Himalayan balsam and framed by trees, the purple heather-covered hills rising in the near distance. I guess if Em was in any sort of position to be able to see outside the windows of the carriage in which she was trapped the best she'd manage was the sight of another train held up at this infamous bottleneck on the south London suburban lines. Or perhaps she'd be lucky. Perhaps she'd be further up the track and be able to see the old Sarsons' vinegar factory in Bermondsey.

I dressed quickly and went outside. It was a dank, drizzly morning, but even so there was a freshness in the air which was invigorating after all this talk of London. The canal was unusually quiet, though, as it had been for a large part of the previous day. Normally on waterways – any waterway, whatever the weather – there's a constant stream of dog walkers or fishermen or joggers passing the time of day. Here there was no one. It was completely deserted, not another human being to be seen. I was beginning to wonder if I'd made a big mistake. Perhaps I'd got my dates wrong and the canal wasn't open after all.

Being alone like this put me in a vulnerable position. It meant that I couldn't rely on anyone else for help, so in this predicament it was important I kept my head and didn't do anything which would make matters worse. I was well and truly stranded, that much was clear. But how badly stranded? From what I could make out I seemed to be wedged against some sort of shoal or mudbank. I needed to apply enough power to get me over this obstacle, but not so much that I'd dig myself in if it proved insurmountable. Cautiously I started the engine and engaged gear, edging the boat gently forward in the hope that the depth might have improved overnight. Sometimes this happens on canals. Sometimes water runs off the summit and leaks through lock gates to flood the lower pounds. Not this time though. If anything, the reverse had happened and water had drained *from* this pound to the one below. If anything, I was in a worse position than I had been the previous night.

Gradually I increased the engine revs, sending a thick plume of acrid exhaust fumes floating off down the canal. This had the effect of churning up a lot of water and causing a lot of mud to swirl around, but it did nothing to move *Justice*. The weather was getting worse, which didn't help matters either. By now the light drizzle I'd woken to had become a steady downpour. Foolishly, because I'd been keen to get going, I hadn't bothered putting on a proper coat and I was already soaked. I hadn't put on a hat either so my hair hung across my face, lank and dripping.

The irony of being unable to move because of lack of water, while at the same time being relentlessly dumped on by the stuff, did not escape me. Nor, as I felt the first dribble of it down the back of my neck, did it make me feel any better about myself or the world.

The only thing going my way was that the stern of the boat – the serious bit with the propeller attached to it – was at least in the water. This was fortuitous. When your propeller is not in the water and is pushing air, it's not just a matter of not being able to go where you want but of not being able to go anywhere. As things stood I could at least activate Plan B – though Plan B was not exactly what you'd call a sophisticated stratagem. It was not one of those manoeuvres born of years of canal experience, not one of those bits of cunning navigational subtlety that would get bystanders gasping in admiration if there'd been any bystanders around to see it.

It basically consisted of trying to reverse the boat to see if there was another way round the obstruction.

This time I opened the throttle with more confidence. At first the boat shuddered and then she shook a bit as if stretching herself lazily after a nap on some sun-kissed tropical beach. Finally, and very gently, she began to edge backwards, inch by inch. Eventually she moved far enough in reverse for me to risk taking her forward again, steering another course, this time a little to the right of where I'd been before. It was all going, well, swimmingly I guess you might say, when I heard a sound I was familiar with from the previous evening. It was the boat grinding to a halt on the canal bed.

Again I reversed and again I edged her forward on a different line.

Seven or eight times I must have done this – maybe more. Until I began to lose hope that I would ever get through. Until

I started to believe it was impossible to navigate this canal with a boat as deep as *Justice*. Until I began to think I hadn't been exaggerating to Em and that not only would I never get to Huddersfield but that I'd have to abort the whole trip here and now.

But just then, on the umpteenth attempt, when my expectation was at its lowest, I felt *Justice* slide effortlessly over the obstruction as if it hadn't been there at all and I'd just been making a big fuss about nothing. Immediately, as if to celebrate my success, the clouds parted like a curtain and the sun came out, the temperature rising until I was soon basking in the heat of a Mediterranean morning...

Well, no, I made that last bit up about the sun. This was Lancashire, after all, these were the Pennines, the spiritual home of rainwater. But all the same it felt good to be on the move again, very good indeed.

Once beyond this stoppage the going got easier, though there were always the locks, the infernal, incessant locks, one after another, and another after that, and another yet. They're relentless. There's barely a spot on the whole of the Huddersfield Narrow Canal where, going through one lock, you can't see another one ahead of you, giving you the finger, like some bloke in a pub who thinks you've been looking at him a bit oddly and wants a ruck. It could be dispiriting except that after a while you get into the routine of it and you shrug off even the difficult ones, enjoying them as much for the challenge they pose as the wonderful countryside in which they lie. And it is wonderful countryside around here: not twee or pretty;

not wilderness; but hard, functional and utilitarian, a landscape of swelling hills tipped by dark moorlands and threaded with rows of stout grey houses built of stone to withstand proper weather, not that mollycoddling stuff they call weather south of the Trent.

I went through the short Scout Tunnel and a couple of locks later reached the outskirts of Mossley where the spire of St John's Church in Roughtown towers over the canal. Oddly, Roughtown used to be in Yorkshire until 1885 when it was incorporated into Lancashire. In 1974, the part of Mossley through which the canal runs, which used to be in Cheshire, became part of Tameside Metropolitan Council. No doubt this bit of bureaucratic paperwork tidied up what was an administrative anachronism, but in my old-fashioned way I can't help regretting it happened.

Mossley, with its steep streets and characteristic stone houses, once used to pride itself on the fact that it was split like this between counties: the peculiarity of the arrangement was part of its identity, part of what made it what it was. Something similar characterised Shepshed, the small village in Leicestershire where my family hails from, which once used to exalt in the fact it was the largest village in the country. I'm not sure that this was ever actually true, but the matter was settled finally when some government report or another defined what a village was, and whatever it was, it didn't include Shepshed which, as a result, lost the very thing that made it special to itself. Perhaps it had to happen. Perhaps the modern world demands that the concept of a village is clarified, as it demands of Mossley that its administrative boundaries be more rational.

Me, I remain unconvinced. Idiosyncrasies like this, insignificant and probably meaningless claims to the exceptional, mark out places and distinguish them. They become part of the character of towns and villages and taking them away – reducing everything to homogenous blandness – may make some penpusher's life easier but it destroys an essential part of the relationship people have to the place they live. And it is this relationship which roots people to their home; it is what *makes* a place home. Redefining the relationship can destroy those roots in the same way as replacing the soil around a plant can kill it.

Being idiosyncratic was once part of what being English was. We dressed idiosyncratically in funny bowler hats and strange flat caps, we spoke idiosyncratically with vowel sounds like strangled birds, we had bizarre idiosyncratic customs like queuing for buses which the rest of the world couldn't understand, and an idiosyncratic system of government that bequeathed power to people for no better reason than that some ancestor of theirs had once slept with a king. We were an island race, yes, and proud of our isolation from other nations. But more importantly, we were a country of regions, as proud of our isolation from each other. This allowed our institutions to grow around us organically, developing in their own particular way rather than being engineered centrally which is what countries like France did, believing somehow that they could marshal the human spirit by an edict from Paris.

And oh, how we mocked those foreigners for it, how we laughed at them for their hubris. Nowadays, of course, the smile is on the other side of our face because we're all in the same European boat. Today we're all modern. We all wear the same mass-produced clothes and eat the same mass-produced food and enjoy the same mass-produced entertainment. And all our county boundaries are tidy and organised; all our villages counted and categorised to the last detail.

Why can't I help but feel we're poorer for it?

Beyond the magnificent old cotton mill at Woodend, and its single massive chimney like a mountain obelisk, I stopped at the Roaches Lock Inn for a pint in the shadow of the splendidly named Noon Sun Hill – though sadly there wasn't much of either noon sun or hill – evident through the murky, remorseless rain. The place lies adjacent to Roaches Lock, the fifteenth lock in the four and a half miles that I'd travelled since Ashton. Four and a half miles? Four and a half miles! It's a distance you could walk comfortably in an hour or so, and yet already it seemed a world away – a classic example of that strange phenomenon of 'canal time' when you only have to step on a narrowboat for the clock to wind back to the eighteenth century and a time when a journey from one small town to another was an arduous trek, the passage from one county to the next as momentous a trip as crossing a continent.

This was the pub I'd hoped to reach the previous night and I felt some sense of achievement actually getting to it, though I'd been warned off the place by some grumpy old sod in Stalybridge who'd advised me not to go there. He said it was always empty at lunchtime, and too full in the evening. Either way, according to him, the place was cold and unwelcoming because the locals wouldn't talk to you unless you'd been born in Mossley and your grandfathers had fought in the war together. The First World War, he meant, not the second.

I can't imagine what experience he'd had in the pub for it to upset him so much. Except that, as I learnt later when I called wanting to check out a detail for this book, no one there ever answers the phone. Perhaps that's why this bloke felt so strongly about the place. Perhaps he'd tried to ring it once too and, like me, got this infuriating recording of a woman telling him that 'this number is not accepting calls at present'. Things like that can send you over the top. Well, they can send me over the top. After all, why have a phone at all except to talk to people? If you don't want to talk to people, then get rid of the phone. That way you won't need an infuriating recording.

I had a decent enough pint there, anyway. And although I've no recollection of the clientele being particularly friendly, they weren't by any means standoffish either. And at least there was a clientele, despite the dire warnings I'd had to the contrary. No, it was outside when things became disagreeable. After I went back to the boat and found this bloke sitting on my front deck, hunched over a fishing rod surveying the water. I surmised he was a fisherman. Call me a smart arse, but it was the rod that gave him away.

'You're on my boat,' I said.

'It's on my fishing spot,' he replied.

To which there was no real reply. Astonished by his audacity I went into the cabin and made myself a sandwich.

Now, I am not one of these boaters who feel an instant antagonism towards fishermen. Far from it. It seems to me that anyone who pursues, as I do, the sort of hobby that involves spending a lot of time on your own in the rain getting freezing cold and soaking wet can't be all bad. Even so, it's fair to say that fishermen can sometimes be cantankerous old buggers. And they are very unpredictable in their mood. One day, you'll nod to them as you're passing and they'll launch into a long conversation about the weather, or the waterways, or the state of American foreign policy in South America, which you know they'll be banging on about long after you've turned the bend and disappeared from sight. Another day, you'll wish one good morning and that'll be enough for him to start pelting you with maggots from those catapults they use.

After my sandwich I said, 'I'm leaving now.'

'Please yourself,' he replied with the sort of curtness that made me think he was a Yorkshireman still not over the shock of finding himself living in Lancashire.

Of course, I could see where he was coming from. It must be frustrating to have fished in a derelict canal for fifty years or so only to wake up one morning to find that it wasn't derelict any more and that your favourite spot was occupied by a sixty-foot chunk of floating steel. Even so, there were limits to my sympathy and this conversation was getting very close to them. Eventually I started the engine and began to untie my ropes.

This seemed to unsettle him.

He said, 'Hey you, what do you think you're doing?'

I said, 'I'm just going, like I said I would.'

'Well, you can't take me with you.'

'No,' I agreed, 'that wouldn't be my preferred option either. Perhaps you should think about getting off. What do you reckon?'

I pulled the boat in again while he disembarked but he was most indignant that he had to. I was accused of ruining his fishing and when it became apparent that this did not greatly trouble me, of destroying the environment and polluting the countryside. I'd probably have been accused of starting the war in Iraq too if I'd stuck around much longer. Frankly I'd had enough.

He'd probably had enough of me too.

As I cruised off up the canal, I heard him fire off a volley of the worst insults he could muster. 'Bloody selfish dickhead,' he said. 'Bloody stuck-up twat. Bloody... bloody... bloody southerner...' he said finally.

Now don't get me wrong, I have nothing against fishermen. I used to be a fisherman myself once. I had a tin Oxo box for my maggots, and an old wicker picnic basket my mum bought me from a jumble sale, ostensibly to carry my kit in. Since I didn't have much kit apart from the maggots, I used it mainly as a seat, one of which I was inordinately proud since in those far-off days every self-respecting fisherman had a wicker basket to sit on.

Not nowadays though. I mean! Have you seen fishermen nowadays? The gear these guys have is worth thousands of pounds. They're all kitted out like professionals with layer after layer of lightweight waterproofs emblazoned in the colours of angling teams none of the rest of us has ever heard of. Team Diawa Dorking. Team Maver Barnsley. Team Kamasan Starlets. These are all genuine. There's even one in Scotland called Team Arctic Monklands.

All their kit is tagged with labels like designer clothes, most of it made by a company called Shakespeare which advertises itself so much on its products you could send a group of fishermen into the auditorium at Stratford-upon-Avon and they wouldn't look out of place. Their tackle-boxes are remarkable. They're made of indestructible moulded plastic, so resilient to misuse, or vandalism, or the elements, that at a push you could probably use them as nuclear bunkers. And as for their capacity, well, on a *Which?* consumer test they'd beat the Tardis hands down. Open them up on one side and there's a series of cantilevered shelves with compartments for hooks and line and bait. On the other side they've got fully fitted kitchens, some of them with a through-lounge.

These guys do not rough it any more, take it from me. They have long since gone past sitting on wicker baskets – which is perhaps understandable since, as I can attest from my own experience, they did have a tendency after a couple of hours to leave an impression on your bum like a garden fence. These days, though, fishermen have purpose-built, fully padded recliner chairs with integral parasol, drinks cabinet and probably underfloor central heating, for all I know. These guys don't just fish from the towpath nowadays; they colonise it. They've so much kit they have to use special all-terrain trolleys to get it into position. Believe me, a group of fishermen walking up the towpath is worse than the Army on manoeuvres.

But it's the rods that have changed most. In my day they used to be modest, unassuming instruments from which much satisfaction could be derived simply by developing the skill to use them properly. That mainly meant learning how to cast your float onto that bit of the water you thought most likely to yield a fish. Today they've dispensed with all that nonsense. Now they use fishing poles which are great fibreglass contraptions twenty or thirty feet long that allow them to place their float in exactly the spot they want to. This is usually in the most inaccessible patch of water on the opposite bank to where they're sitting. As a boater, coming across a stretch of canal where one of them is being used, it's like suddenly being confronted with an old Eastern European border post. If you're unlucky enough to pass a fishing match, then they'll be miles of them, one after the other, like an Olympic steeplechase track.

As you pass they will occasionally be withdrawn across the towpath into the hedge, but more often than not they will be lifted like a reluctant guard of honour, leaving half-drowned maggots dangling so tantalisingly close to your face that you can't help but wonder if the fishermen are hoping you'll bite at them.

They're pretty dangerous things too, these poles, since they conduct electricity. This does not make them the safest of objects in the vicinity of the many electricity lines that criss-cross the waterways; and regrettably there's been more than one example of fishermen frying themselves (though this is perhaps no bad way to go for fish-lovers). Even so, in this world of health and safety obsession, nothing of this sort can be left to itself, and so over the previous few years there have appeared a rash of warning signs to add to the rest of the ugly signage littering the towpath. There are thousands of them aimed at fishermen – millions, it sometimes seems! Jeez, what is it with these guys? They spend large parts of their life peering through the rain for the slightest movement in a tiny float bobbing about in the water. You'd think they'd have eyes like hawks, wouldn't you? Yet they seem congenitally incapable of seeing an electricity pylon twice the size of a house unless there's a sign telling them it's there.

Thirteen

It got shallow again. Very shallow. I went under Division Bridge which used to be the old county boundary between Yorkshire and Lancashire. I crossed Royal George aqueduct which takes the canal over the River Tame. I was hoping to get to Uppermill before the afternoon was out, but after the lock at Royal George Mills it got so bad I could only make headway by using a novel cruising technique which I developed myself and named in my honour as testament to the slog this stretch had become.

I christened it the Steve Haywood Innovative Transit Style on the basis that its acronym would indicate how difficult it was. It came about because it was impossible to control the boat with the tiller. The tiller did nothing at all. It was as useless as a disconnected steering wheel in a car. All it did was make waves in the water. It had no effect whatsoever in determining the direction of the bow of the boat which went wandering around all over the place with a will of its own until finally it ran itself up a shoal similar to the one on which I'd spent the previous night. The only option then was to go through another of those *Come Dancing* routines with the bottom where I had to do that whole forward–backwards, backwards–forwards thing again until I could wriggle free.

It was exhausting. Mentally and physically draining. Eventually I just let the boat go its own way. I set the engine to the gentlest of tick-overs and went to the front with a barge pole which I employed to steer the boat by pushing off from the banks and the bottom. It only worked because there was no other boat on the canal to get in the way, but it did at least work. *Justice* seemed to find her own water and inch by agonising inch, painfully slowly, she edged up the canal. As the day progressed, a few more people appeared on the towpath, but despite the outlandish nature of my progress, I excited remarkably little attention. Either locals were used to idiots sporting a bargepole in the manner of a high-wire artist, or maybe, because the canal had been closed for such a long time, they'd just forgotten what a boat moving properly actually looked like.

One bloke along the way did ask if I was OK and whether I needed help. But he didn't look a well man. He was limping along on crutches with his leg in a splint and one arm cradled in sling. Even if I'd needed a hand, his wouldn't have been the best choice since it would almost certainly have fallen off before he could have done anything useful for me. But I appreciated his offer and I hope he recovered quickly.

Adjacent to one of the suburban gardens bordering the cut, in a place I now know as Friezland, I got involved in another, less amiable exchange with a woman in one of the houses. She'd been washing up or something, gazing out of her kitchen window; but on my appearance she was out of the house faster than a goldfish down a plughole, flapping at me with a brightly coloured tea towel as if she was trying to wave away an irritating wasp.

'Go away! Go away! You're destroying my garden with that pole of yours,' she said.

This was a tiny bit of an exaggeration. After all, I hadn't driven across her garden in a JCB with the bucket down; I hadn't taken a tractor to it and ploughed it up. However, her comment wasn't entirely divorced from the truth. The fact was, the cruising was getting tougher. I kept getting grounded every few yards. Most times I could shift myself by pushing off from the towpath, but sometimes there was no alternative except to work my way along from the other side which, on each attempt, left a pole-shaped hole in the grass of the adjoining garden lawns where they had been allowed to grow down to the waterline.

Unless I lied through my teeth and claimed the holes were nothing to do with me (blaming their existence of some innocently sleeping mole, perhaps? One with a degree in civil engineering which might possibly explain the regularity of its excavations?), there was nothing I could do except to put my hand up, admit liability and throw myself on her mercy. But she wasn't having any of it. There were mutterings about the police and about making complaints to 'the authorities'. There were dark hints about legal proceedings. Eventually she disappeared into the house, only to re-emerge a moment or two afterwards with a notebook into which she carefully inscribed *Justice*'s name and licence details.

Of course, I never heard anything from her again. Despite her threats, I guess she decided on reflection that with all the barristers and solicitors and bureaucracy it would entail, the protracted and expensive business of issuing proceedings against me in the civil courts might just be a tad too much trouble. Perhaps she'd decided that it might be easier after all to tamp a bit of soil into the holes to repair them. Which is what I'd have willingly done for her if she'd given me the opportunity.

Still, the episode taught me a couple of valuable lessons. The first was not to expect much sympathy from anyone making this journey. Even people who were boaters themselves didn't always understand the problems that a solo trip along this canal entailed at this particular time. Even Em didn't understand it, so why should I expect people living adjacent to the canal to have any greater insight? It taught me a bit about English social manners too. It was clear that the woman had flown at me, not for the tiny amount of damage I'd done, but because in doing it I'd invaded her personal space. And personal space is an inviolable right of English life these days. Where once we prided ourselves on our national spirit – which was just another way of saying we were social animals working together for the common good – now it's everyone for themselves. This is as much the case in the North, which was once lauded for its sense of community, as it is in the South where it's always been devil take the hindmost.

Or maybe I'm just making too much of this. Maybe there never was a period when people were just good-hearted, generous souls, selflessly concerned for the welfare of others. Maybe suggesting there was just ages me, betraying me as the sentimentalist I am. Perhaps the woman had just had a bad day. Or perhaps she was naturally just a grumpy old sod and if it she hadn't been having a go at me, it'd have been the postman. At the end of the day, I guess, it's all it's all about people not sociology. You can try and generalise but you're doomed to fail.

I finally got to Uppermill about eight o'clock in the evening, hours later than I'd estimated. As you enter the town from this direction you pass through the portal of High Street Bridge which has been widened to accommodate the main road passing overhead so that it's almost a tunnel in its own right. Emerging into the lock on the other side and coming up into what is virtually the centre of the town was an odd experience after the journey I'd had. In my own mind I'd faced such a struggle to get to this point, such a relentless battle against the odds, that I was disappointed not to find the bunting out for me, or a brass band in the street playing in my honour, or at least the mayor in full regalia waiting in welcome.

Instead, the town seemed completely uninterested in me or my doings. I moored adjacent to Saddleworth Museum, just above the main road which seemed unusually busy after the stillness of the canal. The traffic hurried by without so much as a gesture to my heroic achievement, and in the museum car park a family with a couple of kids unloaded bottles into a recycling bin, indifferent to my existence. In the pubs, too, people went on drinking in the same way they had before I'd appeared; in the restaurants they went on eating. It was incomprehensible. I felt like screaming for attention. I've arrived, I wanted to shout. Now I've got this far, at least come and congratulate me.

Strangest of all was that after a day when I hadn't seen one single boat in either direction, here were two or three moored together as if this were just any old spot in any old town anywhere. But as I soon learnt, Uppermill is the last staging post on the canal before the Standedge tunnel and one of the first feasible places to moor after coming out of it. It's a natural stopping place, and as one of the first sections of the HNC brought back into use, it's wide and deep, and well... normal, the way canals are supposed to be.

On the boat next to me were a young couple who heard me arrive and came out of their boat to help me tie up. Snuffling around the towpath with them was a doubtful creature which, first chance it got, threw itself on me and started having it off with my ankle. It was a narrow-eyed black thing, small and shifty, with a snout like a rat. In fact I was convinced it was a rat, although they claimed it was a toy Manchester terrier. A Manchester terrier? A *toy* Manchester terrier? This had about it the euphemism of a 'Glasgow kiss'. I have heard of criminals selling shorn sheep to the Japanese as poodles; it is only a small step to sell rats as toy terriers. The world is full of wicked people who prey on the feelings of dog-lovers. And there are a lot of people who love dogs on the canal. Even when their dogs don't much look like dogs. Even when – like this one – they aren't really dogs at all.

Whatever its species, I bent down to make friends, the way you do in these situations. But it had my fingers down to the bone before I knew it – which confirmed matters for me since this is exactly what you'd expect of a rat.

'Oh my God, I'm sorry about that, he doesn't usually bite people,' said Prune. 'Can I get you a plaster?'

CHAPTER THIRTEEN

Prune was in his mid-twenties with dreadlocks and a penchant for coarsely knitted rainbow tank-tops. He was a fender maker – which is to say that for a living he travelled around the country on a narrowboat making those rope coils and buttons us canal types use to protect our hulls. Why he was named Prune I never did find out. His wife didn't feel the need to associate herself with dried fruit. She wasn't called Raisin or Currant. She had a perfectly normal name, and preferred to be addressed as Heather.

After first aid had been administered, Prune and Heather and I went for a drink. I was hoping that out of deference to my injuries they'd leave the Rat on the boat, but they seemed to have no control over it, and it trotted along beside us as if it knew it. Once in the bar it immediately developed a fixation on someone else's leg. As far as I was concerned this proved the point once and for all since everyone knows rats are notoriously promiscuous.

The guy whose leg it was eventually kicked it off, but not before it had peed on his shoe.

'Oh my God, I'm sorry about that,' said Prune. 'He doesn't normally do that. Can I get you a tissue?'

We sat in a corner cradling pints around a small table. Prune and Heather were from Rochdale and had been in Uppermill for a few weeks now, both of them looking for work because, although they liked the place, they weren't going to be able to make much of a living from fender-making given the dearth of boats passing.

'Business is dreadful,' they explained. 'There's just not enough water in the cut. No one's coming down here.'

'Is it as bad on the other side?' I asked.

'The other side?'

'The other side of the tunnel. Is it as shallow? Is the going as hard?'

Heather sipped her beer and shook her head morosely as if their passage had been so bad she hadn't yet got over it. 'Worse,' she said, 'much worse. The locks are much harder too. Some of them are dreadful. You can hardly get them to move.'

I bought another drink, even though strictly speaking it wasn't my round. I bought crisps too. I thought nibbling a savoury something would make us all feel better about the world. We got no chance to find out. At the first sound of the packet opening the Rat appeared from nowhere and had them off me, snatching them from my hand in a single, vaulting leap that took it from floor to eye level and back again as if it was bouncing on a trampoline.

'Oh God, I'm really sorry about that,' said Prune. 'He doesn't normally do that. Can I get you another packet?'

Now it was my turn to shake my head. Nothing to do with crisps; I was just amazed. This was one of those Madagascan jumping rats I'd read about. Even its ears were the same shape.

After a few more drinks during which the Rat, thankfully, kept its distance, I made the decision to stay for a few days in Uppermill. It would give me time to recuperate for the next leg of the journey. Besides, the place is one of what are known as the Saddleworth villages and a perfect base from which to explore Saddleworth Moor itself. For outsiders, especially those of a certain age from the South, Saddleworth Moor is still one of the most emotive place names in the country, forever associated with Myra Hindley and Ian Brady, the Moors Murderers as they came to be known. But for locals it's still what it always had been: one of the beauty spots of Yorkshire and a feature of this part of the country. I wasn't going to miss it.

Immediately Prune offered to be my guide. Apparently he and Heather were keen walkers and knew all the routes across the hills. I was sceptical. Prune was one of these slightly built blokes born without hips, let alone the sort of beer belly it had taken me more than fifty years' hard work to develop. There was barely enough weight on him to hold him down in a breeze, and my fear was that up on the hills one good gust would be enough for him to finish up in Sheffield. With Heather my concern was whether she would be able to get to the hills in the first place. She was not a svelte woman. She had a frame designed more to trudge along the lowland valleys than dance ibex-like among the craggy rocks.

My reservations about them weren't quelled the following day when we set out on an expedition together. They were wearing paper-thin trainers and light plasticky jackets as opposed to the hiking boots, walking pole and Norwegian all-weather anorak with which I'd come equipped. OK, the weather forecast hadn't been bad but it was hardly expected to be tropical either. And this, anyhow, was the Pennines. It was bound to rain, wasn't it?

The Rat at least inspired me with more confidence. As they led me uncertainly towards the outskirts of Uppermill, getting lost and having to double back on themselves somewhere around the cemetery, it bounded off in all directions with untrammelled reserves of energy, hinting that it had at least done this sort of thing before. Twenty minutes or so from the canal we hit a public footpath and the route suddenly turned vertical. Or that's how it seemed to me. For all my designer gear I was soon an oozing ball of sweat, gasping for air, shown up as the lazy metropolitan slob I was. The same one I still am, as it happens. Heather and Prune, however, were in their element. They were gambolling upwards in paroxysms of rapturous joy, occasionally bursting into a chorus of 'The Hills are Alive' as if to underline how much they were killing me.

The Rat, too, was suffering in a way that made me feel almost sympathetic to it. After its first wild cavortings, it had tired itself out and was now trudging upwards behind me, following in my footsteps with the sort of expression that made you understand where the word 'hangdog' came from. When I paused for a breather, it paused too. And when I stopped for a drink from the bottle of water I was carrying in my rucksack, it looked at me with such beseeching eyes that I couldn't be such a bastard as not to share it. Even though it meant using my hand as a bowl while it drank from my palm. Even though it meant giving it a second chance at my fingers.

Way above me, I saw Prune and Heather emerge onto the crest near an obelisk-shaped war memorial, part of the hill which is known hereabouts as Pots and Pans. They waved at me and began shouting for the Rat to come to them. But rats don't run about at everyone's beck and call. To do that would be to concede to the idea that they are owned by human beings – an idea which is totally alien to them. At first it showed a sort of willing by spurting ahead for a few yards; but then it stopped, defeated by the gradient, and fell back to its position behind me panting like an asthmatic in a dust storm. Finally it collapsed into the shady crevice of a rock, where it stubbornly refused to move.

Nothing I was able to do could get it to its feet again and eventually I had no choice but to tuck it under my arm and carry it the rest of the way up the slope. Well, I wasn't going to wait for it, was I? And I couldn't just leave it. I felt somehow responsible.

On the top I caught up with Heather and Prune and we walked the short distance across the summit on a meandering path which led us to Alderman's Hill. Meanwhile the Rat had miraculously revitalised and was running about madly in ever decreasing circles, determined to wear itself out once more. The view from here would have been remarkable in poor weather, but since walking it had turned glorious and the grim clouds of the morning, which to my untutored eye promised rain, had melted away to reveal a clear blue stretching to the horizon. The light now was as sharp as the edge of a broken bottle. A range of great hills stretch in a plateau from Broadstone in the north across Saddleworth Moor to Alphin Pike in the south. At points it is cut by the valleys – or cloughs as they're called round here – of Ashway Gap and Chew Brook where tiny watercourses feed into a series of huge reservoirs, the two largest of which, Dovestone and Yeoman Hey, are like English versions of Italy's northern lakes, sparkling and glinting in the sunshine as if they'd been scattered with sugar.

We gazed at it for while; even the Rat seemed to pause its frolicking in wonderment. That's when I became aware for the first time of other people around us. And other dogs too. At least a dozen of each, all of them appearing as if from nowhere. And all of them – not the dogs, of course; don't be ridiculous! – were dressed in the same sort of informal clothing that Heather and Prune were wearing. The sort of stuff you might put on if you were just popping round the corner: slacks and cardies, sleeveless jackets and flowery dresses, tracksuits and shorts. One woman – believe me, this is true – was even wearing a pair of fluffy mules. Not pink fluffy mules, I grant you. But mules all the same. Raised-heel slip-ons with a sort of furry bit round the top. How she could have got up the hill in them I'll never know. But how most of the people could have got up it in the footwear they were wearing I'll never know either, since most of them were in stuff equally ill-equipped for the job. Sandals or flip flops or soft-soled loafers of the sort you'd think wouldn't get you across a decent road, let alone up a sizeable slab of the Pennines.

That's when it began to occur to me that perhaps they weren't as underdressed as I thought. Perhaps the problem was me. Maybe I was *over*dressed. People who live in these sorts of landscapes have a natural sense of the climate in a way that those of us who live in other places don't. They don't rely too much on weather forecasts, that's for sure, judging these things by the small clues they've learnt to read in the world about them which we call instinct. I suppose I'd done the same sort of thing when I'd identified them as looking like people who'd just popped round the corner. That was because most of them *had* just popped round the corner. They were locals and this much-loved beauty spot was where many of them came to stretch their legs.

I climbed up to Pots and Pans on three or four occasions while I was staying in Uppermill, and every time the weather was different. Yet whatever the conditions, the locals I found there were invariably dressed in the appropriate clothes, a process that seemed to happen by magic. It wasn't a trick I could have pulled off. And though I knew I was making myself stand out as a foreigner, I was loath to dispense with my gear on the basis that once I did the weather would turn nasty and I'd be left depending on the mountain rescue team to get me back to the boat.

It did turn bad one afternoon I was out. A storm blew up from nowhere as I was walking over Tooleyshaw Moor. Or at least I thought it was Tooleyshaw Moor though after an hour of driving rain I didn't know where I was, being barely able to see my hand in front of my face. It would have been difficult enough on my own but I had the Rat with me after Heather and Prune, desperate for a break from him, had bribed me with the promise of beer to take him for a walk. Of course, the minute he felt the rain on his head, he did his usual trick and stopped walking altogether so I had carry him. It was at that point, with him under my left arm, a sodden map in my right hand, and rain running down the back of my neck, that my brother rang.

My brother rarely finds good times to call, but this was one of the worst. Mind you, what could he have done? There's never a good time for news of the sort he had to impart.

'It's Mum,' he explained. 'She's had a fall. They've taken her to hospital.'

Fourteen

You always have to wake up afterwards, that's the problem with dreams. Especially when they're good dreams and you're lost in them. Especially when they're the type of dream that's taken you out of yourself, away from the real world to one where's there's no pain or suffering and where everyone you meet is young and healthy and has a smile for you. But a man can't live in dreamland for ever. There are other worlds beyond the bedpost. And there are worlds beyond the towpath too: altogether harsher places where playtime has to stop, and where the game suddenly isn't a game any more.

I got a train to the Midlands from Piccadilly station in Manchester and that evening I was at her bedside trying to pacify her as she demanded to be discharged immediately. I hadn't expected this. When my brother had telephoned she'd only just been found on the kitchen floor, unconscious, in a coma, call it what you will. Now, miraculously, she was her normal stubborn self, obstreperously demanding that we bring her cups of tea, or grapes which she fancied, or a fresh nightie from home to replace the one the hospital had given her.

'I can't understand it,' Jay said. 'When she was first admitted, she was totally out of it. The doctors thought she might have had a stroke or something.'

'What do they think now?'

'They're going to do tests. That's why they want to keep her in overnight. As things stand, they haven't got the first idea. But that's what you'd expect, isn't it? We like to believe the medicos have got all the answers but nine times out of ten they're stumbling around as blindly as the rest of us.'

It was a Friday and the following day Em drove up from London. After we'd been to the hospital we went for a walk in Bradgate Park, the 850-acre estate north of Leicester which was the birthplace of Lady Jane Grey, the 'Nine Days Queen', who got caught in the machinations of Tudor politics and paid for it on the scaffold at the tragically young age of sixteen. Today the house lies in ruins, a moody reminder of the transitory nature of life and ambition. But it's a great place to blow away the cobwebs when you've things on your mind, a much kinder and gentler landscape than the one I'd been travelling through on the boat.

We climbed the rocky, bracken-lined path to Old John, a granite-built folly shaped like a great beer mug which stands on the top of the highest hill in the park and commands a spectacular view over the county. It was erected in the late eighteenth century to commemorate a loyal retainer of the Grey family which by that time — notwithstanding the execution of an ancestor on a charge of treason — had risen to become Earls of Stamford. I was brought up in a small village very close to here and I grew up somehow absorbing the history of the thing although I can't ever remember anyone sitting me down and telling me about it.

The folly is believed locally to have been put up following a dreadful accident at a party to celebrate the coming of age of one of the earls. The story goes that a bonfire had been built on the summit around the trunk of an old pine tree which, in the middle of the drunken reveries, burnt through, falling on Old John and killing him outright. This was terrific stuff for a local kid with an over-fertile imagination. I used to stand at the spot fantasising what it must have been like as the tree gradually began topple. I pictured it disturbing the bonfire so that it flared up, throwing flaming fragments of burning timber into the dark night sky. I could visualise the screams of the women and the cries of alarm there must have been as people finally realised the tree was falling, and scrabbled to get out of its way. I could almost hear the fear-inducing sound it must have made as it finally cracked and gave. My impressions were so vivid that even now I can fancy I was actually at the event myself. I'd certainly convinced myself by the age of eight that the tree landed directly on Old John's head. I liked to picture the splintered bone and the gore this would have involved. Kids are funny that way, aren't they?

The monument built afterwards by the remorseful earl is a pointless edifice, good for nothing except looking at, and not even that really since it's not what you'd call an elegant or beautiful structure. Yet it's an icon of this part of Leicestershire, as important a symbol as the county emblem of the fox. And being from round here, it always lifts my heart when I see it since I feel in some spiritual way that whenever I do, I've come back home.

CHAPTER FOURTEEN

Whether this account of the Old John story is true, or whether the whole thing's just a fantasy, I don't know and I can't even be bothered Googling to find out. The fact is, I don't much care. In my life I've been told too many tales that have captivated my imagination only for them to turn to dust later under scrutiny. From Father Christmas to the Tooth Fairy. From Richard the Lionheart to Good Queen Bess. Stories of inspirational heroes with feet of clay, or stirring battles for truth and justice which turned out to be grubby affairs of nationalism and self-interest. Personal stories too, stories of the kindness of women and the loyalty of friends. Stories of the strength of men and the love of God. And most of them have proved to be a deception, a flimsy amalgam of myth and propaganda that falls apart in your hands at the first cursory examination. Nowadays I don't care to have any more of my illusions shattered. At my age I just don't have many of them left intact. I've come to prefer the stories to the reality, I suppose. Stories have at least got meaning, which most real life hasn't. They've got a beginning, a middle and an end too, whereas life's a sorry old business with a plot you can't follow however hard you try. It's like one of those interminable accounts of journeys you read in bad Victorian travel books. But a journey to nowhere. A journey with no purpose except its dreadful, final end.

I never had any sympathy with Old John anyhow. He can't have been very bright to have stood under a burning tree trunk while it fell on him. And he was old too, wasn't he? He had to go sometime – we all do. And not many of us get his sort of monument, do we? Or such a glorious goodbye either, with the bonfire blazing, and the booze flowing and people around loving us enough to mourn us when we're gone.

'What are you going to do, then?' Em asked. We were standing under the monument, against a low granite cairn about three feet in diameter, capped with a bronze disc engraved with the points of the compass and the direction of local landmarks. In front of us, in the far, far distance, three or four massive columns of belching cloud rose from the cooling towers of Ratcliffe on Soar power station in Nottinghamshire, spreading across the Trent valley like vaporous gases of hell.

'There's not much I can do, really. I'll hang around until the results of her tests come through but I'm not confident they'll show anything. They'll discharge her as soon as possible after that. They want the bed and she wants to get back home. Maybe I'll stick around until she settles in, make sure she's got food, milk, that sort of thing. After that, it's back to the boat, I guess...'

'Panic over?' Em asked.

'If it's ever actually over.'

She looked at me uncomprehendingly.

'Well, explain to me how can it be over?' I said. 'As long as we live we all know how it ends. Most of the time we just try and forget it and get on with other things, don't we? But it's always there. In the back of our minds.'

'As we live our lives of quiet desperation, you mean?' Em said, quoting Henry Thoreau or Pink Floyd, I'm not quite sure which.

Prune and Heather had promised to keep an eye on *Justice* while I was away but when I got back to Uppermill they'd gone and the space they'd occupied was empty. The only sign they'd ever been there was a tennis ball on the towpath which had been chewed almost beyond recognition by the Rat. Seeing it, I couldn't help feeling melancholic at their absence. Well, not so much their absence as the Rat's. The fact is (and I don't understand how it happened either) I'd got rather attached to the thing. Indeed, I started thinking about getting a Rat of my own. Well, not a rat, of course. But maybe a dog. Maybe a dog with a more reliable pedigree and a better sense of self-discipline. One that wouldn't have your finger off at the first opportunity. One that wouldn't play dead at the first sign of rain.

Later that evening as I sat hunched over a book on dog breeds which I'd brought from Leicester, there was a knock on the door. It was a bloke called Fly from a boat which had moored over the other side of the canal while I'd been away. I don't know what it is with people on the cut that so many of them feel compelled to christen themselves with bizarre sobriquets. Why can't they call themselves Mike or Jim or Roger or something? It was bad enough when it was dried fruit but now it was insects. Where would it stop, I wanted to know. Building materials? Aquatic invertebrates?

'Hey there, Breeze Block, how you doing?' 'Not so bad, Lobster, life's good.'

I'd seen Fly's boat the moment I got back. It would have been difficult not to notice it. Canal boats – certainly new ones – are generally brightly painted and shiny. Fly's wasn't. His was a new boat but it was battleship grey. More than that, it looked like a battleship. And it wasn't just the colour either. It was built like the proverbial brick shithouse. It was tug-style with portholes and a long, steel foredeck. It was bulky, heavy and industrial, every part of it thicker and broader than it needed to be, everything reinforced and strengthened.

The most extraordinary thing about it was its draft in the water. *Justice* is deep, but Fly's boat was even deeper. Given the problems I'd had, he must have had more. He must have been ploughing the canal to have got this far. I invited him on board and he gave me a roughly wrapped parcel. Inside was a tiny knotted fender, a sort of baby version of the rope protectors we use on boats to prevent us scraping against the bank when we moor. It was an intricately worked object, made out of silk chord, and because of that, I suspect, a good deal more difficult to make than the real thing.

'It's from Prune,' Fly explained. 'A gift. He asked me to give you it. He said he was sorry to have to leave like this but he got the chance of a job somewhere – Stoke, I think he said.

'Stoke?'

'Yeah, Stoke. Or maybe it was Stevenage. Somewhere like that down South, anyway. He asked me to make sure you got this – as a sort of token, you know. Of his friendship.'

The two of us went for a drink. This is the way it works on the cut. You meet someone who meets someone else and before you know where you are, you've got a new friend.

Whether or not you want a new friend is a different matter, of course.

'Your boat's pretty low in the water,' I said when we'd got pints in our hand.

I sensed immediately that this was the wrong thing to say. Fly's draft was clearly a sensitive subject with him and he immediately became very prickly. 'It's just a tug-boat,' he said curtly. 'Tug-boats are meant to be low in the water, that's the way they are. Nothing wrong with that.'

CHAPTER FOURTEEN

'No, no, of course not. But you must be deeper than me and I'm three foot. I was just wondering how you've managed up here?'

'It's not been a problem,' said Fly, in a tone of voice that suggested he was surprised anyone might have thought it was a problem. 'No sweat at all. It's been a bit shallow in places but nothing to worry about. In fact it's been easy. Much easier than I thought it would be. Much easier that I was told it would be.'

He smiled in a way that suggested that if I'd had any difficulties then they were of my own making.

'Perhaps... well... do you think that might have had something to do with me?' I said, hesitating to express an idea which had been forming in my mind since I'd raised the subject.

'You?'

'Being ahead of you, I mean. Perhaps I cut a channel? You might just have naturally followed the line of it.'

The idea evidently irritated him. 'Oh no, I don't think so,' he said. 'I'm a much bigger boat than you. There's no way my boat'd follow any other line except its own. And I've probably got a much bigger engine too. And a much bigger propeller.'

I shrugged my shoulders and changed the subject, resisting the temptation to point out that without water, a big engine and propeller were useless.

With someone like Fly I could already see it wasn't worth appealing to logic.

When I set out towards the Standedge tunnel the next afternoon I was surprised to discover Fly behind me, almost as if he'd been waiting for me to go. We both coincidentally had a passage booked in a few days time but I'd had enough of Uppermill and for a change of scene I'd decided to cruise nearer to the point where boats are asked to assemble before they're assisted through. It's a short section which is probably the best-maintained stretch of the entire canal. The locks were among the first to be rebuilt as part of the restoration and a trip-boat has run regularly from Uppermill ever since. Even so, I hadn't even got through Dungebooth Lock before I was scraping the bottom; and not long after I'd passed under one of the arches of the impressive Saddleworth Viaduct towering above me, I found myself slowing down as the canal became predictably shallow again. Soon afterwards I ground to a halt.

By the standards of some of the hold-ups I'd had on the trip, this one was inconsequential, almost routine. It was the sort of grounding you might get on any canal anywhere and it was just a matter of jigging the boat around a bit before I was on my way again. Behind me in the battleship, however, Fly was having a much harder time of it. He got held up at the same spot but, try as he might, he couldn't get over whatever minor obstruction it was. I hung about twenty or thirty yards ahead, reluctant to leave him in difficulty. This was no great hardship since this part of the canal is a delight visually and, despite its difficulties, well worth dawdling over to prolong the period you can enjoy it. But the same's true of most of the canal. Indeed, the difficulties add to the pleasure of cruising it for, like so much else in life, you appreciate things more when you have to struggle a bit for them.

From where I found myself, hovering about in mid-channel, looking back towards Uppermill, I could appreciate the enormous scale of the viaduct in a way I hadn't been able to going underneath it. In the railway world it's known by the prosaic name of Bridge 31, but this sells it short. It's almost 900 feet long, more than seventy feet high, and with its twenty-three spans it dominates this section of the Tame valley, lying on the landscape like an enormous buttress supporting the sky above. It is brutal, primitive and uncompromising, a monstrous construction overshadowing the countryside. Yet at the same time it is surprisingly light and delicate, ineffably satisfying in its form, like the frontage of the Parthenon, or a Nash terrace. The canal passes under it at an unusual skewed arch, which has the effect of highlighting the line of the rest of the arches in a peculiar way, making them seem like a row of immense gothic windows with the scenery stretching out into an unfolding panorama beyond.

I reversed to where Fly was still thrashing about, making no headway whatsoever, and offered to give him a tow. This was a mistake. Unintended though it was, I could tell he saw my proposal as an unforgivable slight on the battleship which in his eyes was a boat built to dominate the waterways, one designed to travel fast and true, along wide, deep watercourses. Not one to need a tow after getting stuck in a Pennine ditch.

The boat was his pride and joy. Any minor defect with it would have embarrassed him enough. This – the somewhat fundamental defect that it couldn't move – mortified him. You could tell how he felt about it by the look on his face. By the grimace around his mouth which had developed as a result of him gritting his teeth. He waved me away, told me he would catch me up later.

Just around the corner from where he was having his problems is the rendezvous point for the tunnel adjacent to the former canal transhipment warehouse. A little way before there I managed to get close enough into the bank to moor comfortably. After half an hour there was no sign of Fly. Every now and again, when the wind was in the right direction, I'd hear the low growl of his engine echoing across the water. From time to time I'd become aware of telltale signs of exhaust fumes wafting gently along the canal. What should I do? Should I go back and offer help again, risking antagonising him further? Or should I just wait for him to make his own way? It was a difficult call to make. As a single-hander myself I know how much of the pleasure of boating this way is the personal challenge it poses. Sometimes you just want to be left alone. Sometimes you don't want help.

Even so, I couldn't leave him stranded. Eventually I walked back up the towpath to find him. He was on the bow of the battleship, his face an incandescent purple as he heaved on his barge pole, vainly attempting to extract from the boat the slightest sign of movement.

'You OK? Can I give you a hand?'

'No, no problem, I've cracked it now, thanks all the same…'

I went back to *Justice* but after another half an hour and a good deal more exhaust on the canal, he still hadn't showed. I walked back once more.

'Are you sure I can't help?' I said.

'No, it's OK, mate, thanks. Appreciate the offer, but I've worked out what's wrong now…'

CHAPTER FOURTEEN

At this, I gave up and went off to explore the transhipment warehouse which for twelve years between 1799 and 1811, while the Standedge tunnel was being completed, was the terminus of the western part of the canal. Here cargo was offloaded onto pack horses prior to being taken over the hill and loaded back onto boats again on the other side of the canal for its onward journey. Warehouses of this sort are a regular feature of canal tunnels since they took such a long time to build that canal constructors would invariably open their waterways and charge tolls on the lengths which were navigable in order to get some sort of return on their investment as soon as they could.

The one here at Dobcross is of natural stone: a very simple, single-storey construction, with eves overhanging the canal to afford some basic shelter in bad weather. I'd like to think that this was done out of concern for the welfare of the workers but I suspect it was more to protect the cargo coming from the boats – though a lot of that on this canal was wool which, like the local sheep it comes from, is hardly affected by a bit of water dropping out of the sky.

It was getting on a bit now and there was still no sign of Fly, so eventually I decided to risk a further rebuttal and ventured on another expedition to search him out. I crept up the towpath and peeked around the bend to where I'd last seen him. The battleship hadn't moved an inch. It was exactly where it was before, the only difference being that Fly wasn't on it. He was up to his knees in the water close to the hull, hacking at the canal bottom with a shovel. What he was doing, I couldn't fathom. But it wasn't only me who was puzzled at his behaviour. This is a popular stretch of towpath for locals and at this time of day, with the dog walkers out in force, his antics had attracted a small crowd which was engaging him in lively banter. From where I was I couldn't make out clearly what was being said but the drift of it was clear. I heard the words 'silly bugger' uttered by one bloke. I heard another ask with some exasperation, 'Why don't you just throw us a bloody rope so we can help you?'

Fly, of course, was having none of it and was waving them away with the same arrant confidence he'd shown to me.

In terms of Fly's inability to accept the realities of the material world, it was difficult not to think of the Black Knight in Monty Python's *Holy Grail*. If his boat had been sinking, Fly would doubtless still insist it was nothing. If it had been breaking up about him, his engine room exploding, he'd have dismissed it as a minor technical problem. If it had been in flames, he'd probably have claimed it was a new form of cabin heating. In any case, he wouldn't want help.

I crept away and left him to it. It must have been after five o'clock before I heard him moor up behind me. It had taken him the best part of half a day to travel a mile or so.

Fifteen

I was living with two obsessions now. It was no longer just a matter of taking this damn boat across the mountains, battling with the locks and the lack of water and the idiots I was meeting along the way. Now it was dogs too. Dogs fixated me. I dreamt about them at night; I thought about them every waking moment of the day. Though to be fair, it was difficult *not* to think about them. You won't have noticed this – you only do when it's pointed out to you – but once you become aware of dogs, you see them all over the place. They are everywhere you look. Black dogs, white dogs, brown dogs, small ones, large ones, fat ones, thin ones, short ones, long ones.

I read a book once which argued that the world belongs to bacteria because bacteria had arrived on the planet shortly after the Big Bang and are all over the place. Apparently a kilo of our body weight is composed of them. But bacteria have got nothing on dogs, believe me. You don't notice bacteria, for a start. You don't see them wandering around the street with their tongues hanging out when it's hot, or flopping over the floors in pubs looking at you with doleful eyes because they've noticed your crisps. Once you get attuned to dogs, you realise how completely they have colonised the world, especially the waterways. The towpath is overrun with dogs and everybody on a boat seems to be carrying a lead like some form of prosthetic attached to their arm.

And curiously, once you begin to notice dogs, they begin to notice you. Before the Rat I was very suspicious of them. I'd been brought up with dogs, and so their ways weren't completely alien to me. Even so, age had made me more cautious of them. Their teeth had somehow become larger, their turds somehow bigger. Since the Rat, however, I'd softened in my attitudes. And dogs knew it. I was dozing on the deck in the sunshine that first morning back from Leicestershire and I woke to find a spaniel nuzzling my hand. It had been walking along the towpath and just taken a fancy to me. The next day, moored up near the transhipment warehouse, I was fiddling around doing something or other to the batteries when I looked up to find a labrador gazing at me through the engine-room doors. They have such deep, expressive eyes, labradors. They can talk to you with their eyes. This one wanted to know why I wasn't out playing. He wanted me to come out and throw a ball around for him. Or maybe I got that wrong. Dogs spend a lot of time thinking about food. Perhaps he was just wondering if he could eat the batteries.

As I began to notice dogs more, I began to become more aware of their relationship to their owners. Dogs are like daemons in Philip Pullman's *Dark Materials*: they are extensions of their owners, they are the visible parts of their souls. It is no coincidence that young men with big boots and an attitude to match are attracted to pit bulls and rottweilers. No accident either that small people have big dogs and lazy people have active ones: their choice of dog complements what they lack in themselves. But it works in different ways too. That's why Prune and Heather had the Rat. It wasn't to supplement something they felt they were lacking, more to reflect something about themselves they wanted to highlight. They were doing the same sort of thing as the guys with the dangerous dogs. But at least the guys with the dangerous dogs knew what they were doing. Prune and Heather didn't have a clue. They couldn't have had, or why would they have chosen to have a dog as much of a mess as the Rat? I mean, what does a dog like that say about you to the world?

I called Em that lunchtime and inevitably dogs came up in conversation.

'Steve,' she said in that reproving tone she reserves for those occasions when she thinks I'm about to come off the rails. 'Is there a pub near where you are?'

'A pub? Yes, I guess so. Why do you ask?'

'Because I think you ought to go there now. Immediately. Or if not a pub, then a tea shop – or any shop for that matter. Somewhere there are other people you can talk to. People you can engage with in civilised conversation. All this dog talk, Steve; you need to know, it's just not healthy for a bloke your age. You really do need to get out more…'

As it happened I did get out to the pub that night. But not because of anything Em said. It came about because later that day the canal, which had been virtually deserted since I'd been on it, suddenly became busy. Before, there'd been only me and Fly on this stretch; but over the course of the next five or six hours, three more boats appeared, each of them scheduled like us to do the passage of the Standedge tunnel the following day.

The reason for all this activity was that a major waterways festival was scheduled for Huddersfield and boats planning to attend it were already beginning to descend on the town from all points of the compass. Arranged by the Inland Waterways Association – the most important of the organisations representing canal users – the location had been chosen to encourage use of this and other recently opened canals in the North; although disappointingly few people from other parts of the country had risen to the challenge of these new waters. The HNC's reputation for being difficult had put many off, as had the distance needed to cruise to the festival site from the South and Midlands where most narrowboats are based.

But the biggest disincentive for many was Standedge where because of safety rules – ostensibly the lack of ventilation – boaters had been forbidden to take their diesel-powered craft through the tunnel themselves. Instead, they had to be towed through in convoy by an electrically powered tug and crews were compelled to travel separately from their boats in a specially constructed passenger module. As if this wasn't sufficient to make the passage a big enough deal, each boat in the convoy was allotted an individual British Waterways' worker whose job was to protect it by fending it off the tunnel walls.

It was a system that struck at the very heart of the relationship of owners to their craft. A lot of people thought it was a liberty; they thought it was health and safety gone mad. Why should they have to get off their boats for a bit of diesel smoke when there were other tunnels which were choking with the stuff? Why should they leave someone else to take their boats through when they could just as easily do the job themselves? They saw it as an insult, an affront to their navigational skills. Some objected to it on more personal grounds. For these owners, people who felt for their boats like the woman in Friezland felt for her house – as private, inviolable space – the idea of abandoning their craft to the care of others was unreasonable. Like handing over their kids to strangers.

A lot of apocryphal stories about Standedge suddenly began doing the rounds. These generally featured boats which belonged to friends of friends, or which someone had heard of along the towpath – boats which weren't easy to check out and which you'd probably find didn't exist if you tried. They'd had windows broken. Or been scratched or dented. The propellers had been knocked out of alignment, their rudders unseated. The rumours were legion.

Because the rules required that craft were left unlocked for easy access in case of emergency, there was talk that some boats were being robbed while they were in the tunnel. There was even a rumour that some of the waterways' workers charged with protecting the boats were actually taking the opportunity of the long trip to have a nap on board. As far as I know, there wasn't a scrap of evidence to support any of these allegations – although to be fair, there were one or two mishaps in the tunnel which did lead to boats sustaining minor damage. But you'd expect as much taking boats into such a hostile environment, and the level of damage was anyhow probably less than if we'd been allowed to steer through ourselves, which there is talk of us soon being able to do.

Among the new arrivals that day was one boat I recognised immediately. *Progress*, owned by waterways' activist Chris Coburn, has earned a reputation over the years as a result of a series of high-profile cruises to places where narrowboats haven't been before and wouldn't normally go. These include improbable trips around the coast of Devon, across the Channel and even over the Irish Sea — all pretty challenging stuff for boats that are essentially flat-bottomed coal scuttles designed to trudge up inland ditches. Chris uses his voyages to highlight various restoration and waterways projects which he supports, but I'm sure he'd forgive me saying that his major incentive for doing what he does is good, old-fashioned adventuring, most of which is filmed by his friend, waterways cameraman Laurence Hogg who runs a video and DVD marketing company.

Laurence was along on this trip too but the whole thing had turned into something of a disaster for the pair of them. Originally they'd planned another of their crazy journeys along the coast to Inverness but bad weather had forced them to abort the voyage and they'd put in at the Manchester Ship Canal. After that, they'd gone back to the drawing board and come up with the idea for a cruise across the Pennines. But even the chances of meeting this more prosaic objective was now in doubt because Chris wasn't sure his boat would get through the tunnel.

'We might be a bit wide on some of the bends,' he said. 'BW are worried we'll get stuck. And to be honest, so am I.'

CHAPTER FIFTEEN

We were moored adjacent to each other – literally tied together – outside the transhipment warehouse where we'd been instructed to gather so that the following morning BW gangs could take us up the remaining locks to the mouth of the tunnel. It wasn't a pleasant place to be situated. As part of the restoration, the stone shed next to the warehouse had been converted into a sanitary station, the function of which you can probably work out for yourself, given the unsophisticated nature of boat toilet arrangements. The trouble was, this sanitary station wasn't particularly sanitary. Something inside had blocked and was spilling over the towpath into the water. The place smelled like a military latrine after curry night.

That this should have happened here, at this time, makes you think not only that God has a sense of humour, but that he has a pretty perverse one too; for in real life Chris Coburn runs a sanitation company. No doubt, had he been able to get access to the plumbing, and had he wanted to do it, he could have fixed the problem himself in an hour. Instead, it being that time of day and he not being inclined to take a busman's holiday (and who can blame him?), he suggested we all abandon ship to a nearby pub for a meal. Which we all did except for Fly, who probably thought fully prepared food was too much of a challenge to his sense of his own independence.

But perhaps I'm being too harsh on Fly. Maybe the smell had put him off food. It certainly hadn't done much for my appetite.

'So what are BW going to do with you?' I asked Chris later, after we'd sat ourselves down over a beer. He'd just been served a great mound of something with chips and with the smell of sewage still in my nostrils, the sight of him tucking into it was enough to make me want to throw up – though I guess things like that don't worry you too much when you're in his line of business.

'I think they're going to leave the decision to me,' he said. 'If there's a risk of getting stuck, they don't want to be blamed. But even if I decide to go through, they won't take me tomorrow with the rest of you. There's too much of a risk of blocking the whole canal – which wouldn't be a clever idea with the festival next week. They're offering to take me Sunday instead.'

'So you'll just hang around until then?'

'We've got no choice – but we thought we'd go along in the observation boat with you tomorrow and recce it. Maybe do some filming while we can,' said Laurence, who was sitting opposite, tucking into an indeterminate mound of food himself.

'Are you sure you're not hungry?' he asked. 'You're not sickening for anything, I hope?'

'Not anything in the way of food,' I said. 'I think I may have developed an obsession with dogs though.' He looked at me a bit oddly but didn't pursue the matter. Perhaps he thought I meant that I harboured ambitions to eat one.

Later he told me this joke involving dogs. Or maybe I told it to him, or perhaps somebody else altogether told me it at a completely different time. Anyway, there were these two blokes out walking their dogs when they came across a pub. They were going to go inside for a pint until they saw a sign saying that only guide dogs were allowed.

'No problem,' said one of the blokes, who had a Labrador. He took out a pair of sunglasses and put them on and went inside and got served. The other bloke thought he'd try the same trick, but he'd got a poodle which the barman clocked as soon as he walked through the door.

'No dogs permitted in here,' he said. 'Sorry.'

'But it's a guide dog,' the bloke said.

'A guide dog?' said the barman. 'Pull the other leg. They don't train poodles as guide dogs.'

'Poodles?' said the bloke. 'They gave me a poodle...?'

We'd been alerted to be ready at 8.30 a.m. the next day and at 8.30 a.m. on the dot a waterways team arrived to take us up to the tunnel mouth.

The odd thing was that by then the smell seemed to have gone. Or at least I thought it had. Then one of the waterways gang wrinkled his nose and said how whiffy it was. He was amazed any of us had been able to stand the stink through the night.

Maybe the smell was the incentive the team needed to get to work. They broke up into gangs, one to a boat, and took us each separately through the last nine locks to the summit level, working the paddle gear as if their lives as well as their livelihoods depended on it. For me, used to boating alone, it was like travelling in fifth gear after weeks of grinding along in first. The locks disappeared behind me effortlessly and I rose through the landscape like a helium balloon released into the air. The water situation helped a lot. The rest of the canal may have been shallow and virtually impassable, but between Dobcross and Diggle it was wide and deep and the going was easy. This was no coincidence: nothing to do with canal maintenance ever is. The simple truth is that a canal is the way it is because it is kept that way. Indeed, the reason for this whole palaver of being met and accompanied up to the tunnel is part of that process. It's to conserve water, to make maximum use of a valuable resource which becomes increasingly precious as you get closer to the summit.

A lot of people, even some who spend considerable time cruising the waterways, don't realise how critical this question of water supply is to a canal. If they think about it at all, they assume that as with rivers, water runs into the canal from tributaries or seeps into it from the ground naturally as if by some fortuitous act of God. But it isn't like this. Canals are man-made structures; every mile of them has had to be carefully planned and surveyed; everything about them is the result of some engineering decision. Water supply was always a primary problem. It's true that along the way a canal will make use of various streams and culverts which drain into it naturally; but even so on many canals – especially the high ones – the summit has to be fed artificially through reservoirs. From here water drains down, lockful by lockful, with every boat that uses it.

Crossing the Pennines as it does, the Huddersfield Narrow Canal had particular water supply problems from the outset. At first it was thought that two reservoirs would suffice to feed the summit, one on either side of Standedge. But building them properly was problematic in an era when engineering was in its infancy. Tunnel End reservoir was completed in 1798 but it breached a year later, devastating the village of Marsden below it. Diggle reservoir was washed away the same year. In practice what this must have meant was that boatmen in the early period of the canal faced exactly the same water problems navigating their craft as I'd done with *Justice*. Much worse really, because at least I wasn't trying to carry cargo with my job depending on it.

It wasn't until 1848 that the problem was finally sorted with the completion of the last of an astonishing network of ten reservoirs which had a total capacity of almost 350 million gallons. They were a constant maintenance problem though, always leaking, silting up, or threatening to collapse. Keeping them operational is still a problem today, though nowadays most of the remaining ones don't feed the canal at all, but Yorkshire Water's huge reservoir at Scammondon adjacent to the M62 ten miles away. Meanwhile water from Scammonden – and how crazy is this? – is used to feed the eastern part of the canal. This is an arrangement dating from the 1960s when Scammonden was built and when the idea of the canal ever being used again for boats was just a pie-in-the-sky fantasy of the mad and the deranged. On the plus side it earns BW money, since they charge Yorkshire Water for the privilege. It also prevents the problem of having to restore all the old reservoirs to full working condition which would be horrendously expensive. But these benefits are far outweighed by the disadvantages, for these days what BW is allowed to take back under the agreement for its own use just isn't sufficient for the traffic on the canal, sparse though it is. It's the main reason why anyone going across the canal has such depth problems.

On the way up to the tunnel, with my own personal crew of professionals working me through the locks, water management was the last thing on my mind. Travelling like this so effortlessly and so fast was an exhilarating experience, and all I had to do was sit back and watch the world fly by. The canal here clings to the side of the gentle valley below Broadstone Hill; and though overshadowed by Standedge which looms ahead, the landscape nevertheless appears to widen out as it climbs the meticulously tended flight. Everywhere you look, up or down the valley, the fields stretch around you in a gentle patchwork nibbling at the hills. The lock sides are carefully mown but beyond them the grass has been allowed to grow wild, and when a breeze blows it ripples like a field of corn.

It is all quite lovely, the only thing spoiling it the sculptures which are scattered around as they are on so many stretches of canal nowadays. I don't know why they persist in doing this. Canals are lovely enough as it is without having to 'enhance' them with odd chunks of wood or metal offcuts – or football-sized red seed pods on sticks which is one I remember particularly that day.

Perhaps it's because twenty-first-century artists are so out of tune with the idea of art as beauty and they hope that by placing their art in a natural context, the landscape will somehow compensate for what they're unable to deliver themselves? Perhaps they site their work in these sorts of places because they have a captive audience. Perhaps it's a way of force-feeding us art?

We eventually arrived at the tunnel mouth which was already bustling with people and getting busier as other boats began to arrive from the transhipment warehouse with other BW men. There were a sizeable number of spectators milling around too, caught up in the general sense of anticipation that was in the air. In the period it had been open the tunnel had become a tourist attraction, and I guess this daily preparation of boats for the passage had become a local equivalent of the Changing of the Guard, or the raising of Tower Bridge. Among the small crowd I caught a glimpse of the familiar lumbering frame of Laurence Hogg from *Progress* who was filming as much of the activity as he could keep up with. There was certainly enough of it to keep him occupied. Gangs who had worked the locks had transmuted into new roles. Some of them were now strutting about with massive set squares which they were using to measure the profile of boats to ensure they'd get through the tunnel; others were pulling boats together in a line, roping them together between great plastic floats until they were rigid.

Most extraordinary though was the process of covering the boats with thick rubber matting to protect them against the tunnel walls. In the space of a few minutes these brightly-painted icons of folk art were reduced to looking as if they were all encased in black condoms ready to play their role in some unspeakable perversion. Poor *Justice* looked a sad sight when it was done, almost embarrassed at the transfiguration, as if I'd burst into the bedroom and caught her indulging herself in some private fetish.

Eventually everything was prepared. Everything that had to be done was done. Everything was ready to go. That, of course, being England, was the point at which all activity stopped. It took me a while to realise why but then it struck me it was lunch, and lunch is still a powerful concept among those who earn their living by physical labour.

As a gesture of sympathy I went off to make myself a sandwich. Inside the sheeted boat it smelt of old Second World

War gasmasks and was as black as midnight. I was tired after my disturbed night so it was an easy thing to drop off to sleep. A minute later – though I knew an hour had passed – there was a knock on the outside of the boat.

'Could you all move into the observation boat as soon as possible, please? We'll be entering the tunnel presently…'

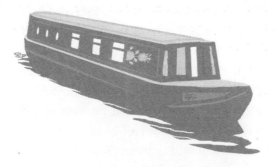

Sixteen

*L*et me tell you a secret about the Standedge tunnel. One they know but won't even whisper.

They'll wax lyrical over the fact that at 5,500 yards, a bit over three miles, it's the longest canal tunnel in Britain. And they'll try to get you excited, as you should be excited, about the fact that at 645 feet above sea level, it's also the highest canal tunnel in the country. They'll attempt to impress you, and you should be impressed, by telling you that it lies 638 feet below Standedge Hill which makes it the deepest tunnel in the country too – about as deep as some early coal mines.

They will awe you with how astonishing an engineering structure the thing is. And you should be awed. From the minute you go under the portal, going in either from the east side, near Tunnel End cottages, where the entrance looks like 'a mouse hole in the wainscoting' as someone once memorably described it; or from the west as I did, entering under the 200-yard extension which was built in Victorian times so as to be able to build railway lines over the canal, you are in a unique environment, one which is remarkable in every way. In places the tunnel can be suffocating and claustrophobic and at others wide and cavernous. Sometimes it is close and stifling, sometimes chill and damp. The construction changes too as you go through it. Sometimes it is lined with brick, occasionally it's sprayed with a grey, unappealing concrete. In places it's just bare rock, hewn by men who've left pick marks you can see on the hard millstone grit as their signature on life. All this they will tell you. They will tell you that the Standedge tunnel is a truly wondrous thing – and they are right, it *is* a truly wondrous thing.

What they won't tell you, the secret they keep to themselves, is that it's also very boring.

Well, it's bound to be boring, isn't it? It takes more than three hours to get through it. Three hours stuck in a hole in the hill with a chunk of the Pennines balanced on your head. Three hours in the dark staring at a tunnel wall. You could drive half way across the country in that time. You could fly across Europe.

But they don't tell you that. Instead what they do – or at least what they used to do until they stopped doing it a year or two after it opened to save money – is to provide entertainment to while away the time. Not, however, entertainment of the in-flight movie variety. Not draw-the-cabin-blinds-and-plug-in-your-headphones type entertainment. At the time I'm talking about, not long after the tunnel was opened, British Waterways used to provide guides for the trip. The one on duty that day was called Mel or something like that. He was a personable, rather delicate-looking young man with short, well-tended hair, and it was clear from the outset that he relished his work. As soon as we'd settled into our seats in the

CHAPTER SIXTEEN

glass-roofed observation module and been swallowed up by
the hill, he launched into an account of the tunnel's history
with all the relish of an actor starting a one-man stage show.

The name Benjamin Outram figured a lot in his script.
Outram was the first tunnel engineer, either a hero of the canal
age or a bit of a shyster, depending on your perspective. In
many ways he was a very modern man, a partner in a prominent
ironworks company which bore his name, yet at the same time
a freelance civil engineer – what we would nowadays call a
consultant. Whether having two jobs led him to cut corners,
and whether this in turn led him to off-load too much of the
work on the Huddersfield Narrow Canal onto the shoulders
of his inexperienced young surveyor Nicholas Brown, is a
matter of conjecture even today.

But what is beyond dispute is that the job eventually went
pear-shaped. And the way Mel told it, Brown and Outram
were like Laurel and Hardy. They'd started digging the tunnel
from both ends – but one end turned out to be higher than
the other. And the tunnel was crooked too – at one point near
the centre it was twenty-six feet out of alignment. Eventually,
like the cavalry appearing over the hill to save the day, the
canal company had had to employ the iconic Thomas Telford
to sort out the mess they were in, which by then had cost them
the equivalent of millions of pounds in today's money and set
back the tunnel opening by years.

Yes, Mel was entertaining enough at the start; but so he
should have been because his core material was good. After
that it began to fall off a bit though. He just couldn't keep it
up for three hours. Nobody could keep it up for three hours.
You'd have had to have been a Soviet leader in the days of the

Berlin wall. You'd have had to have been the president of some banana republic with a chestful of medals. Someone with either a big ego or a big army. Trust me on this, three hours is a very long time. I have some small experience of public speaking myself. After an hour the eyelids of any audience will droop in desperation. After two hours they lose the will to live and are screaming to get out of whatever room you have locked them into.

OK, I grant you, on a boat in a narrow tunnel 600-odd feet below the moors, there aren't exactly many places for an audience to go. But this is no excuse to presume on them as Mel started to do. Away from Outram and Brown, he seemed to lose it completely and go off on a track of his own. At the start, his story had at least been compelling. It had plot. It had narrative. Now it disintegrated into a series of lurid facts. He told us about the number of times the tunnel had collapsed during construction, about the volume of water that leaked into it, about the fifty people who had died building it.

None of this, it has to be said, was designed to make us feel particularly confident about being in the tunnel at all. It was like an airline steward lecturing you on plane crashes. And it was wearisome stuff too, a catalogue of unadulterated detail which after a while made you feel so hopeless you wanted to shoot yourself. Soon – it was only a matter of time – Mel would tell us the exact number of bricks used in the construction. The exact amount of rock removed from the tunnel calculated to the last pound.

Or should that be the last stone?

Eventually I couldn't stand it any longer and I left the inside of the module for the front deck where I could chat to the tug

CHAPTER SIXTEEN

pilot. He was controlling the convoy from an external steering position using a couple of joysticks similar to those you might employ playing a computer game. This made it hard to take him seriously. His clothes didn't help either. Presumably, in case there was the danger of anyone failing to see him in the gloom, he was dressed in a fetching hard hat of pixie green with a matching yellow fluorescent jacket. He only lacked pink boots to complete the outfit.

With him I found Chris Coburn and Laurence Hogg who had used the filming as an excuse to make their own escape some time before. They were trying to capture the unique ambience of this hole in the hill although this was not an easy task for them. It wouldn't have been an easy task for anyone. Even Steven Spielberg would find three hours of the Standedge tunnel an artistic challenge.

Laurence's solution was to focus in closely on the walls to try to get a sense of texture and movement. Now he was trying the same trick on the tunnel roof, though the pilot was becoming concerned for his welfare.

'It gets a bit wet at this stage,' he said. 'I'd watch out.'

Laurence waved him away.

'No really, it is pretty bad…' said the pilot.

But Lawrence wasn't listening. He was an artist in search of his vision. Not only that, but he was an experienced canal traveller too. A drop of water from a tunnel roof wasn't going to put him off.

'I'll be OK, all I want to do is…' But he got no further. He was suddenly submerged beneath a torrent from a Pennine stream which was gushing into the tunnel through the roof with the force of a burst water main. Luckily Chris and I were well out of the way and hardly got touched by it. The pilot, knowing what was coming, had only to move a little sideways to avoid the deluge.

But poor Laurence copped the full whack. He was drenched and his camera all but destroyed.

He was not a happy man, not a happy man at all. I recall him trying to mop himself down inside the module, expressing as much in a few choice phrases. It was a shame there wasn't a second camera to catch his performance.

It was X-rated stuff but it was worth seeing.

There are actually four tunnels at Standedge, the canal one being the oldest of them. A second was built as a single-track train tunnel in 1848, a couple of years after the canal had been bought up by the Huddersfield and Manchester Railway. But, like the canal, which was so narrow it could in practice only be used in one direction at a time despite having passing points built into it, the single-track railway proved to be a bottleneck too, and a second track was built in a separate tunnel in 1871. Finally a double-track tunnel was built by the London and North Western Railway in 1894. This is the only railway tunnel in use today and passing through Standedge on the canal, you can constantly hear the low rumbling of Manchester–Huddersfield trains like a faraway creature trapped in the mountain growling in frustration.

The 1848 railway tunnel has been adapted to take vehicles and it's used now as an emergency escape route for both rail and canal. It lies parallel to the canal tunnel, though a little higher, and is linked to it by a series of connecting passages called adits. These were originally used during the construction of the rail tunnel to transport spoil away by canal, although today their main function is as monitoring points where British Waterways can track boat convoys as they are taken through. There's a couple of blokes who drive along the old rail tunnel in a Land Rover checking out the convoy as it passes and it's a curious experience witnessing these assignations. There you are, hundreds of feet under the hill, feeling yourself a world away from anywhere or anything, when suddenly the wall of the tunnel opens out and there are beams of flashlights dancing all over the place like fireflies, and blokes chatting to each other about time-sheets or the match the previous night. It's all over very quickly. In an instant, or so it seems, the convoy has moved on and the silence of the tomb prevails again, only the strangled screech of the tug's electric motor and the occasional hollow boom of boat hulls striking the tunnel wall punctuating the quietness.

This happens five or six times along the way. The first time it was interesting to see but the second time it was less so and the third not at all, like watching ads on television when you can't even remember the products they're supposed to be selling you. Eventually, bored out of my skull by now, I went back inside the module where at least it was warmer and where, after a while, the monotony of the tunnel and the constant, droning commentary on our progress through it lulled me into much-needed sleep. It had the same effect on most of the other people in there too because when we finally emerged blinking into the bright sunshine on the other side it was like the waiting room in a station at some quiet branch line somewhere with everyone slumped about in various stages of torpor waiting for something to happen. Even so, Mel was still rabbiting on about something or another – although by now even he must have realised the game was up and that this most captive of captive audiences would soon have to be liberated.

Not that it turned out to be much of a liberation; for in the same way we'd had to queue to be taken up the last locks to the tunnel, so we had to wait to be taken the first few locks down from it. This didn't happen until the following morning, which meant we were all trapped at the top overnight. The prospect wouldn't have been too bad if we'd been allowed to moor around Tunnel End which is a picturesque spot with a little row of natural-stone cottages and grass towpaths which are kept like bowling greens. The trouble was that if we'd all done this, we'd have blocked access to the tunnel for the tug and any convoy travelling the opposite direction the following day, so instead we all had to squeeze in beyond the bend past a visitors' centre where the canal enters a shallow cutting which leads to the first of the downhill locks on the western section. There was barely enough towpath space for one boat, let alone half a dozen, which was the size our convoy had finally ended up. We tied up to each other as best we could, spreading ourselves across the canal in whatever space we could find so that we had to trek across each other's boats in order to get to our own. It was a scrubby destination for the end section of a trip which in so many ways, though dull, had been so memorable. The canal at this point seemed strewn with rocks and overgrown with straggling brambles hanging down to the water's edge. It was gloomy too, the sort of place that's shaded from the sunshine even in the middle of the day so that it smelled dank and putrid like a… well, like a sanitary station when something's blocked.

It was too much even for Fly who suggested going for a drink. I didn't really fancy it, but since Chris and Laurence had gone back to *Progress* and everyone else had been reduced to zombies by the tunnel, I went along to keep him company. At least it gave me the opportunity of surveying the dogs hereabouts. Perhaps I would light upon a local breed which Em would take to her heart? One which smelled of Issey Miyake and bought her chocolates on her birthday. Or one which enjoyed shopping expeditions to Bluewater.

We ended up around the corner at the Tunnel End Inn where we sat inside on a couple of settles, stayed longer than we should have done and drank more beer than was good for us. We were probably talking too loudly as well if truth were told. Or too loudly for a small place like this where you felt everyone was listening to you anyhow.

On one of my trips to the bar I was confronted by a customer who must have heard my accent. He was in his early thirties, with blond streaks in his hair and a face as bronze as a Marbella sunset. He wasn't a local himself but he seemed to know the pub well – a regular from Leeds or Huddersfield, I guessed. Maybe even from Manchester. One of those people attracted to country pubs in the summer when the weather begins to brighten up. Why did I just know that the Porsche I'd noticed walking up the lane from the canal was his?

'You from the South then, mate?' he asked. His familiarity should have alerted me. But hey, I'm a nice guy. I'll talk to anyone.

'Er, yes. Sort of,' I said. 'I'm on a boat. I've just come through the tunnel.'

'Where you from then, Camberley?' he asked.

This was not at all what I'd have expected. Why of all the places in the South which he could have chosen had he picked out Camberley? It didn't make sense. No doubt Camberley is a pleasant town. No doubt it's green and attractive, criss-crossed by elegant boulevards and scattered with genteel squares. It probably has excellent restaurants and a low crime rate too, and I'm sure the people who live in Camberley love it dearly and would live nowhere else. But even they, I'm sure, would hardly number it among the great urban centres of the South East. I mean, it's hardly Brighton, is it? Or even Gillingham? It's barely even Croydon.

Who knows, perhaps he'd visited Camberley once and taken a shine to it? Or perhaps he'd taken a shine to me, despite an animosity I thought I felt from him. Perhaps he knew that Camberley was near Sandhurst and had me down as a military man. But it's near Broadmoor too as well, isn't it? Perhaps he had me down as a lunatic. Or perhaps he just thought that everyone who lived in the South had to be mad.

'No, erm, actually. I'm from Leicestershire originally, but I'm living in London now,' I said hesitantly.

I could see his eyes widen.

'London,' he mumbled as if the concept was new to him. 'London, eh? Do you know, I've never understood what people see in London. It's supposed to have all these cinemas, yes? Well, where I live, we've got cinemas too. A bloody great multiplex, more films than you'd ever want to see. And theatres too. Well, one theatre but it's closed for refurbishment at the moment. And museums, we got a museum and an art gallery, two art galleries in fact if you count the community centre where they're always showing paintings and pottery and stuff...'

'An interest of yours, is it?'

'An interest?'

'Art. Art shows. That sort of thing?'

He looked at me as if I was bonkers. 'No. What gives you that idea?'

'It was just what you said about where you lived, about it having two art galleries.'

'Yeah, but you wouldn't catch me dead in them. Not my gig, is it?'

I nodded, partly in agreement, partly in mollification. I was waiting for the barman to get beer for me and Fly. I only wished he could have got it quicker. Back at the table I could see Fly looking at me, curious about the conversation I was having. Or maybe impatient to know where his drink was.

'It's the scenery, isn't it?' Marbella man said, apropos nothing at all. 'It's the best in the world, God's own country round here, isn't it? Now look at you, like. As an example. You've come all this way up from London just to see it. That's because you don't have countryside like this in London. You don't have hills like this, or moors like these. Beautiful,' he concluded, taking a sip of his lager, 'bloody beautiful. Unmatchable. You've got nothing to compare with it down London way.'

'You do a lot of walking then, do you?'

Again he looked at me incredulously, as if my brains were in my bum. 'We've got cars up here, you know,' he said belligerently.

'No, I didn't mean that. I meant, you know, hiking, trekking, that sort of stuff. Outdoors stuff.'

He laughed. 'Oh yes, lots of outdoor stuff. When I was a kid, I spent a lot of time outdoors on the moors.' He nudged me in the ribs. 'Courting, you know. Used to drive up there with me girlfriends after closing time.'

'Great views,' I mumbled.

'Yeah, but it was dark, wasn't it? Besides,' – he nudged me again – 'I wasn't up there for the views. Or not them sort of views, anyway.'

The barman finally arrived with the beer and I paid him gratefully.

But Marbella man stood barring my way back to my table. 'And that's another thing,' he said. 'How much would you pay for that in London? A couple of pints – what? Five pounds, six…?'

'No actually…'

'And what would you get for that money? Piss-water, that's what. Fizzy pop you could give to kids.'

'London has some good beers, you know…'

'That's what I mean,' he went on, 'It's overrated, London. Overrated and overpriced. I went there once. I had a meal near Leicester Square, two of us and a bottle of Chardonnay – good stuff though, mind, not your cheap rubbish. Even so, it was more than forty quid. Forty bloody quid for a couple of steaks and a bottle of wine! There's places round here you can get that for a fiver on Monday nights. No, London's not what it's cracked up to be. Myself, I can't see what people see in it…'

Back at the table at last, I handed Fly his beer. Fly was from Bradford, something we'd established not long after meeting.

'What was all that about then?' he asked.

'Oh, nothing,' I said, not wanting to have to go over it. 'North against South stuff, flat caps and bowler hats. You've heard it all before.'

'Did he have anything new to say on the topic?' Fly asked, nodding towards Marbella man and lowering his voice.

'Look at him, Fly. Does he seem the sort of bloke to have much new to say about anything?'

Fly laughed. 'Old school, eh?'

'Yes, but in new clothes. It surprises me.'

'Not me,' said Fly. 'There are a lot of them around.'

Seventeen

I'd had enough socialising. Sometimes on canals it's nice to do it, but that's not what you come to the waterways for… well, not if you've made the decision to go across the Pennines single-handed on a newly opened canal. If you do that, you've got to expect a certain amount of solitude. And you've got to embrace that solitude. Canals are good for that. They're good for daydreams that last a whole day; they're good for fantasies that aren't fantasy at all. Most of all they're good for getting lost in yourself when you're fed up with the rigid road map of your life.

So the next day, after the British Waterways' gang had arrived and worked us down through the Marsden flight and after the rest of the convoy had rushed off, breathless to reach Huddersfield, I broke away and moored at the first reasonable place I could find. It was where the canal widens into a small lake adjacent to a lock where there is an imposing stone house standing alone on the water's edge commanding a view for miles around.

CHAPTER SEVENTEEN

Travelling east towards the tunnel, the canal had been in the valley of the River Tame; but now, dropping down from the summit, the River Colne was its new companion, the gentle hills around enfolding them both in its embrace. Looking back from the direction I'd come, the canal and river arced past a small row of cottages and a disused mill with a single dominant chimney rising from it, pointing to the sky. In the other direction, the fields melted into the two waterways so gradually that if you squinted your eyes it was as if they had flowed over them like a stream of liquid lava, obliterating them entirely. It was a beautiful location.

Unfortunately I shouldn't have been there.

This little lake (as I have so very carefully termed it) was actually a 'winding hole'. Winding holes – pronounce them like you'd pronounce the wind whistling in the trees – are actually turning points for narrowboats, so-called because the old boatmen would use the wind to do their work for them to avoid the sweat of having to haul their craft around manually. Winding holes are critical for canal boats. They solve the problem of how a long boat turns in a narrow channel. And this, of course, is why you're not supposed to moor in them. If you do, you leave no room for boats to use them for what they were made for, which rather defeats the purpose of making them in the first place.

Normally I'm quite a stickler on these canal rules, many of which aren't 'rules' at all, in that they're not written down, but are really just accepted codes of behaviour. This doesn't make them any less important, though – the opposite if anything. They're a form of courtesy, and courtesy is just a way of oiling social behaviour – an increasing necessity on the waterways since there are more boats using them nowadays than there ever were in the past. You've all heard the statistics about how there are more boats on the canals now than at the height of the Industrial Revolution. And it's true. But figures like that don't really mean much, do they? None of us was around in the Industrial Revolution to experience how busy the canals were.

However, I *was* around at the beginning of the 1980s when there were a third fewer boats on BW waters than the 30,000 there are now; and at the beginning of the 1970s when I reckon there were perhaps half as many again. This level of growth has had a terrific effect on an environment as sensitive as the waterways. Despite the dearth of boats I'd experienced on my travels, waterways generally have become busier, especially in the hotspots of the Midlands and the South. Increasingly those of us using them find ourselves getting in one another's way, with all the frustration this can cause. There have even been examples of what it has amused the newspapers to call 'canal rage'.

This phenomenon is difficult to explain to anyone unfamiliar with the pace and tenor of the waterways. It's hard to explain it even to the waterways' authorities who sometimes seem determined to wring every last penny they can from the canals by sardine-ing as many boats as they can onto them. For them, busy is a concept defined by roads. Busy is a jam on the motorway because of excessive traffic. It's crawling at a snail's pace through a city or not being able to park because there are too many cars.

But on a canal, even a single boat ahead of you, or one following you too closely, can make you feel claustrophobic.

It impinges on your space, and space – along with tranquillity – is one of the major attractions of the canals. Overtaking happens, but it's subliminally rather frowned on because there's a consensus speed in operation which keeps us apart and acts as a far more efficient check on our progress than the 4 mph official limit in force. This is determined by the conditions: by the depth of the canal, by how straight or how bendy it is, by how many people are using it, or even by how many people are moored on it (since it's considered bad manners to go too fast past stationary boats as well). To overtake on the canals is therefore to challenge the consensus. It means someone's travelling either too fast or too slow, and when it happens (which is less than you'd think) it's strangely unsettling for both parties and is always accompanied by elaborate semaphores of intention by the overtaking boat and profuse apologies by the boat being passed.

It is as if both realise they're confronting a shibboleth, breaking a taboo.

The same is true of the rules that determine the way you pass through locks. If the lock is 'against' you – that is, if the water level is not in your favour – it's the height of bad manners, not to mention a dreadful waste of water, to fill or empty it in the face of an oncoming boat. If someone does it to you, it's an affront on a scale difficult for an outsider to grasp. It's as if someone has wilfully jumped in front of you at the bus stop or wheeled their trolley to the front of the queue at the supermarket checkout. You feel outraged, incensed; at one and the same time indignant and resentful. It's a personal affront and you feel it socially too because they are defying the structure of values you take for granted. It's like people who drop litter. Or park their cars on double yellow lines with the hazard lights on as if this somehow gives them permission to break the law (rather than just mark them out as the dickhead they are).

Sadly more and more of this sort of thing is happening on the canals. Newcomers are either unaware of how things are done, or contemptuous of the traditions of the cut. They bring the habits of roads to the water and go speeding past moored boats, ripping out their lines and causing mayhem. They camp for weeks on end on twenty-four-hour mooring spots and set up home on water-points where they're only supposed to stop long enough to fill their tanks.

This last one irritates me the most. What part of 'You Do Not Moor on Water-Points' don't they understand? 'Ah,' they always say apologetically when I pull them up on it, 'I thought it was too late for anyone to want water.' Or sometimes they say they thought it was too early. Or that it was the wrong day of the week. Or that it was the age of Aquarius or the Year of the damned Pig.

It makes me want to scream. Don't these people realise that it is *never* too late to want water, that it is *never* the wrong time? Personally, if I see someone moored on a water-point, I am *always* going to want water. It may be the middle of the night and my tanks may be full to overflowing with the stuff. My boat may be sinking with the weight of it, in danger of going under – but even so, if I see someone moored on a water-point I will always stop to fill up because well… the rule is you don't moor on water-points and that's an end of it.

So, upholder of the true canal creed, priest of all that is perfect in good canal practice, what was I doing moored at a winding hole? Wasn't that a rule too? Or was it too late or too early for it to apply to me? Was the moon in the Seventh House and Jupiter aligned with Mars?

Well, actually no. But in mitigation the canal was empty. There were no other boats on it, let alone ones that would want to climb up from Huddersfield only to turn round and go back again. There still wasn't much water either, which was really the nub of it, since my decision to stop where I had wasn't so much choice on my part as necessity. The fact is, I hadn't been able to pull up anywhere else. It was so shallow at the edges I just hadn't been able to get close enough to the bank to make it practical. Even mooring where I did meant I had to tie up three or four feet out from the towpath which involved a precipitous jump every time I embarked or disembarked.

And that wasn't the least of the drawbacks, for as I subsequently discovered, the lock-gates on this part of the canal leaked badly and overnight, as water drained through them, it emptied the pound I was in and began to gradually tip *Justice* over sideways, bit by bit. I woke at 3 a.m., my head so far below my feet they were blanched white because all the blood had drained from them. Not that there was much I could do in the middle of the night to rectify the problem, except change position in bed. This way at least my head didn't explode, though such was the angle of the boat, it meant I spent the rest of the night sleeping virtually upright.

At first light, first chance I got, I jumped to the bank and pushed the boat further out into deep water to level it off. This turned out not to be the cleverest decision I ever made in my life. The boat was now so far out I couldn't get back onto it without rolling up my pyjamas and paddling. And paddling is not to be recommended in canals. The bottom is soft and squidgy. It squeezes up through your toes and feels like creatures are sucking your feet. Or worse you put your foot on something rusty and it feels like they're biting you.

I had no alternative. I soon realised that if I was going to stop on the mooring then this process of having to adjust the boat's position on an almost hourly basis, day and night, dependent on the water level, would have to become a pattern of my stay. Still, at least it got me noticed by the local dog-walking fraternity who are thick on the ground in these parts. In pursuit of my new interest in dogs, and ever hopeful of being able to find a way around Em's intransigence on the subject, I was happy to natter with them for hours about the characteristics of different breeds, exercise regimes, food intake and vets' bills.

Even so, it's not easy as a boater to continue serious conversation with anyone about anything when your boat's looking like the wreck of an oil tanker grounded in a storm on some beach in Cornwall.

Eventually, sooner or later, whoever I was talking to would break off from explaining the relative advantages of Iams over Eukanuba to comment on the fact that *Justice* appeared to be listing at an odd angle, and wasn't I worried she'd tip over.

The weather changed. Up until now it had been a typical English summer – which is to say not summery at all: cold and windy with odd days of insipid sun managing to penetrate the blanket of cloud that always seemed to hang over the hills. From time to time this same cloud would open to release odd showers of warmish, half-hearted rain which the locals seemed not to notice at all (or, if they did, they refused to accept as rain, reluctant to grace this bit of dampness in the air with the same noun they used for the cat-and-dog downpours of the winter, that being real rain: glum, bleak stuff falling from the sky for weeks on end in drops the size of dinner plates).

Suddenly, though, it all changed. On my first morning at Marsden I woke blinded by beams of sunlight embarrassed to be so intrusively invading the dark privacy of my cabin. They were like sharp shards of steel cutting through the gloom, so substantial I could have held them and yet at the same time ephemeral too, frail and illusory, dancing with delicate motes of dust. Outside, in every direction I looked – towards Huddersfield where I was heading or back towards Manchester from where I'd come, up the hills on one side or down the valley on the other – was a clear, cloudless sky as blue as thin ice. The sun shone relentlessly, and where a gentle breeze occasionally rippled the surface of the canal, it caught it and turned it into crystal which it shattered against the bank. At 8 a.m. it must have been sixty degrees. By the early afternoon it was in the high eighties and by 4 p.m. it seemed hotter yet, well into the nineties. I opened up both of *Justice*'s roof-windows; I threw open all her doors and her side hatch. But it made no difference to the temperature. It became so hot it hurt. There was no escape from it, no way of getting away from the close, sultry air that had descended without warning on the valley, as palpable as a heavy cloud.

That first day of the heat wave, craving relief from this sudden onslaught and thinking I might get it around a greater expanse of water than the one I was on, I walked back up the towpath to where the canal passes between the straggling length of Sparth reservoir on one side and an old millstream on the other. There I found the local kids out in force splashing about, their bikes left higgledy-piggledy along the towpath, lying where they'd been dropped in their enthusiasm to get into the water. But even here it was blisteringly hot – worse, if anything, because it was unshaded. I went scurrying back to *Justice*. Its steel top was by now too hot to touch, but at least it was insulated and as efficient against the sun as it was against a frosty night. And at least there was a fan on board. I showered and sat in front of it in my underwear, draped modestly with a towel so that at least I could still chat with those towpath dog walkers intrepid enough to venture out in such conditions.

In fact, these Yorkshire folk seemed as resilient to the heat as they were to every other sort of weather. Some of them, fair to say, had cast off the customary top-coats they wore in concession to the conditions, but beyond that there seemed to be as many jackets, collars, ties and cardigans in evidence as normal. I thought for a while I was making too much of the heat, just another demonstration of how much of a namby-pamby I'd become living so long in the capital of namby-pambyism. But the dogs gave it away. Despite their owners looking as if they'd just stepped out on a chilly November night, the dogs confirmed that it was, in fact, hot. Very hot indeed.

Dogs sweat through their tongues, everyone knows that. But these dogs didn't just sweat, they steamed. Their tongues waved in the air like great flags, searching out the slightest stale draft of air. Or they'd drag along the ground listlessly, great floppy flaps as pink as plastic and speckled with spume and slime.

'Bit warm today,' I'd say by way of a conversation opener to the blokes passing on the towpath.

But dressed like that, in a towel and not much else, they were always going to be mistrustful. They'd look me up and down as if I was the encapsulation of some permissive culture somewhere, all free love and nudity. Certainly not from Yorkshire anyhow.

'Aye, 'appen,' they'd say.

While behind them, some great spaniel or little whippet on a lead, being towed along like a sledge, would wave its weary tongue at me in solidarity.

'Take no notice of him,' they seemed to be gasping between laboured breaths. 'Don't listen to a word he says. It is hot. In fact, it's scorching. And while we're on the topic, can you persuade this lunatic to get off home so we can get a bit of shade this afternoon?'

The next day I brought a sun-lounger out onto the towpath and sat under an umbrella with my trousers rolled up dangling my feet in the water. I don't know if folk up that way thought I was loopy; I certainly thought some of them were. That afternoon I watched a young bloke in his twenties walk straight into the canal. He was dressed in posh jeans and a spotlessly white T-shirt and was having a conversation on his mobile phone at the time. When I say he walked straight into the canal I don't mean that he strayed over the edge and gave himself a wet foot, or that he slipped and went tumbling. What I mean is that he literally walked straight into the cut, as if it was part of his route, striding into it with such purpose you'd have thought he'd got an appointment with the bottom.

He was lucky there was water in it at the time. An hour or two later after it drained and he might have broken his neck. One moment he was chatting away with all the confidence you have when you're young and think you've got things worth paying thirty-six pence a minute to say; the next, he was up to his waist in water, still chatting away to whoever was on the line as if nothing had happened. Mind you, he didn't look so cool afterwards. But I could hardly talk about cool, looking as if I'd just wandered in from Blackpool beach, only a knotted handkerchief short of the full image.

I blame it on technology. Technology's given us too many opportunities for sane people to look mad. In the past, if you saw someone walking along a street talking to themselves you'd know they were three sheets to the wind. You wouldn't mind that they were like that; you wouldn't hold it against them. But you'd keep away from them. You'd walk round them and avert your eyes from theirs. Nowadays, though, you wouldn't bat an eyelid: you'd know immediately they were talking hands-free on their mobile phone. Even when there are groups of people together, you know they will still be talking on their mobiles. Sometimes they will even talking to each other on them.

This is mad, isn't it? You see people sitting in pubs with each other desperately texting their friends. Presumably to arrange to meet them in other pubs somewhere where they will sit and text other friends. Or you see people together engaged in animated conversation, talking loudly, laughing and joking. But not with each other. Oh, no, that would be too simple. They are talking on the phone. To some faraway person on the other side of the country.

'Hello, hello… Are you there? Can you hear me? I'm on the train. I'm in the car. I'm on the bus. Hello. Can you hear me? I'm in the next room. I'm standing next to you.'

I wonder how much money the mobile phone companies have made out of this sort of drivel. Millions, surely? It is as if at any stage, separated from our friends, we are timorous of the world and terrified of the eternity in which we exist. It is as if by fetishising our phones, which we do more and more, we are seeking reassurance that we are never going to be alone.

I don't blame this all on the young either. It's not exclusively young people who are driving into rivers or finishing up in supermarket car parks on the way to Inverness as they slavishly follow directions on their sat navs. Neither is it just young people who are collecting friends on Facebook like sad philatelists, or emailing each other on the move from Apples or Blackberries or whatever the trendy technological fruit of the moment is. There's a general impatience about the world in the air at the moment. As if what people have to say is of such importance it can't wait an hour or two before it's uttered.

As if – if it's not uttered now – there won't be time to communicate it at all.

Late one afternoon on the third or fourth day of my stay when it had cooled enough to move, I packed away the sun-lounger and finally made it into Marsden, the suburbs of which I'd skirted coming down from the tunnel. It was only a step or two from the canal but it could have been another world; and Marsden itself, though just a small village of some three thousand or so people, was like a massive metropolis after the seclusion of the towpath. The streets weren't exactly teeming with people, but all the same Marsden's a busy enough place with its shops, its Mechanics Institute topped with its characteristic red-striped wooden clock tower, and its pubs, one of which brews its own beers named after the reservoirs that fed the canal.

Marsden's an old cloth-manufacturing town, and like several such places hereabouts, some of the old grey grit houses rising up the steep streets have wide back windows positioned so as to catch maximum light for the weavers. I fell in love with it the first time I visited some years ago, before the canal was re-opened, when I was a TV producer and took an away-day from London to meet Mike Lucas who for many years ran the Mikron Theatre Company, a small troupe which toured (and still tours) the waterways on a traditional narrowboat, performing plays on waterways-related themes.

There was talk then of a sort of real-life soap about the trials and tribulations of the company, and though the idea never came to anything – TV commissioning editors not being interested in much outside of the South East, and definitely not in any idea that hasn't been done at least once before – the visit was nevertheless far from being a wasted trip. Indeed, my ambition to one day cross the Pennines on the canal, even if it meant walking it on the towpath, probably dates from that time.

The weather that day was about as different as it could be with snow thick on the ground, so much of it that at one stage I was sure I wouldn't make the meeting at all. Seven or eight miles outside Manchester, where I'd made my connection, the train stopped for a quarter of an hour or

CHAPTER SEVENTEEN

so because of drifting, and when it started again it went at a crawl, advancing through the hills in a series of abrupt jerks, like a learner driver uncertain on the clutch. When it eventually pulled in at Marsden station it was more than an hour late and poor Mike, who'd been on standby most of the morning, and had been regularly slithering up and down the hill to the station to see whether I'd arrived, showed himself as a man of some graciousness not to send me straight back where I'd come from. In fact he took me down to his local and we ate sausage and mash and drank good beer in front of a roaring open fire.

The town was enchanting that day, more Alpine than Pennine and not at all what I'd expected of Yorkshire. The boughs of the bare winter trees were heavy with virgin snow and the precipitously hilly streets, which were virtually impassable, were unsullied by traffic of any sort. A sort of heavy, flat silence lay over the place, a deep muffled quietness which was comforting and consoling after the clamorous hysteria of London which I'd left behind that morning.

Walking to the village from the boat during the heat wave, the late afternoon sun still hot enough to burn the back of my neck, it was difficult to believe that this was same place I'd visited that day. I bought fresh milk and vegetables, and some pulses from a health food shop. The presence of a health food shop in a small town or village on the canal is always a good indication of its social composition. It means there's a New Age urban overspill population, or a demographic with a higher than average percentage of ageing hippies. I always feel comfortable in places with a health food shop. It makes me feel I'm with my own people.

Eventually I found the pub that Mike had taken me to on my first visit, but it was messy and unloved and had a floor so tacky my sandals stuck to it, so I didn't stay long. There was no reason to anyhow; there's no shortage of pubs in Marsden. Eventually I found one on the main street backing onto a weir, with large, wide windows and an open door that seemed designed to catch every breeze visiting the valley. I drank a couple of pints, so rich and full-bodied they made me feel rapturous, as if I was in another of my dreams again, disjointed from the real world, separated from reality.

It's called getting tipsy.

Afterwards I walked back to the boat the long way, by the lock flight, which was deliciously cooling in what was now the early evening. The air was heavy with the smell of honeysuckle, and I sat for a while on one of the lock-beams, the river gently rippling on one side of me, and the canal gates dripping at the other. Gradually, filtering through the trees I began to make out the faraway hypnotic sound of a brass band rehearsing in the distance. It was like the sirens of Marsden calling to me.

I could have sat there all night listening to it. Indeed I could have moored in Marsden all summer except that it would have been a form of shipwreck, as damaging to the trip I was on as if I'd dashed *Justice* onto the rocks. It wouldn't do. I was involved in a journey after all, a journey which until now had been a pleasant enough, though aimless, affair – but which very soon was going to take an unexpected turn.

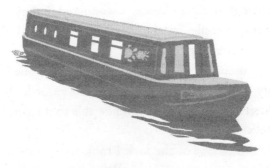

Eighteen

A boat woke me the next morning. I heard it coming a mile off, travelling towards me from the Huddersfield direction, and I was so excited to discover that I wasn't alone on the canal anymore that I pulled on a pair of shorts and a T-shirt and went out to greet it. It was another lovely day, a cloudless sky as far as you could see, the sun as bright as a meadow buttercup. I had hope in my heart and a spring in my step.

'Had a good trip?' I asked the helmsman as he came through the lock. He was with his wife and must have been in his mid-fifties, I guess. Around my age. The sort of bloke you'd have seen working in a bank or a building society a few years back before they started clearing them out for younger men with sharper haircuts and a different attitude to client relations.

He looked at me fearfully with eyes that spoke of horrors they had experienced of which I could but dream.

'No. It's been dreadful,' he said. 'Bloody awful.'

I felt my stomach lurch on their behalf. My God, what could have happened to them? It was only nine o'clock. What could have happened before nine o'clock? Nothing ever happens in England before nine o'clock. I wondered if they were just exaggerating. People on the canals can do that. They get divorced from reality. Things get out of perspective. Maybe they'd just run out of tea. Maybe the milk had gone off?

'Twenty-odd locks from Slaithwaite,' he gasped. 'And every one of them a bastard. You'll never be able to manage them on your own.'

As they pulled out of the lock I took their place and I was soon on my way, happy to be on the move again despite their warning. The first three or four locks were OK. I couldn't see what their problem was. I began to think it was because they were past it that they'd found the going so hard.

But then the paddles got stiffer and the gates became almost impossible to open. And I began to realise exactly who it was who was past it.

At one gate I pushed and pulled for about half an hour without results, and I'd probably still be there now if it hadn't been for one of those streaks of Lycra that ride up and down the towpath on bikes. He stopped and helped me. He only weighed about eight stone and I thought the effort would kill him. But they're a tough breed, these cyclists, despite the need they have to dress like technicolour frogmen. The gate swung open at his first push.

The next lock, thank God, was easier and I was closing the gates behind me when habit made me look up the canal to check for approaching boats. I was astonished when I saw one. A second boat of the day! It was unprecedented, the first time since coming through the tunnel that I'd really been aware of other people using the canal.

CHAPTER EIGHTEEN

It was another single-hander like me, a young bloke in his mid-twenties, certainly no older. And another deep-drafted boat too, I noticed. I considered maybe warning him about the difficulties which lay ahead, but then I had second thoughts. It's better to travel hopefully than to arrive, they say. But on the Huddersfield Narrow if you don't travel hopefully you don't stand a chance of ever arriving.

I opened the gates I'd just closed and went back to *Justice*, but something had happened to her in the interim. She'd grounded herself on a ledge, or run herself against the bank and was wedged solid. Eventually I had to enlist the help of the approaching boat to tow me off the obstruction, but immediately I was out of the lock and over that difficulty, another equally tricky one presented itself. The channel was too narrow. We couldn't pass. We couldn't get by each other. Boats tend to find their own deep water. The trouble with these two boats was that they were fighting for the same deep water. It was a stand-off with neither of them able to make any progress.

'Mmmmm, tricky one,' Pete said as we stood surveying the situation. Pete was the bloke on the other boat. He had long dreadlocks to his shoulder which was the first think you noticed about him. The second thing you noticed was his eyes. They were steely grey. Or at least one of them was. The other seemed to be blue, but the pupil was so distended you couldn't really tell. 'Fancy a cuppa while we think about it?' he suggested. 'Hop over, I'll put the kettle on.'

The inside of his boat was furnished like an up-market junk shop, put together from stuff which he proudly admitted he'd salvaged from council recycling centres. Mind you, he was a bit like that himself. He had one leg that seemed thicker than the other, a left arm that seemed longer than the right – and those odd-coloured, odd-shaped eyes, of course. Maybe God had assembled him from the recycling centre too.

The tea arrived in old china cups. They weren't from the same set, but they were beautiful all the same, Wedgwood, Crown Derby or something like that.

'You didn't get that stuff from a council recycling centre, surely?' I asked.

'No, that was my ex-girlfriend,' he admitted. 'She's got a nose for a bargain. But sadly she had a nose for other blokes too. She could sniff them out at twenty paces, especially ones with narrow hips in tight trousers. She left me a year ago, went off with a welder from Stockport. They've got a couple of kids and a mortgage now. Twins,' he explained before I could ask. 'Fancy a beer?'

Why on earth I agreed to drink beer at that time of the day, I'll never know. Perhaps it was the weather. It was already oppressively hot, definitely beer weather. But perhaps part of it was the ludicrousness of the position we found ourselves which called for beer to make sense of it. Our two boats unmoored, bow to bow, floating free and blocking not just each other, but the rest of the canal too.

One beer, of course, led to another and in the process I learnt more than I needed to know about Monica, the wife of the welder from Stockport, the woman with a nose for a bargain and for men in tight trousers.

'The problem with her,' Pete explained, 'was love.' But then he corrected himself. 'No it wasn't, it was the boat.'

CHAPTER EIGHTEEN

'The boat?'

'She thought I loved the boat more than her. She was always complaining how I never brought her stuff back from the tip. I said, "Monica, let me get this right, you are belly-aching that I don't bring you back stuff from the tip? From the tip? Would you really *want* stuff from the tip?"'

We had another beer.

'And the welder from Stockport?' I asked.

'He probably buys everything new. Probably pays a fortune for it too, though I doubt it's any better than the stuff she had here. I mean, look at that table there.' He pointed it out. It was the table my beer cans were on. All three of them – two empty and one just opened.

'Nice table,' I said.

'Yes, it is nice, very nice,' he agreed. 'Mahogany. I had an antique dealer on the boat once – well, not an antique dealer, not as such, but a bloke who does a bit of trading on eBay. He said a table like that might have fetched £100 before I cut the legs down. Did you notice I cut the legs down?' he asked.

'It did strike me it was a bit low,' I said. 'Well, not low, just lower than normal, lower than I would have expected for a mahogany occasional table,' I added, not wanting to upset him.

'She doesn't love him, you know.' he said. 'The welder, I mean. Not like she loved me, anyway. With me it was something special.'

I nodded. 'You sound as if you had something precious between you.'

'It was different,' he said.

'It certainly sounds that way,' I agreed.

He reached over and put his hand on my arm. 'I can talk to you, Steve, you know. You're an old bloke but you're not like other old blokes. Not like me dad, fr'instance. Me dad thinks I'm a waste of space. He never liked Monica. He said I was bonkers getting involved with her. Or maybe it was the other way round…'

At length we decided to try to get past each other again. We'd come up with this crazy idea of backing up the boats until we'd got space for a good run at each other. If we accelerated as much as we could, opening up our throttles, we reckoned we could just about do it. He would steer to one side of the canal and I'd steer to the other. If we were lucky we thought we could squeeze past. OK, with the benefit of hindsight I can see now if we hadn't been lucky we'd probably have hit each other head-on and killed ourselves. But after a few drinks these sorts of details don't seem important.

In the event, thank God, we didn't need to try it. We emerged into the sunshine to find that the boats had practically drifted past each other under their own steam so that all we had to do was push them apart. Would that all of life's difficulties could be like this, I thought. Would that every time there was a problem we could have a few beers and it'd solve itself.

When we were clear of each other we started our engines. 'What's it like further down?' I asked before I moved off. 'Easy going?'

'No sweat. You'll fly through it. What's it like up there?' he asked, indicating the canal ahead.

'Not too bad at all. Hard work, but nothing you won't be able to handle.'

CHAPTER EIGHTEEN

'I heard tell it was a bit low on water.'

'Ah, just towpath talk,' I said. 'Just rumour.'

I set off for Slaithwaite with a vengeance. I suppose at the beginning of the day I had some notion I might be there by lunchtime. I'd heard tell of a pub where a guy bred dachshunds. And there was a church I fancied seeing with an interesting ceiling, and a old mill that was still working which I hoped I might be able to talk my way into.

But it was clear the going would be slow. It was the old familiar problem again. Oh, the depth, the depth, the damned depth. I felt like Quasimodo tormented by the bells. It was worst at the locks. Once I'd let *Justice* down to the level of the next pound, there just wasn't enough water to take her over the concrete edges of the bottom, the cills as they're called. Every time I came out of a lock she would grind over them, scraping her bottom with such an excruciating noise you felt someone was filing your teeth. I knew it was only a matter of time before I came to one that would be impassable. Pete must have known that too. He had a deep-draughted boat. He must have had the same trouble coming up the locks as I was having going down them. But he'd been discreet. He'd not told me what to expect, any more than I'd told him what lay ahead. There'd been a conspiracy of silence between us, a conspiracy of kindness.

It happened a couple of locks further down. Coming over the cill *Justice* stopped dead and there was nothing I could do to get her moving again. I used the engine, I used the barge pole, I used ropes. I pushed her, I pulled her, I rocked her. Eventually, with an agonised screech, I managed to move her forward a yard or two. This represented some sort of progress, I thought. Until I realised that the only thing it had actually achieved was to take me away from the lock ladder which was now just out of reach.

It was a serious problem. When you are in a lock single-handing a boat, the ladder is your only contact with the outside world. Without it, you're trapped. And I *was* trapped. Trapped miles from anywhere at the bottom of a dank and slimy lock chamber. I tried throwing up ropes blindly in the hopes I could lasso a bollard at the top and climb out that way. I tried shouting for help, attempting to attract the attention of someone passing on the towpath. But there wasn't anyone passing on the towpath, not even a dog walker. It was a weekday afternoon in a middle of a heat wave and the world had gone off to sit under a shady tree.

I must have been there an hour before anyone registered my existence. I heard a voice and soon afterwards a pale, suspicious face peered over the lock side. It was a boy. Twelve years old or thereabouts. He was wearing raggedy-arsed short trousers which surprised me because I didn't think that kids today wore anything except designer jeans.

'You OK?' he said.

Part of me wanted to tell him that I was perfectly fine. That I was just taking tea at the bottom of the lock, cooling off; doing the sort of thing that narrowboats do in the middle of the summer and hadn't he ever noticed before? But facetiousness would not have been a good move. My wellbeing depended on this child. Without him I would be stuck on the Huddersfield Narrow for ever and ever. Without him I would die and be found as a bleached skeleton when next a boat ventured onto these waters.

So, as best I could – given that he was on the lock side and I was in the lock eight or nine feet below him – I explained what had happened.

Eventually the penny dropped. 'You mean, the bottom of the lock's made of concrete,' he said, 'and you're stuck on it because there's not enough water to float off at the bottom?'

'Got it in one,' I said. 'Now what I want you to do is this. I'm going to throw you a lock-key – you know what a lock-key is, don't you? I want you to wind open those metal things over there for me…'

'What's that going to do then?' he wanted to know.

'It's going to release water from the top of the canal,' I said. 'It's going to flush me out.'

'What, like a lavatory, when you pull the chain?'

'Yes, I suppose so, if you must put it that way,'

He shook his head. 'Can't do it,' he said.

'Can't do it? Why on earth not?'

'Me dad.'

'Your dad? What's your sodding dad got to do with it?'

'Me dad's told me not to play with locks. He says they're dangerous.'

'But you're not playing with them, you're helping me.'

'I still can't do it.' he said again. 'It wouldn't be right unless…'

'Unless what?'

'Unless you were willing to pay for it,' he said.

Pay for it? I couldn't believe what I was hearing. What had happened to altruism? What had happened to doing someone a good turn?

'Well, you're stuck, aren't you?' he explained. 'That's what you've just told me. So without me, you're not going anywhere. That must be worth something.'

'OK, a fiver,' I said. I wasn't going to quibble.

He, however, was.

'Not enough,' he said. 'Make it a tenner and it's a deal.'

'Watch yourself,' I shouted, 'these lock-keys can be heavy…'

It was when he bent to pick it up that I noticed the label on his raggedy-arsed short trousers which weren't short trousers at all but long shorts which are a very different thing when you're twelve years old and trying to be cool. It said Diesel. Diesel is a hip multi-national Italian design company much favoured by the young. Their stuff costs a fortune.

At least now I had an inkling of how kids could afford to pay their prices.

Regardless what it looks like on paper Slaithwaite is pronounced Sloughwut. I understand this sort of thing. I was born in Loughborough which some people call Lugerboruga which is the same sort of assault on language. Just before you get into Slaithwaite there's a factory with a lock near a bridge which was widened in such a way that it didn't leave space to swing lock-beams any longer. The solution was to build a lift gate – or a guillotine lock as they are sometimes called for obvious reasons. They have an outer framework of steel, and the gate which rises inside it is like a blade which goes up or down to let boats through. This is made of steel too and it's very heavy so that in order to be able to manoeuvre it, it has to be counterbalanced. The spindle which controls this is geared so highly that opening or closing it seems to take forever.

You could read a book while you're doing it. You could write one. It isn't heavy work but you just have to keep going at it and try not to lose concentration which would be an easy thing to do because turning a spindle for what seems like an eternity isn't exactly an intellectually engaging thing to do. It's too easy to just drift off onto another astral plain and forget what you're doing and why you're doing it. Too easy to let your mind wander so that you lose all sense that you're approaching Slaithwaite and begin to think you're close to Sloughwut instead, wondering what an earth you're doing spending your life turning a handle on a guillotine-lock.

This happened to me. I'd been winding the spindle for so long I'd lost all track of time. I wasn't really noticing what I was doing and I certainly wasn't watching the gate. I think I must have been suffering from too much sun. It was early evening by now but it was as hot as it had been all day. I felt I was getting too old for these sorts of games. I was overheated, thinking about how late it was, and whether I would get to the shops on time, and what I might buy if I did, and what would I eat that night if I didn't...

Then this bloke tapped me on the shoulder. I'd been half-aware of him out of the corner of my eye watching me. In fact, I'd found him a bit irritating, looking at me as if I was an idiot who didn't know what he was doing. Blokes like that get on my nerves. If they think they can do better they should do it, not stand on the sidelines sniping at those of us who are getting on with the job.

I snapped at him. 'What do you want?'

'I hope you don't mind me saying this, mate,' he said. 'I mean, I'm not being funny or anything. But you're turning it the wrong way.'

So I finally got there. OK it was hours after I planned to get there, and I was on my knees with heat exhaustion. But I'd finally made it; I was in Slaithwaite.

I thought Slaithwaite was terrific, however they pronounce it. It was a town like Stalybridge which had lost its canal and then found it buried under the high street. Or in this case under Carr Lane where a row of lovely cherry trees had been planted on top. It was a loss that these had to be cut down as part of the canal redevelopment – but it was the only downside of the deal which has benefited the town enormously. The Huddersfield Narrow as it passes through Slaithwaite is as impressive an example of canal restoration as you'll find anywhere: thoughtfully planned and beautifully executed with lots of natural stone and solid cast-iron railings that would stop a football crowd in its tracks, let alone a drunk stumbling about after a night out. Some people feel the channel's too narrow and too much like a culvert but I think this brings it into scale with the town, and the two seem to embrace each other effortlessly. Passing through, you immediately begin to feel a part of things.

It was a Friday night and although people were still shopping, the pubs were beginning to fill up and the fish shops were starting to fry, covering this part of Yorkshire with the smell of heaven. I couldn't wait to get off the boat.

But it wasn't to be. Soon after I'd moored up I got a call from Em in London.

'Your brother's been ringing you all afternoon,' she said.

'The phone's been in the cabin,' I said. 'But I've seen that there's messages from him. I was going to call him back after I had a shower.'

'It's just that something's happened to your mum,' she said.

'Oh my God! Another fall?'

'Yes, that – but something worse too. It's just that they think they might know why it's happening.'

Nineteen

I was on the train to the Midlands first thing the next day. That afternoon, and again in the evening, I visited the hospital. The prognosis was not good. Afterwards I went home to London, and on the Sunday Em and I went for a walk in Kent across the North Downs to Hollingbourne where at the top of the ridge at Cats Mount the county lies in creased folds below you like an unmade bed. We drank coffee we'd brought with us in a flask; we ate some chocolate biscuits we'd picked up at a service station. It was a bright day with only the occasional cloud to sully the sky. But it's high there, and windy, and every now and then we'd catch a blast from the south blowing full in our faces as sharp and tart as a lemon.

'So they're continuing with the tests at the hospital then?' Em asked, picking up from where she'd left off the previous night when I'd got back late and tired and tearful and she'd only been able to talk to me long enough to get the headlines.

I shrugged. 'I guess so. But they seem pretty certain of their diagnosis, even now. She can't remember what happens, you see, after she falls. They're pretty certain it's this vascular dementia thing I was telling you about.'

Em stared into the distance, her arms resting on her knees, cradling her coffee in her hands. Above the shallow valley where we were sitting a couple of gulls from the coast were circling silently, buffeted by the gusts.

'Is it different from Alzheimer's?' she asked at length.

Again I shrugged my shoulders. 'At the end of the day I don't think there's much in it. Either way you lose your mind. But Alzheimer's is more of a gradual decline, more predictable. Vascular dementia's like having a series of small strokes. It can be stable in a person for months on end, but then the next time you see them they've gone into decline.'

'And there's no cure?'

'Well, there might have been. Thirty years ago. If she'd have stopped smoking and joined a gym and started eating greens. But hey, this is my mother we're talking about here, not Kelly Holmes.'

We walked on to Hollingbourne, where we had Sunday lunch, a meal as traditionally English as a bulldog, and the beef – sadly – about as tough as one too. Afterwards, on our way back to where we'd left the car at Thurnham, she raised the topic again.

'So when are you and your brother meeting social services? Thursday, did you say?

'Yes. They're going to look at organising a care package for her so she can live at home as long as possible. But after that…'

'Yes?'

'After that I suppose she'll have to go into a home. She's going to need specialist care, twenty-four hours a day. I suppose we're going to have to start preparing for it now. There's going to be a lot of work arranging things, visiting places and checking them out.'

'So where does that leave your trip on the boat?' she asked.

'My trip on the boat? I haven't thought about it, to be honest. Not once. Not since I left Slaithwaite. All that seems a million miles away now, like another world. I guess the straight answer is that the trip's over.'

'What, finished? Just like that?' We'd come to a stile and she stopped and looked at me, puzzled, as if she could hear what I was saying but couldn't quite believe that I was saying it.

'What I find the strangest thing,' she said later, 'is that you don't seem particularly worried that you've given it up. You don't even seem to care.'

I found myself shaking my head.

'No,' I said eventually, weighing my words deliberately before I replied, 'I don't think I do.'

Over the next few weeks, weeks that I spent driving up to Leicester on the M1 and driving back down to London again; weeks that I spent going to meetings with social workers or with doctors or with occupational therapists; weeks that I spent visiting care homes at the rate of two or three a day, reporting back to my brother on them in the evening, discussing them late into the night; weeks that I spent visiting my mother every chance I got so that hospital became, bizarrely, almost like a second home to me, a home from home, a bitter unhappy home filled with tears and regrets, my mother's memories – even at this early stage in her illness – beginning to fade and lose their edge; during all this time I thought a lot about why

I was so unconcerned that a project I'd embarked upon with such anticipation and enthusiasm should now hold so little attraction for me that I could put it behind me with scarce a regret.

Of course, compared with what was happening, nothing of the rest of my life really seemed to matter much anymore. But then life itself didn't seem to matter much either, when it was so transitory and could end in this whimpering way. Yet it was more than just what was happening to my mother that made me feel disillusioned, I realised that. There was something specific to the trip that had been a disappointment to me too, something I'd hoped to get from it which it hadn't delivered, something it could never deliver. I'd begun it in such expectation – but expectation of what, I kept asking myself? At the beginning I'd harboured some bonkers idea that I might find the North. Find the North? What was I thinking of? Had the North suddenly gone missing? Had it dropped down the back of a bus seat somewhere in Bolton, or been misplaced in Gateshead on a trip to the MetroCentre? No, it never was the North I was out to discover, but me. I'd been mistaking something external for something inside. What I'd really wanted to know was where, with my background, I fitted into all this. What I'd really wanted to know was where I belonged.

And the truth was that judged by this criterion my months on the waterways had been a waste of time. I'd not been on a journey, not a real journey, not a journey of genuine discovery where you find out things about yourself and the world you live in. No, I'd been on an extended holiday, a sort of indulgent amble through England without either a purpose or a philosophy to justify my movements. OK, I'd had a great time. I'd been to places I would never have visited otherwise; and I'd met people I'd never have met either. But it was no use trying to pretend to myself that it meant anything when all that really mattered, I'd learnt, was that overweight, chain-smoking old lady from Leicester whose brain was dying before the rest of her body.

I tried to explain all this to Em one night over dinner but it came out badly and she finished up getting the wrong end of the stick.

'I got the impression you didn't even like the canal,' she said. 'Some nights when you called, you sounded as if you hated it.'

I couldn't believe what I was hearing. 'Hated it? What? The Huddersfield Narrow Canal? No, I don't hate it, I love it. It's the most interesting canal I've ever been on: it's got a grandeur about it, a dignity, that's unmatchable. And it's beautiful beyond compare. You can keep your Oxfords and your Llangollens. Compared with the Huddersfield Narrow they're just insipid and prosaic. The Huddersfield Narrow is truly amazing. It's amazing not just because of the landscape it passes through but because of its history and what that represents in terms of man's triumph over his environment. It's amazing because of what it is and the demands it makes of you.

'OK, it's a challenge, I grant you that,' I went on. 'It's not an easy canal to cruise. I'll confess at the beginning I thought it was a pain. But it's grown on me – like the idea of having a dog has grown on me. I don't like it any the less for being cussed. If anything, I like it more. It reminds me of the old days of canalling when the two of us got our first boat. You know what it was like then – everything was much more unpredictable, closer to the edge somehow. You didn't know then when you started out on a trip that you'd ever arrive, or what you'd have to go through if you did. The Huddersfield Narrow's like that: it's gritty and provocative. Sometimes, in the sunshine, it can seem benign. But I've been in that part of the world in the winter, I've seen what it's like. I know it wouldn't take much to make a canal like that angry.'

Em poured herself another glass of wine. 'You should go back and finish the trip,' she said. 'You'll regret it for the rest of your life if you don't.'

'Maybe. But it doesn't seem worth it any more. I can't see that I'll ever have anything worth saying about canals any more.'

She laughed. 'Perhaps not. But sometimes the wisest thing to do is to just go to places and let them say things to you.'

'No,' I said. 'It's not going to happen. Too much has changed.'

Yet as the weeks passed and the summer ebbed away, August turning into September, I began to think again about the decision I'd made. I had to go back to the boat sometime soon anyhow; I'd left it on sufferance at a temporary mooring in Slaithwaite and it had to be moved. Either I'd have to find a more permanent home for it over the winter or I'd have to bring it south again. Yet if I was going to do that, it was as easy for me to complete the trip I'd started as to turn around and go back the way I'd come. My mother's situation was less of an issue now, or at least for the moment: her condition appeared to have stabilised and what plans that could be made for her future were already in hand.

A decision had to taken quickly. The canals close over the winter for essential maintenance and if I didn't make up my mind soon there simply wouldn't be enough time to travel the distances that lay ahead. Even as things stood, I was cutting it tight, for ahead of me lay the Rochdale Canal, the second of the two Pennine waterways to have been opened after restoration.

And the Rochdale is a far more physically demanding challenge than even the Huddersfield Narrow. It's thirty-three miles long and has ninety-two locks. In just fourteen miles between Sowerby Bridge and the summit there are thirty-six of them, rising 350 feet before dropping down into Manchester. But these aren't narrow locks of the sort that gave the Huddersfield Narrow Canal its name. These are big locks, double width: great cavernous things with heavy gates that you have to walk miles to operate because you can't step over them like you can narrow locks. Single-handing they cause you no end of trouble because when you empty or fill them your boat heaves around uncontrollably because they use so much more water. The weather wouldn't help much either. The heat wave was long since over and when I checked on the Internet, the forecast for the next month was for wind and rain.

What finally made me decide to finish the trip – apart from Em nagging me that I should do it and complaining that if I didn't do it, could I please do something else because she was sick of having me moping about the house getting under her feet like a bored teenager – was a canal book I came across on one of the shelves at home. It was an old book that we'd had for thirty years or so. I was looking for something to read when I just picked it up without thinking and it fell open at some pictures of the Rochdale.

Planning the trip, I hadn't really thought much about the canal except that I noticed it went through Hebden Bridge, a place that looked interesting and where I'd made a mental note to stop. One of the pictures in the book was of the canal before restoration. It was taken not far from Todmorden on a late autumn afternoon when the sun was low in the sky so that it picked out the burnished copper colours of the moors as they tumbled down steeply to the water's edge. There was a row of small grey cottages backing onto the canal which was so still and smooth it was like glass. And there was a man walking along the towpath following what at first I took to be a dog but which on closer examination, incomprehensibly, turned out to be a duck. It was, without doubt, one of the most evocative pictures I'd seen of any canal in a long time. Lyrical, alluring, slightly surreal. And it made my heart lurch, like seeing an old lover across a crowded room.

'I think I'll leave later this week,' I said to Em that night when she got back from work. 'It'll mean a rushed trip – but that won't be any bad thing. It'll be a different sort of cruising to what I've been doing so far, but probably one that's more honest to the original. After all, I can't see that the old working boatmen would have been particularly impressed with my rate of progress so far.'

In fact, I left the next day; there just didn't seem any reason to delay further. I got up early and I was in Slaithwaite and ready to go before lunchtime. *Justice* was in a sad state. Her brass was tarnished and the summer had left her covered in a layer of dust. Old chip-papers littered her deck where the kids had been messing around on her. Inside, she smelt musty, abandoned. I'd left so quickly I hadn't cleared her out properly and potatoes I'd forgotten under the sink had begun to sprout. Her whole demeanour seemed reproving, as if she was disappointed that I should have left her forsaken like this in this unfamiliar place.

I was washing her down, trying to make amends, when a bloke passed on his way back to work at a joinery factory over the way.

'Everything OK, I hope?' he said. 'We've been keeping an eye on her for you.'

It was just the sort of polite thing people say on the towpath and I barely took any notice of it. But not long afterwards someone walking in the opposite direction with his Jack Russell snapping around his ankles said the same thing. Except that he added something else, something that made me break off from my work with astonishment.

'Your mum's not been well, has she?' he said.

And he wasn't the last to mention it. I was there a couple of hours while I got *Justice* shipshape again, and there must have been three or four people that alluded to the 'trouble' I'd been having or the 'difficult times' I'd been going through. It was ridiculous. I know Slaithwaite's a small place, and the canals are a close-knit community. But did everyone know my business? Did everyone know about my personal life? What was I to expect next? Comments about my underwear? References to my sex-life?

I could only assume that someone at British Waterways who I'd spoken to about leaving the boat had mentioned it to someone local who had passed it on in a pub or some such place.

Or perhaps so little happens in Slaithwaite that they'd written a piece about me in the local newspaper. Perhaps they'd even got the town crier onto the job. *Oyez, oyez, oyez. Steve's mum has now stabilised and Steve will soon be leaving his lovely Blackheath home to resume his trip…*

One way or another, the way word had got out was designed to strike fear into the heart of a Londoner, even an adopted one like me. After all, we don't do things this way in the South. It's not that we don't care about other people, or even that we don't notice them. It's just that there are so many of us living together that we have taught ourselves to be blind to one another's lives. If I were to catch sight of my neighbour in thigh-high boots and leather suspenders, it wouldn't cross my mind to acknowledge the fact in any way, let alone talk to anyone else about it. Stuff like that is her business. Or his.

But privacy's indivisible. You can't factor it out for one part of life but decide you actually rather like it in another. In London we've bought into the complete package and this makes us seem stand-offish, as little concerned about our neighbours' welfare as we are their peccadilloes.

And it's actually not true. It's just that this personal stuff frightens the hell out of us. We can't deal with it and we prefer to keep it at arm's length. That's why we're so dreadful at this continental kissing thing that's become fashionable recently with us not knowing whether to embrace once or twice and which side to start and which to end, so that we finish up bumping our noses and giggling and looking complete idiots and not at all chic like the French, which is how we'd like to look.

It's because at heart we're uncomfortable with crossing that line of removed detachment that keeps us separate from one another. We have been imbued with the idea that physical contact is somehow distasteful, and so it's never been natural to us. And because of this we're not being honest to ourselves doing it.

In this part of the world things are different. Here they touch as easily as they gossip. You see women constantly putting their arms round one another's shoulders in reassurance; you see blokes slapping each other on the back.

Just before I was about to cast off and leave Slaithwaite for good, a woman passed on the towpath pulling a shopping trolley behind her. Along with everyone else in the town she'd obviously heard about what was happening in my life and she stopped to pass the time of day.

'It'll all work out well in the end, luv,' she said. 'I wouldn't fret too much.' And she laid the fingers of her hand on my arm with the very gentlest of touches, a gesture so fleeting and inconsequential, the weight of the contact so light and insubstantial, that I hardly registered it was happening until it was over.

It is difficult to explain the effect this had on me. I went through the bottom lock towards Huddersfield, and soon afterwards near Linthwaite I passed the derelict Westwood Mill, said to be the oldest surviving woollen mill in the Colne Valley. Very close is the larger six-storey high Titanic Mill built in Edwardian times. It was in the process of being developed as luxury flats, surrounded by hoardings on which were advertised the luxury hotel and a restaurant it would contain, the swimming pool it would have, the steam room, the sauna.

But I could hardly focus on any of this. It was my eyes, you see. I kept finding them misting over with tears.

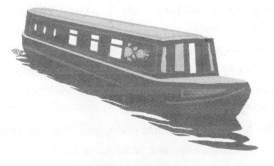

Twenty

I arrived at Huddersfield – the terminus of the Narrow Canal – that night after a trip that was unremarkable by the standards I'd come to expect of the canal. There were only four occasions I was grounded and only one moment of sheer terror at the locks in Milnsbridge, when I was convinced I was sinking. This was after I'd found the engine room a foot deep in water. It turned out to be the locks leaking through my open side-doors.

But hey, this is the sort of thing you have to get used to on the Huddersfield Narrow. It's a canal with a sense of humour.

It was true, as I'd said to Em, that I loved it. But you can love your kids and still be pleased to see the back of them. I was relieved to be shot of the Huddersfield Narrow. My nerves felt as if they'd been through a paper-shredder with it. I needed a respite. I needed a complete break with canals to get over it. Actually, what I probably needed was counselling, but show me a therapist who'd take you seriously if you told them that cruising through the Pennines at 3 mph could reduce you to a nervous breakdown?

So I decided to reinvigorate myself instead with a Yorkshire night out. I would carouse with the locals. I would drink foaming pints of ale in local hostelries and break bread with them in local inns. Well, either that, or I'd get totally pissed in a pub on my own.

I was moored in Aspley Basin adjacent to Sainsbury's and just around the corner from the elegant old mill which has become Huddersfield University.

After so long in the countryside, being in the centre of a big city in such an exposed position made me feel nervous. I'd seen a gang of teenagers, you see. Well, I'd seen a couple of teenagers which is the beginning of a gang and just as bad. I won't say they were up to no good, but they were breathing and that was enough for me. I am not keen on teenagers. They are sullen, unpredictable creatures with spotty faces and dubious views on property rights. So when I left the boat I double-locked it, chained the inside of the hatches and put up the security bar up on the front door.

Huddersfield proved to be a dull town for a visitor on a midweek bender, although I don't blame it on Huddersfield. Or not Huddersfield personally. It's just the way towns are recently all over the country – just cloned versions of one another filled with the same old Marks and Spencer and Next, with a McDonalds on every street corner. Visit one and you've visited them all. Even the pubs in towns look similar nowadays: they're all chains or theme pubs, all decorated in the same way with stuff bought from auctions which is supposed to make them look unique but which finishes up making them all look identical.

The pubs in Huddersfield all seemed to be the size of dance halls, and for all I know they might actually have been dance halls. This would at least explain why some of them seemed reluctant to sell beer and kept me waiting around for so long before they'd serve me, even though I was sometimes the only customer in the place. What they weren't was warm and welcoming, the way pubs should be. There was one close to Aspley Basin with its own microbrewery which someone had recommended to me, but I didn't know its name and no one seemed to have heard of it, so I spent a large part of the evening walking fruitlessly from one sad bar to the next. One I stumbled into was freezing cold, colder than outside. As soon as I got through the door I could feel ice beginning to form on my nose. I wondered if the landlord had mixed up his heating and his air-conditioning, or whether he kept it like that as some sort of statement of cultural independence, as in Newcastle, where it's a point of principle when the temperature drops below freezing for young people never to wear anything heavier than a cotton T-shirt.

Huddersfield prides itself on having the third largest number of listed buildings of any town or city in the UK and there's no doubt that architecturally it's a handsome place. The railway station reminds me vaguely of Buckingham Palace, although it's much better designed and has a rather jaunty statue of former Prime Minister Harold Wilson outside which sets it off a treat. The football ground's something else too. It has four roofs like sails so that you half-expect to see it floating off in the wind – of which there does seem to be rather a lot in Huddersfield, positioned as it is at the bottom of two river valleys.

But you can't sit and look at the outside of buildings all night (even though I understand that's more entertaining than some of the football you see in Huddersfield on occasions). I was cold and grumpy and I couldn't find the pub I wanted, or even an Indian to have a meal which made me even more bad-tempered because there is nowhere in this country of ours – *nowhere* – where there isn't an Indian restaurant if you only know where to look. Finally, I had to make do with a kebab house I stumbled across, and grateful I was for it too. I bought a takeaway doner with chilli sauce and picked up a few cans from an offy across the way before calling it a day and going back to the boat.

That's when I found I'd locked myself out.

At first I thought I must have dropped the keys out of my pocket as I'd been walking around. Or that maybe I'd left them in the arctic bar. Yet the more I thought about it, the more I could remember tossing them onto the table inside the boat just before I left. I stood for a few moments horrified at my own stupidity. Could I really have done something that dumb? Could I really have been such an idiot? Now what was I going to do? There are spare keys for the boat, but they're kept at home. I had visions of having to go back and collect them the next day, as I'd had to do once when I left my passport in Manchester and was flying off from Heathrow on holiday.

I could feel myself beginning to panic. I put down the kebab and beer on the roof of the boat and forced myself to think carefully about the events of the evening, desperately trying to remember any small detail that might help. Yes, I had thrown the keys onto the table inside the boat. But I'd picked them up again, hadn't I? I must have picked them up again because I'd put the security bar across the front door, and that meant using the keys to open the padlocks on it. Afterwards I must have put them down somewhere…

CHAPTER TWENTY

Somewhere convenient, surely. Somewhere close at hand, certainly. Somewhere possibly like… er, like the roof of the boat where I'd just put the kebab and the beer.

When I looked, they were there. Of course they were. It was incomprehensible that I hadn't seen them before. For heaven's sake, I'd almost put the beer and the kebab on top of them.

But you do this sometimes, don't you? You don't see things for looking.

Just as astonishing as my blindness was that they hadn't been taken. They'd been on the roof of the boat, on a key ring attached to a rather desirable Swiss Army knife that you'd think would have been nicked as soon as seen. Yet streams of people must have passed on the towpath that evening. No one had so much as touched the keys, let alone used them to break into the boat. Not even the teenage lads I'd been so sniffy about.

It was enough to restore your faith in human nature. Or maybe not. Maybe there are some inanimate objects like keys and wallets and spectacles which have the ability to disappear at will, just to exasperate us. I know it sometimes feels that way. That would certainly explain why I hadn't seen the keys, and why they hadn't been taken. It was because they had gone off for a walk. Because they'd gone back to have tea with their mum or gone to the pictures for a midweek matinee.

Yes, it's a barmy idea. Typical of the sort of thing that goes through your mind when you're tired and need to eat.

And when you've done something so dazzlingly foolish you can't accept what a bonehead you've been.

I was up and gone before five the next morning on a schedule that I was now going to have to keep to regularly now if I was to have any hope of completing my journey before the winter. Huddersfield was empty, the city streets barely lit. The canal was calm and silent, a thin covering of mist hovering above the water giving it an unworldly, ethereal feel. Canals are like this in the early morning; it is when they are at their most beautiful, even in a city. It's a gnawing, haunting beauty, difficult to describe because even up some backwater in Birmingham or on some rubbish-strewn industrial estate somewhere, a little of that beauty survives despite everything.

It could be just the alchemy of a new day, any day, anywhere. But I think it's something special to canals, a magic in these grey ditches that has the power to weave spells. It can bewitch you at any time. But in the early mornings when you're alone, no other boats about and the world your own, you're at your most vulnerable. It becomes intimate then, this thing between you. Like lovers together, the two of you in thrall to each other, your lives bound together in propeller patterns. Call me a romantic, an old sentimentalist, but all I know is that when I'm cruising anywhere at that time in the morning I can sometimes find myself lost in reverie, not on a canal at all, or not a real canal, but transported to that fairytale world of roses and castles where I steer around the painted battlements, under turrets bedecked with flags, towards the sunrise in the mountains beyond.

I slipped under the first bridge of the day, just up from where I was moored. Its name was Locomotive Bridge, so called, it's said, because it was thought to look like an early steam train. As explanations of names go, this one seemed a little fanciful to me. It was under restoration at the time, and if it looked like a train at all, it looked like one that had come off the rails with wheels and pulleys lying around all over the towpath. It was a strange sight glimpsed through the dawn gloom at that time in the morning. Like the sort of thing Dali might have painted after he got fed up with melting clocks.

I was soon past it and making good progress, taking advantage of a water depth I hadn't experienced for some time. Lock followed lock with remarkable uneventfulness. I passed Red Doles, the highest of the nine locks on the Huddersfield Broad Canal on which I was now travelling. I passed Falls Lock and Fieldhouse Green; Reading and Turnpike Road. Just after Longland Lock, the canal runs parallel to a large park and playing fields where the mists, which had by now lifted from the water, seemed to have coalesced into a great cloud, swirling about with currents and eddies like a troubled lake.

Until now I'd been totally alone, no sign of life on the canal at all except the odd coot scratching about in the reeds or a blackbird playing peek-a-boo in the hedgerows, regaling me occasionally with a burst of song. But at Ladgrave Lock, next to what seemed like a derelict chemical factory, I came across the first person I'd seen that morning. He was a youngish bloke, not even thirty, but with a corrugated face that made you think he'd seen a bit more of life than his years suggested. He was sitting on the lock-beam, cradling a brown plastic bottle between his knees, staring into the empty chamber.

'Oh, come on, it's not that bad,' I joked. But as soon as I'd said it, I could see that it was. That bad and probably a lot worse too. He looked as if he hadn't slept that night. In fact he looked as if he hadn't slept for a week.

He gave me a smile so weak it died before it was born. 'It's unusual to see a boat on the move this time in the morning.'

'It's unusual to see anyone hanging around the towpath too,' I said.

He moved over to allow me to get to the paddles.

'It's just that I like the early mornings, before everyone else is up,' he explained. 'The world always seems so much more hopeful, if you know what I mean. Everything's new, perhaps that's all it is. It makes you feel better, doesn't it? I can't sleep anyhow, so I might as well get up. No use stewing in bed, eh?'

I sat on the gate with him, and while the lock emptied he lit a cigarette, its smoke hanging in the air between us along with the smell of the alcohol on his breath. It was cider: rancid, pervasive.

'Do you live round here?' I asked.

He nodded towards the centre of town and mentioned some place I'd not heard of before. 'That's where the house is anyway, where the wife and kids live, you know. But I'm staying up with me mum and dad in Deighton for a week or two until, well… you know how it is…' He trailed off, aware he'd said more to me than he'd intended.

After the lock emptied, the two of us pushed open the gate. It was much heavier and more industrial than any on the Narrow Canal, which by comparison seemed like miniatures made for kids.

'Do you mind closing it for me after I've left?' I asked. 'The gate, I mean. It's the most irritating job there is travelling on your own on a boat. You have stop and moor up and walk back…'

'No problem,' he said. 'In fact, if you want I'll come down to the next lock with you, give you a hand there as well.'

It was a bit of a hike so I gave him a ride down. Maybe that's what he was after all the time. Or maybe it was just the company he needed. We stood together on the back deck in companionable silence, neither of us feeling the need to say much to the other. I've met people like him before on the canal, casualties of the world who use the waterways to escape their troubles. You see them most often in towns, as I'd seen them on the Ashton Canal coming out of Manchester, groups of drinkers congregating on the towpath for solace. But there are also a lot of loners too like this bloke, people fighting with themselves or the world over some crisis or another, people in pain, nursing hurt at how their lives have panned out.

There's nothing you can do for them, of course. Except perhaps share the moment and hope they'll find some comfort in that. But there are limits to what any human being can do for another met randomly like this along the way, a brief intersection of two lives, two journeys, each going in separate directions.

After the next lock we parted and I watched for a while as he walked back up the towpath to where I'd met him and where I knew that he'd soon be sitting on the lock-beam where I'd first seen him, staring distractedly into the lock chamber again, waiting for someone else to intrude on his life, or perhaps hoping that they wouldn't. Who knows? As I cruised away I gave him a wave of futile farewell like the one Liza Minnelli gives Michael York at the end of *Cabaret*. It was only a gesture; I knew he wouldn't see it. Already he was as lost in his world as I was in mine.

The Huddersfield Broad Canal was opened in 1776, the same year as the United States Declaration of Independence. It was built to link with the older Calder and Hebble Navigation, which it joins at Cooper Bridge and which for a while was called the Cooper Canal as a result. Later it began to be more commonly referred to as Sir John Ramsden's Canal, after the major owner of the land across which it passed. This was an act of sycophancy which might not have impressed Sir John as much had he known that in ensuing years the family name in these parts would be associated less with water transport than with fish and chip shops.

Personally, I regret the passing of the old name in favour of the unimaginative one the canal has now. Yorkshire folk have always had a talent for bringing the high and mighty down a peg or two. Had Ramsden's name still been associated with the canal I'm sure they'd have re-christened it by now.

The Huddersfield Chip Canal, almost certainly.

I had breakfast at the junction and afterwards I cast off into the deep waters of the River Calder, where the tenor of the waterway changed immediately. Although it was only a short hop before the river became canalised again to take it around a weir, it was tree-lined and wide, and *Justice* began to react differently, the way she always does on rivers. This is because rivers are natural phenomena in constant movement, and that gives them a life of their own compared to canals which are barren and still, created by man to be controllable. On rivers, boats travel faster and with more purpose. As soon as they feel a bit of deep water under them they get their heads down and get on with the job in hand.

I was soon feathering again – creating that elegant wash from the bow which looks as if you've grown wings but which sometimes, travelling swift and true and steady, seems to carry you along so fast you think you'll fly too.

In no time at all I was in Brighouse – not, perhaps, one of those places you'd put on a list of must-sees in this part of the world but nevertheless somewhere I'd picked out as a place I wanted to stop when I'd planned this trip in London all those months ago. Brighouse has a pie shop, you see. A famous pie shop at that. An award-winning one, no less. And pies being somehow so associated with the North I wanted to see what the best were like. I moored up briefly with the intention of just popping up the high street for one. For some reason though the shop was late opening that day and I found myself in a queue outside with a posse of bad-tempered women whose mood became more ugly by the minute as the pie-maker failed to show.

In the absence of an accommodating husband to be the butt of their animosity, they soon identified me as a handy substitute. They were all carrying enormous amounts of shopping and they used this to work a form of flanker movement on me which I guessed they must have once seen at some Rugby League match. I'd joined the queue at the back, and although at first everything seemed polite and orderly, it soon became apparent that however many people joined the line, I was still at the back, blocked from asserting my position by a couple of bulging string-bags and a shopping trolley which, from its size and shape, looked as if it was filled with King Edwards the weight of a prop forward.

As the only man in the queue I'd been getting some funny looks being there at all. Now I became aware of quizzical glances being thrown my way and of whispers being exchanged, the subject of which was clearly me.

At length one of them let me in on the conversation. 'Are you Maisie Allerton's bloke from Halifax?' she asked. She pushed her face into mine and examined me with the repugnant curiosity of Brian Sewell appraising a modern art installation.

'Er, no,' I said.

'I told you,' announced one of the other women jubilantly. 'Maisie Allerton's bloke is much better-looking than him. And he's not so fat either. Anyway,' she added, nodding in my direction, 'he's not from Halifax, he's local. He's from Rastrick. He were at school with my brother.'

She turned to me, as if I hadn't been party to the conversation so far. 'You're from Rastrick, aren't you? You were at school with my brother, weren't you?'

'No,' I said.

They all looked at me suspiciously, as if I had some alien excrescence growing from my head.

Eventually one of them confronted me. 'Well, where are you from if you're not from Rastrick, then?'

'I'm from Blackheath in London,' I said. 'I'm off the boats,' I added, attempting to give this unlikely story some credence.

They all went suddenly very quiet, as if in shock; but immediately afterwards they exploded in a babble of competing voices, the topic of which, as far as I could make out above the hubbub, was London. The word 'queen' was used a lot, as were 'gracious', 'radiant', 'family', 'embarrassment' and 'disgrace', roughly in that order. 'Cost' seemed to be another frequently used noun, invariably juxtaposed with the adjective 'outrageous'. As in 'the outrageous cost or a cup of tea' or 'the outrageous cost of a sandwich'.

CHAPTER TWENTY

Meanwhile, cleared of any imputation that I might either be from Rastrick or Maisie Allerton's bloke, the blockage ahead of me seemed to clear miraculously so that by the time the pie-maker finally appeared at the shop – flustered, hot and hassled – I had somehow found myself near the head of the queue.

I was anyhow served first, the pie-maker presumably arriving at the conclusion that of all his customers clamouring for attention, I was the one least likely to rip his head off.

This took me unawares and I blurted out an order, the first thing that came into my head. 'Two Cornish pasties, two meat and potatoes, a chicken and mushroom and a medium pork pie,' I said.

Behind me I heard an appreciative murmur of approval from the women.

'Oo-ah, he likes his pies,' one of them said.

'He'll not get pies like this down his way,' said another. 'He'll be treating hisself.'

None of the pies they sell in Brighouse is small. They are the size of dinner plates. When I picked up the bag in which the pie-maker wrapped them, the weight of them all but dislocated my shoulder. Back at the boat looking at them, I couldn't understand why I'd bought as many as I had.

Or when I'd possibly eat them.

Twenty-one

*O*K, twist my arm, I'll admit it. I'd never been on the Calder and Hebble before and I thought it was going to be one of those grim, industrial canals reeking of the nineteenth century. I had visions of cruising on a rubbish-filled oil-slick through a landscape of derelict factories. I thought it would be all brick walls and barbed wire, broken windows and drug addicts under the bridges. But hey, everyone's allowed one mistake in this life, aren't they? And if you look at a map you can see where I went wrong. On a map, the Calder and Hebble looks like a necklace strung with a series of small towns, a bit of greenery threaded in here and there for decoration.

But it's nothing like that, nothing at all. A lot of the time it's surprisingly rural. In some places it even feels isolated. It's not even nineteenth-century either, if you want to be accurate about it. The bit that I was cruising was actually built in the 1770s, making it eighteenth-century, Georgian rather than Victorian.

CHAPTER TWENTY-ONE

After Brighouse I went through Elland, and soon afterwards I arrived at Woodside Mill lock, named after an old factory, the surviving ruins of which look uncannily like those etchings you see of ancient Rome with crumbling arches and columns covered in creepers. It was a delightful spot, magical. I was just beginning to enjoy it when a man cycling up the towpath told me that I'd be better off moving.

'Why would I be better off moving?' I asked him. 'This is a delightful spot, magical. I'm just beginning to enjoy it.'

But he speeded off without telling me anything more, chuckling away to himself like Mutley in *Wacky Races*.

Well, sod you, I thought, getting stubborn about it, I'm not moving anywhere then. I'm like that, the whole family is. You can't tell us anything unless we know the ins and the outs of it. Later though, I wished I'd have listened to him. I was sitting outside on the front deck having a cup of tea. The weather had turned pleasant for the first time that day. There was even a glint of sun forcing its way through the clouds.

Then this immense barge appeared from out of nowhere pushing a wave in front of it so high it was breaking over the banks and washing across the towpath.

The boat was the same length as *Justice*. But that's where the similarities between the two ended because it was twice the width and probably twice as deep. As it got close it sucked *Justice* into the centre of the channel. She lurched and her lines tightened, straining against her mooring-pins until they could hold her no longer and they shot out of the ground like a couple of bonfire night rockets, leaving her floundering in the middle of the canal, ricocheting down the sides of the oncoming boat.

It was a traditional Calder and Hebble barge. Or at least I think it was, though I couldn't swear to it. Given the circumstances I wasn't exactly taking notes on the details of its design. Whatever it was, though, it was big. Most barges this size have been converted for leisure use in recent years but this one was a relic of another age. It was still a working boat – probably involved in canal maintenance – and it had a hold half-filled with gravel. It also had a captain who looked the part – which is to say he looked industrial, the way the canal didn't. He smelt of the nineteenth century too. His jeans were so greasy you could have wrung them out and fried chips in the extract.

As he scraped down my side, he thanked me – although for what I couldn't rightly say. For not complaining that he was going too fast when he clearly was? For not taking out a gun and shooting him for what he'd done to me? Maybe for just brightening up his dull day, since I guess a job like his could get boring and it must make the hours go quicker scaring pleasure boaters out of their wits?

Big boats were not the only navigational hazard of the Calder and Hebble, as I soon discovered. The locks caused me problems too. Most of them, thank God, were normal – a little shorter than the average but operated with a standard lock-key and nothing which would cause any half-experienced boater much trouble. Some, however, had an older style of paddle-gear which you could only use by employing an implement called a hand-spike. People had told me about hand-spikes so I had a good idea of what they looked like before I ever got my hands on one. Nonetheless, my first acquaintance with the real thing was still an eye-opener. OK, I grant you, not much on the British canal system is state-of-the-art technology; not much of it is what you'd call sharp-end science. But even by the standards of the canals the hand-spike is a bit basic. Crude doesn't even begin to describe it.

It's really nothing more than a club. A four-foot cudgel made (if 'made' isn't pitching it too highly) out of a chunk of mahogany tapered at one end so you can get your hands around it. It is more like an offensive weapon than a tool – so much so that there's a whole mythology of stories about boaters who've had them impounded or who've been arrested by the police on the basis that something looking so brutal could never have a lawful use.

You stick the spike in a rudimentary cog on the lock, and a pull or two is generally all that's needed to sink a boat. That's because it opens the paddle so fast it's like firing a shell at the gate. Suddenly a hole materialises out of which a four foot square column of solid water appears. If you're not ready for it – and I wasn't ready for it the first time it happened to me – then it hits you head-on, the biggest water canon you'll ever experience.

The second time it happened I was more prepared for the outcome, but all the same I didn't feel comfortable. *Justice* has an open front deck with nothing to protect her. And I had no other crew member with me who could help control the boat in that sort of turbulence. I finished up by just jiggling the hand-spike about so that water dribbled into the lock. It was a time-consuming process – a bit like filling a bath with a teacup – but it seemed the best option under the circumstances.

The rate of my progress obviously worried some people who were walking up the towpath. One bloke seemed more troubled than most.

'Why don't you open the damn thing properly and have done with it?' he said, as if I was a total fool for doing it the way I was. Maybe it was because I was in a boat from Banbury that he felt he could offer his advice so freely. Maybe he just thought Southerners were too dim-witted to get their heads around the concept of a hand-spike. He probably thought it was all the muesli we ate. All the weak tea we drank. He was one of the flat cap brigade which always spells trouble. Worse, he had a Yorkshire terrier in tow and I should have known from that what he was going to be like.

Yorkshire terriers are normally dogs noted for their intelligence. This one hadn't passed any GCSEs though. It was as thick as a municipal paving stone. I realised that after it had spent ten minutes sniffing a lock-beam thinking it was getting lucky with an Alsatian. The bloke obviously took after the dog. Not that I'm suggesting he got off on Alsatians, but in a crisis requiring an intellectual approach to solving a problem, you'd have been hard-pressed to say which you'd have wanted helping you, him or the dog.

It was afternoon now; I'd been on the move since first light. I was tired and impatient and I'd have been justified telling him to sod off and mind his own business. But at the same time I didn't want to be rude, so I sat down on the lock-beam with him and, displaying a patience I certainly didn't feel, I talked to him about the problems I was having. I explained to him about the cog and the hand-spike and the column of water. I explained how boats sink. I even touched a little on Archimedes' theories of hydrostatics, although this was perhaps taking things a bit further than was strictly necessary. Eventually, however, I seemed to get through to him and he appeared to understand what I was getting at.

But then he said, 'I still can't see what the harm would be if you just opened the paddles full up. I mean, what damage could it do?'

Once more I explained the problems. I showed him the cog which controlled the paddle; I showed him the hand-spike which controlled the cog. I even showed him the water in the lock which controlled whether the boat was going to float or not. At last he seemed to grasp the simple point I was making.

Then he said, 'That's all well and good, but surely if you did the job right you'll get it done a lot quicker.'

I could have screamed. I wanted to throttle him. I wanted to tell the daft old bugger that yes, if I opened up the paddle fast, of course it would fill the lock quicker. But it would fill my boat quicker too and probably sink it in the process. I wanted to take him and shake and ask him which bit of that he did not understand.

But by now I couldn't be bothered. I'd lost interest. The truth was I'd lost the will to live. Any longer and I'd have lost my mind along with it. I grabbed the hand-spike and jerked it towards me. Immediately a blast of water the size of a white van hit the boat like a missile, throwing it to one side, pitching it one way and then the other, crashing it against the lock sides, sending the front doors flying open.

'Oh, I see what you mean,' he said.

And he walked off, the dog trailing at his heels.

In one respect at least the bloke at the lock was typical of the people I saw on the Calder and Hebble. It wasn't just that he had a dog – everyone has a dog once you get beyond the Midlands. What was typical about him was that he had a Yorkshire terrier. Everybody up this way seemed to have a Yorkshire terrier. Everywhere you looked were Yorkshire terriers. Everyone on the towpath had one. Every house you passed there was one. I began to think a prerequisite of living in this part of Yorkshire was that you had to have a Yorkshire terrier. I began to think they didn't let you in unless you had one. That they banned you under some law dating from the War of the Roses.

I had become very keen on terriers since the Rat in Uppermill but even I got a little tired of the Yorkshire breed, ubiquitous creatures that they were. I saw perky little long-faced ones with neckerchiefs instead of collars; I saw arrogant, long-haired show versions with bows between their ears; I saw miniature versions, in bicycle baskets; I saw old ones trailing behind fishermen, young ones strutting up and down the roofs of narrowboats.

Eventually I yearned for the sight of some exotic breed to relieve the tedium. An Affenpinscher perhaps, which is a dog I've never seen but which is supposed to have a face like a monkey. Or a Basenji which yodels instead of barks. Or a perhaps even a Xoloitzcuintli, which would be a dog worth having if for no other reason than its name and the fact you could have a lot of fun in the pub after a couple of pints getting your mates to try to pronounce it.

I guess all I really wanted was to see a dog I could have a reasonable conversation about with its owner – something you could never do with the owners of Yorkshire terriers because the slightest expression of curiosity was like winding up a longcase clock that, once started, would go on for weeks.

Despite my best efforts, a couple of them did manage to buttonhole me as I went up the canal and as a result I learnt more about the breed than I wanted to know. One of them lectured me on their distinctive blue and tan colour, on their history as ratting dogs, on their temperament and their health problems. Another told about their diet, about the exercise they needed, about their mating preferences. Coming through the locks in Salterhebble, one guy even took it upon himself to instruct me in the finer points of their digestion and the factors that made them susceptible to diarrhoea.

'All very interesting,' I said, after he'd finished, 'but are you going to clear it up now?'

Sowerby Bridge marks the terminus of the Calder and Hebble and the start of the Rochdale Canal. By the time I finally arrived there dusk was falling, the temperature dropping with the light. Only a few weeks earlier I'd been sweltering in a heat wave, but that had been the last kick of summer and now it was becoming cold in the evenings, the smell of autumn increasingly in the air. There was the sense of things being over, things dying. In the basin there's a community of people living on their boats; their curtains were drawn and their fires were lit and from their chimneys came soft, reassuring wreathes of coal smoke which hung above the water like the mist had done that morning in Huddersfield.

Huddersfield? That morning? Had it really been just that morning? It seemed to me like another world, another existence, and yet it was only twelve miles away, a journey by car of – what? – half an hour, forty minutes? By boat it had taken me almost twelve hours and I'd had to negotiate twenty-two locks along the way. I was exhausted, wiped out by the effort of it. But I felt exultant too, the way I always do after a hard day's cruising, proud of myself for what I'd achieved. Other people, land-based people, may measure progress in miles, but such crude calibration is not for those of us who travel on water and who've learnt long ago the truth of the old maxim about the journey being more important than the arrival.

The import of that was all falling into place for me now with my mother and the trip, the tunnels, the Narrow Canal and all the people I'd met along the way: travellers passing on their own road, a different road, but in the end a road we all know leads to the same place.

I had a walk around the town to stretch my legs. Sowerby Bridge – pronounce it Sawby Bridge (and don't, for God's sake, call it just Sowerby because that's a separate place up the hill) – lies at the confluence of two rivers, the Calder and the Ryburn. At one time it was a big wool town: rich, important, a force to be reckoned with in these parts. One of the first turnpikes in the country went through Sowerby Bridge, and even as late as the 1970s it was a sizeable industrial centre making clothing for the forces. But the years have not treated Sowerby Bridge well. The remnants of the mills that made the place what it was still cling to the riverbanks, but they've seen better days and buddleias grow in the mortar of their façades. And that turnpike's now a busy road which cuts straight through the town, slicing it in two with an interminable stream of traffic.

The church was in a mess too. The ground around it had moved and the graves had collapsed in on themselves; and the vicar had decided that the entrance was unsafe and he'd unilaterally closed it off with orange tape. The whole place felt shabby and run down, as if it had had a dust up with the twenty-first century and come off worst.

Even so, you can see Sowerby Bridge has a future if only it could decide what that future is. Approaching it from the canal, as I'd done, it seems to rise out of the landscape, clinging to the valley wall in the manner of a Tuscan hill town. When a place is visually that pleasing, not all is lost; and there was clearly something of a renaissance going on. Around the canal basin new flats had been built and the old warehouses were being restored; and in the town there were a couple of restaurants, including one very upmarket one, which hinted at what the place might yet turn into. I went to the shop to buy milk and the headlines in the local paper were about a survey which showed that in the previous six months property prices had risen higher in Sowerby Bridge than anywhere else in the area.

There was also a rather good pub to make up for the one I'd failed to find the previous night. It was just up from the basin, a typical waterways bar with canal memorabilia on the wall and an improbable clientele ranging from young people necking alcopops to crusty old blokes nursing their pints of mild with dogs at their feet. Yorkshire terriers, in the main, but that goes without saying.

It also did food, and I have to confess I was tempted.

Except the boat was sinking with the weight of pies.

Twenty-two

'Where?' Em said, sounding surprised.

'Hebden Bridge.'

'But you said you were in Sowerby Bridge.'

'Last night I said Sowerby Bridge, now I'm saying Hebden Bridge. The world moves on,' I observed. 'Things change.'

'Water under the bridges, you mean?' she said.

Em's good on a feed line like that; as good as any comic. But I could sense that something was on her mind and I was pretty certain I knew what it was. Talking the previous night, she'd given me enough clues, for heaven's sake. Things were quiet at work. She'd got time owing that she'd lose if she didn't take it soon.

'I thought you were rushing to finish the trip anyhow,' she said suspiciously. 'Why are you moored in Hebden Bridge now?'

'It might have had something to do with the hints you were dropping. About fancying a couple of days away from London. Hebden Bridge is a holiday town. I thought you could take a holiday.'

So she drove up later in the day, and that evening we sat over a drink in a pub catching up with each other.

It had been a funny trip from Sowerby Bridge. I'd thought it would only take me two or three hours but I was held up at Tuel Lock where I was kept waiting about by Mr Grumpy, the lock-keeper, who I'd upset by not booking my passage ahead of time as I should have done. The upside of this delay was that above the lock I found a tumbling wall of raspberries, as plump as balloons, and I picked myself a couple of pounds of them which solved the problem of what to have for dessert after the pie that night.

There's a lot of food on the towpath waiting to be picked up for free like this. Strawberries sometimes as well as raspberries, and blackberries everywhere, of course, in the season: apples, plums, damsons and sloes all over the place – although I don't think your average boater nowadays would recognise a sloe to save their life. A lot of herbs too, and mushrooms and edible fungi, and (dare I say it?) a lot of produce in the fields which in the old days, before there were so many of us, I had no compunction about grubbing out of the ground for a meal. A serving of potatoes, a sweetcorn or two, maybe a handful of fresh greens to be lightly steamed and tossed with wild garlic and good olive oil.

Tuel Lock is only a stone's throw from the church at Sowerby Bridge, and it's a monstrous thing – at twenty feet, the deepest lock on the whole canal system, too dangerous for boaters to be left to work themselves. It was built as part of the restoration, an amalgamation of two existing locks; and it lies at the head of the Tuel Tunnel, a concrete culvert formed when they burrowed under Sowerby Bridge to reconnect the broken link between the Calder and Hebble and the Rochdale Canal which had been severed after the Rochdale's closure in 1952.

It had rained relentlessly all morning, although you can't complain about rain in these parts. It would be like complaining about the sun in Spain or about the Saharan winds. The Calder Valley attracts rain; rain is what the Calder Valley is and what made it what it was. At the time of the Industrial Revolution when the Calder was 'the hardest worked river in England', rain was a resource, not an inconvenience. It was literally what made the wheels of manufacturing go round.

I was moving north-east now, the canal clinging to the slope of the valley with the river below me on one side and the hills tumbling down on the other. Despite the weather it was glorious cruising. Although the sky had darkened to a charcoal smudge, in front of me, above the hills, it was still clear, lost beams of sunlight searing the landscape like searchlights, a Renaissance chiaroscuro highlighting clouds crawling across the horizon as big and black as slugs. I went through the bridge at Hollins Mill Lane, which is really a short tunnel; I passed Luddenden Foot where the houses are squeezed so tightly between the road and the cut that their back doors perch on walkways suspended over the water.

Soon I was approaching Mytholmroyd where the town's most famous son, the former Poet Laureate Ted Hughes, used to fish under the canal bridge while lorries from Rochdale and Bradford rumbled overhead making the water tremble. He once claimed to have seen a trout there, which – in water as stagnant as the canal was then – sounds like the sort of tall

CHAPTER TWENTY-TWO

story fishermen tell. Or maybe it was just poetic licence; I don't know which, although I'd forgive him both. But then I'd forgive a lot of any man who could describe the canal's 'gleam-black stagnation' and have me knowing what he meant and feeling it all at once.

But my! it's a grim, austere place in the rain, Mytholmroyd. It reminded me of wet Sunday afternoons as a kid, trapped in the house waiting for the weather to clear so I could go out, tracing the raindrops down the inside of the window until the marks I left in the condensation were like prison bars. It felt constricting, that's what I'm saying. It felt confined and cramped and limited and I felt hemmed in and couldn't wait to get away from it; although maybe that feeling had less to do with Mytholmroyd itself than with Hughes who had something circumscribed about him too, something dark and fatalistic that seemed to hang over him his whole life.

Leaving Mytholmroyd, at Broadbottom Lock, just before the old Clog Factory which had been half-heartedly converted to craft shops, and before the unusually named Falling Royd tunnel with its corrugated roof like a Second World War Anderson shelter, I came across a bloke prodding around in the water with a stick. He was looking for floats.

'Fishing-floats,' he explained. 'There's a lot of fishing up here and if they lose a float, the wind generally brings it down to the lock sooner or later. I sell them down the club, or people'll buy me a drink if they recognise any of theirs.'

It was an insignificant, unmemorable meeting and not one that would normally have made much of an impression on me. Except that even in West Yorkshire it is unusual to meet someone out and about in weather this bad, particularly when they are so unprepared for it. He was dressed in just a jacket and trousers without even a hat to protect him from the rain which was pelting down harder by the minute now, a low rumble of thunder in the distance announcing that it would get worse yet.

There was something about him that struck me as odd, something about his brooding eyes and the angle of his jaw which seemed set like a vice, clenched against his teeth. And there was something about his hair too, particularly his hair. Even with the rain flattening it, sticking it against his face, you could see he had a stray lock like a boyish fringe that was constantly threatening to fall across his forehead into his eyes.

At first I wondered if he might be a member of the Hughes family. After all, there must be a lot of them still around the area. Or maybe it was just the way people looked in these parts, their features determined by the landscape, by the place itself. Eventually I came to the conclusion that it was all in my head. I'd been thinking about Ted Hughes as I came through Mytholmroyd and what could be more natural than that I should delude myself that I'd seen someone like him. He probably didn't even look the same actually, not really, not if I'd had more time to think about it, more time to examine him properly.

But I never got that opportunity. I opened the lock-paddles and when I turned round he'd gone.

It was strange really. Not strange that he'd left. He must have been soaked to the skin; I'd have expected that. But there were two floats in the water at the top of the lock which he couldn't have missed and which I'd have thought he'd take with him.

I fished them out and left them on the lock-beam for when he returned.

'What was it Oscar Wilde said about parents?' I said to Em the next day. '"To lose one may be regarded as a misfortune; to lose both is carelessness" – is that it? It just strikes me that the same might be said of Ted Hughes and his women. It's a misfortune that one should commit suicide by gassing herself. But when two of them do the same thing, the second one taking her child with her at the same time, well, you have to wonder, don't you?'

As a schoolgirl Em had once heard Ted Hughes read his poetry and she'd fallen for him, as most women tended to do. She said, 'You have to differentiate between a poet and his poems. At the end of the day it's the writing which matters.'

We were in Heptonstall. Hughes bought a house in Heptonstall and it's where his first wife, the American poet Sylvia Plath, is buried. We'd walked up that morning from Hebden Bridge, crossing the packhorse bridge after which the town is named, climbing out of the valley by a route that had taken us up the hill on a precipitous path. After the previous day's storm Hebden Bridge was bathed in sunshine which had brought the tourists flocking. Its streets were full of people ambling around; its souvenir shops and tearooms were packed.

Not so in Heptonstall. In Heptonstall it could have been winter. It was bleak and austere and its steep, slate-grey streets were shiny damp, raked by a cutting wind blowing off the moors. It was like a plague town, scarcely a face to be seen anywhere, tourist or local. Heptonstall used to be an important

centre for hand-loom weaving, and among its maze of snickets
and alleyways you can still identify rows of weavers' cottages
by their large top-floor windows which were designed to
catch as much light as possible. The town had its own cloth-
hall where they traded the finished product, and this survives
too, as does its dungeon, its stocks and an unusual eight-sided
Wesleyan Chapel, the foundation stone laid by John Wesley
himself.

It's all strangely attractive, pretty in a rugged sort of way.
But you couldn't like a place like that, not really like it. It's
too fixed in the past, a little microcosm of a Yorkshire hill
town at a particular point in its history; everything flawless,
unspoilt, but somehow dead. With the Industrial Revolution
and the development of watermills and steam power, the jobs
in Heptonstall moved down the hill into the new factories
on the banks of the Calder; and the town bowed out of the
contemporary world for good, never to return.

Dominating the centre are the bare, ruined choirs of the
derelict Church of Thomas à Becket built in the thirteenth
century to a special low design to avoid the Pennine gales
– although eventually it succumbed to one in 1847 and was
abandoned as it stood in favour of the new Church of St
Thomas the Apostle right next to it. Mind you, that took a
lightning hit a few years later, proving that nothing remains
unscathed in Heptonstall. There are said to be 10,000 people
buried in the two churches and finding the location of a single
grave did not prove to be an easy task. There are no clues to the
whereabouts of Sylvia Plath's burial spot, no maps directing
you to her headstone, no tourist authority signs pointing it
out, world-famous poet though she may be.

You get the sense that she must have been a bit of an embarrassment all round to the Hughes family to have tucked her away up here, away from the world as they must have thought, never believing for one moment that in the future people such as us would come trailing up the hill in pilgrimage to her. You get a sense that she's an embarrassment even today, getting on for fifty years after she killed herself. Her sort of morbid emotionalism and the confessional poetry that springs from it hardly plays well in dour Heptonstall. It is altogether too shrill and demanding. A spoilt child screaming for attention in a world where children should be seen and not heard.

Eventually we found another cemetery a little away from the churches. It was a new one with rows of municipally regimented graves like something you might find in a garden suburb. There was a man tidying up and when we asked him if he knew where Sylvia Plath was buried, he gave a surly, contemptuous nod over his shoulder. The grave was unkempt, shabby, littered with tattered remnants of red ribbon and cheap earrings, references to Sylvia's first legendary meeting with Ted at a literary party where he tore off her much-treasured headband and stole her silver earrings before she famously retaliated by biting him on the cheek so hard that he bled.

After the party she went off drunk and slept with another man, and despite the wounds he suffered all Ted got was a poem about lust which she dedicated to him. She described him as a panther stalking her down and wrote that one day she'd have her death of him.

Which I guess, eventually, she did.

Em looked up from the grave where she'd been staring at the name Sylvia Plath Hughes except the 'Hughes' part of it had been scraped away and was barely legible.

Underneath it was the strange and incomprehensible epithet 'Even Amidst Fierce Flames The Golden Lotus Can Be Planted', a quotation from the book *Monkey* written by the Chinese writer Wu Cheng'en in the middle of the sixteenth century.

'Let's go back to Hebden,' she said. 'This place is creepy.'

So why does everyone in West Yorkshire hate Hebden Bridge and everyone in London want to move there?

'It's got a comfortable feel to it, I grant you that,' Em said.

And you couldn't disagree with her. Hebden Bridge isn't a place where you get many shootings and I guess there hasn't been much in the way of riots since the Luddites.

But it's got more going for it than just this. It's got places where you can buy organic meat, or four-grained bread, or vegetables with mud on them; it's got its own alternative technology centre and a cinema that shows art-house films. It has a specialist shops that sell rare comics or 1960s furniture. It even has one that claims to be 'Britain's Number One manufacturer of juggling equipment'. It's got a concert hall where you can listen to world music; it's got its own arts festival and its own Montessori school nearby. It's got its own local paper, of course – everywhere has its own local paper. But Hebden Bridge has got its own publisher as well, and no doubt it will be launching its own television station before long.

Hebden Bridge has banned plastic bags, for heaven's sake – doesn't that say it all?

CHAPTER TWENTY-TWO

I liked it; Em thought it was overblown. Or at least she pretended to.

'So what's to get so excited about?' she asked. 'It hasn't even got an opera house.'

We went out for lunch. We sat in a pub drinking beer which was probably brewed in the backyard using only the finest Fuggle hops washed lovingly in a Pennine stream. We nibbled crisps, each of which was probably hand-crafted locally using recycled Calder Valley warming-pans. In the background the sound of Bronx hip-hop came from the jukebox. The smell of West Indian curried goat filtered from the kitchen. All of which might not have been so unusual except that Hebden Bridge is relentlessly white, barely a suntan in evidence let alone a black face.

'What's it like living here?' I asked a group of young people on the next table.

'We don't live here,' one of them said. 'We come from London.'

At the bar, while I was waiting to be served, I met another Londoner, and when I came back to the table I found Em in conversation with a woman who turned out to be a Londoner too. More than that, she lived in Blackheath. On the Cator Estate. A stone's throw from us.

'I think we should go,' I said. 'Stay here any longer and we'll meet someone living in our house.'

But this is how it all starts. You visit somewhere and it seduces you. You move there and your friends visit you and it seduces them too. Before you know where you are, you've colonised. You're taking over the schools and persuading the locals to bake ciabatta. I caught Em looking in an estate agent's window and had to pull her away bodily despite the dearth of Puccini up the Calder Valley.

Of course, it would be wrong to say Hebden Bridge has been totally taken over by Londoners. It's full of people from Manchester and Leeds too. Even so, there's a curious linguistic phenomenon that commentators have observed in the kids, a unusual fusion of estuary English and Yorkshire which is not easily explained by endless repeats of *Minder*. A friend of a friend of mine claims to be the last genuine Tyke living in Hebden Bridge – but then again, he spends half the week working in London so what would he know about genuine anything?

Hebden Bridge has got no one to blame but itself. A year or two back British Airways' flight magazine *high life* voted it the fourth funkiest town in the world after Daylesford in Australia, Tiradentes in Brazil and Burlington in Vermont. In response, Hebden Bridge should have voted BA the fourth funkiest airline. The award would have been worth as much. After all, BA can't even run Terminal Five so what does it know about funky towns? And thinking about it, what exactly is a funky town anyway? Hebden Bridge should have ignored the label and got on with things as it used to do before the place was fashionable, when it was just another depressed Yorkshire mill town looking for a future. Instead, it put the article on the town's website where it can still be found as a sort of trophy of its trendiness. Next to a sniffy article from *The Leeds Guide*, Yorkshire's *Time Out*, calling it a 'snobs' enclave' and criticising it for its 'all-embracing pretensions' and its 'self-aggrandisement'.

That sort of thing you don't publicise, surely? Unless, on the QT, you're rather proud of your reputation.

Either way, you can't complain if that reputation attracts people. Yet when we finally did manage to track some locals to ground in a restaurant that evening, that's exactly what they did do, grumbling to us about the rise in property prices caused by the influx from outside and bemoaning the fact that newcomers weren't willing to get 'involved' in the community the way they were.

Back at the boat Em made us a cup of tea before bed. She was leaving to drive home first thing in the morning.

'And you?' she asked. 'Tomorrow you'll just press on, will you? Pick it up where you left off?'

'Things seem to have stabilised with my mother,' I said. 'But I can't relax any more. I'm half expecting a telephone call at any time to tell me she's had another turn. I'll probably stay here a day or two longer, but after that well...' I trailed off. 'I guess I'll head back towards Manchester, find a winter mooring somewhere. The stoppages will soon be kicking in and I'm not going to be able to get back to Banbury this late in the year.'

But the next day all my plans were up in the air again.

After Em had gone and I was clearing up, feeling forlorn the way I always do when I've had company and then been left alone, I struck up a conversation with another boater who had moored up behind me. He had come from the direction I was intending to travel.

'There's a problem with the swing-bridge near Smithy Bridge,' he told me. 'I've heard they're planning on closing it

Thursday for the weekend. But you know what the Rochdale's like. Once they've started the job, they probably won't finish it till next year. If I was in your position, I'd get through as soon as I could. It's better to be safe than sorry.'

Twenty-three

Single-handed boating isn't an Olympic sport. There aren't records for the fastest journeys over different routes. Even so, when I was younger I sometimes used to dash around all over the place as if there were medals at stake.

I have logs that are proof of my journeys. Records of trips that I made alone when I'd think nothing of polishing off a flight of locks before breakfast, or haring off halfway across the country to meet some pointless target I'd set myself. And this, remember, was in the days when canals were shallow and you spent most of your time scraping along the bottom because they were never dredged. When locks were badly maintained and you didn't know when you got to one whether it was going to work or not. It was in the days before there were ladders in a lot of locks so that if you were travelling solo up flights like the one at Bosley on the Macclesfield Canal, you had to go mountaineering up the insides of slimy lock gates in order to get through them.

But that was then, and this is now. I've calmed down a bit since, although to put it like that implies I've had anything to do with the process. All I did was wake up one morning to discover thirty-odd years had gone missing. Where they'd gone missing I'm not altogether sure. Maybe I'd left them on the towpath somewhere during one of my mad rampages round the country. Anyway, I couldn't do that sort of thing now. I'm nowhere near fit enough and I worry about my health too much. And this is the thing about being fit – it's ruinous to the health. It leads to sprains and pulled muscles. I have never seen a fit man who isn't nursing some injury or another.

I went back to the boat and looked at the map. Looking at maps is a salutary experience: it marks the boundary between reality and an old man about to make a bad mistake. When I looked I realised that if I had any chance whatsoever of getting to Smithy Bridge before Thursday and avoiding what could be a long hold-up, then I'd have to keep to a crippling schedule. I would have to get across the summit that night, ready to drop down the next day towards Manchester. It wasn't a long journey, only about eight miles or so. But it was twenty-eight locks. About nine or ten hours' solid travelling. It was nearly midday already. Even if everything went according to plan I wouldn't be there before nightfall at the earliest.

This should have been the point at which I tossed the map aside and opted for drinking instead of boating as a far more pleasant way to bring myself to my knees in Hebden Bridge in late summer. Instead I started *Justice*'s engine. I was having a bit of a mid-life crisis, I guess. Other men buy sports cars or get themselves new wives. This was my equivalent. It was like dusting down my old flares and slapping on the aftershave.

At my first lock leaving Hebden I was Jack the Lad. I was the Fonz of the waterways. It was another lovely day, cold but bathed in lurid sunshine and unbearably bright. A small crowd of people walking along the towpath saw me coming and stopped to watch. They were my audience, the lock my stage. I didn't just go through it, I hurdled over it. It was a performance; it was Royal Command stuff: so slick I felt like tap-dancing down the lock-beam juggling windlasses in case they hadn't realised how competent I was.

One down, twenty-seven to go. Now what was so hard about that? Steady, that was the trick. Don't rush it; don't overdo it; don't take any risks. I asked one of the blokes in the crowd to close the gate behind me and he beamed as if I'd just scored a hat-trick at Wembley and given him the ball. As if I'd done him a favour rather than the other way round.

The first half-dozen locks were soon behind me effortlessly. I was into a rhythm now; I was Brian Jones backing the Stones, Joe Strummer with The Clash. I could feel my muscles loosening; I could feel my brain going onto autopilot. There isn't much to do at a lock but it all has to be done in strict order and it all has to be done to a set technique. Especially when you're alone. When you're alone it's all too easy to overlook things, too easy to forget something. You have to get into a routine. But with this comes another problem. Operating like this, it's too easy to become hypnotised by what you're doing and where you are. By the hills enfolding the canal. By the birds gossiping between themselves. By the pristine peace of the countryside which can sometimes be soporific. That's when accidents happen. It's when you lose your footing and fall or fail to see your boat wedged dangerously against a loose brick. It's when your concentration lapses for a second and your windlass flies off the spindle into your face.

A few years back, late one evening in Shropshire, I was cruising with Em when I came to a lock where the kids had jammed the gate with a bottle. I was definitely hypnotised that night, and tired as well. It had been a hot day and we'd been travelling since the morning, and now the sun was dropping, washing the fields with a pale carmine light like a thin silk coverlet falling across the world. Without thinking, I smashed the bottle with my windlass and the lock gate slammed shut with the weight of the water it had been holding. It narrowly missed my hand which it would have crushed to a pulp as red as the sunset if I hadn't managed to pull it out in the nick of time.

I went through Shawplains Lock; I went through Lobb Mill, their very names a poem on the landscape. Soon I was on the outskirts of Todmorden, the river valley beginning to taper now and the Calder little more than a stream beside me. Todmorden is an odd place in that it is in Yorkshire, but has a Lancashire postal code. It also has a guillotine lock similar to the one in Slaithwaite but much easier to use. Soon afterwards is a massive brick embankment, a quarter of a mile long and thirty or forty feet high, which supports the railway passing alongside, virtually overhead. It's so large and dominating and so unremittingly ugly that with a good-natured if facetious humour the locals have christened it The Great Wall of Tod.

I worked my way upwards through Wadsworth Mill, Shade Lock and through the short Gauxholme flight dominated by the Gauxholme railway viaduct standing with its two castellated towers like fortresses guarding the valley, which seems at this stage to get narrower and narrower until it's not so much that the hills drop into the canal as that the canal seems to erode the very base of the hills.

I'd been going for five hours already now and I'd passed through fifteen locks – or was it sixteen? I'd lost count. I could feel myself wearying. At this stage it wasn't anything physical, or at least not overtly physical. My muscles hadn't stiffened, nothing was aching. But I could feel my concentration beginning to drift; I could feel my attention wandering. Above Smithyholme Lock the pound was full and water was flooding over the gates in such a fierce torrent that I had to tie the boat at the back of the lock to stop it getting drawn into the waterfall. One or two locks had already been like this, and they'd posed no real problem. But at Smithyholme I was away with the fairies. At Smithyholme I was thinking of something else, although I don't know what. Perhaps I was pondering the meaning of the universe or ruminating on global warming. Perhaps I was just wondering whether I should floss my teeth. Whatever it was, I didn't notice that as I opened the paddles the rope I had tied was slipping. I didn't notice *Justice* edging towards the core of the cascade…

'Hey! Watch out!'

It was a woman walking her dogs. Basset hounds, I seem to remember. She'd seen what was happening and had wits enough about her to grab the rope and secure it with a couple of quick turns round a bollard.

I felt mortified.

'You all right?' she asked, probably more aware than me at that stage of how dangerous a position the boat had been in, how close it had been to taking water and sinking.

I shook my head incredulously. 'I wasn't paying attention,' I admitted. 'I guess I'm just tired.'

After this I decided I'd better rest for a while and I stopped at the small village of Walsden a little further on. Already the afternoon was fading into evening. I was beginning to wonder for the first time if I hadn't made a bad mistake and whether I shouldn't just call it a day and take a risk on the bridge repair being a short job that wouldn't hold me up for long. But stubbornness made me press on, and in one respect at least I was right to do so. The Rochdale Canal restoration had only been completed a matter of a few months before – reopening on virtually the 200th anniversary of its original inauguration. But there were to be a series of small, niggling problems that would keep it closed on and off for years afterwards, sometimes for lengthy periods. Some of these would be just teething troubles; some more significant engineering failures; and some, sadly, the results of vandalism, to which the Rochdale seems particularly prone.

What is it with these guys? I can just about understand it when someone strips a lock of its paddle gear so they can sell it for scrap. At least there's money in that. But grown men sawing off two-foot-square lock-beams? For heaven's sake, that's just vandalism for the sake of it. And it's hard work too. It's the same with farmers on adjoining land bulldozing the banks because they don't want the canal there. What sort of madness is this?

These aren't attacks on boats. They can't be explained away by saying they're the revenge of the poor on the wealthy. Farmers? Poor? I don't think so. No, these are attacks on the canal itself. Or at least what the canal represents. Perhaps people see the reopened Rochdale as a violation of their space. As a sort of invasion which opens them up to outsiders. Perhaps, deep down, it's part of that same gene that makes people resentful of others with different coloured skins or different religions. And maybe we all harbour this to some degree: that fear of difference, that aversion to change.

When eventually I cast off again I felt at least partly rested. The weather, thank God, was still holding up and I was anticipating a pleasant evening. The few boats travelling in my direction had moored for the evening so I felt I had the water to myself. Most of them would anyhow have been going only as far as the summit, where they'd turn round and thus avoid the most difficult section of the passage down the more industrialised west side of the canal into Manchester.

I started to enjoy the cruising again. The air was heady, filled with that intoxicating evening cocktail of the countryside: the smell of bruised grass under my feet when I stopped at the locks, the dampness rising from the canal, the fragrance from hedges bathed in evening dew. The light too was exhilarating, dusk beginning to fall, a brume of gentle darkness settling on the world. The landscape was becoming more and more attractive with every mile that passed and for me Lightbank Lock was its crowning glory. If Lightbank Lock had been a food it would have been freshly picked English strawberries with whipped Jersey cream. If it had been a drink it would have been a honeysweet mead. Pastoral hardly gets near to describing it. It was an archetype of English arcadia with its picturesque humpbacked bridge set against the soft curve of hills covered with grazing sheep.

But it hypnotised me. It was smashing that bottle in Shropshire all over again. I had let my concentration slip, hadn't I? I had let myself become distracted. Coming out of the lock I hopped off the boat to close the gate but I can't have looked where I was stepping and my foot found a hole. Immediately my ankle twisted underneath me and I keeled over.

At times like this, you feel shock as much as hurt. Shock that you can have been so stupid to have done what you have. Shock that what you always feared might happen has happened. Shock that ultimately the human body is so frail and unreliable.

Then the pain kicks in for real and there's no room to feel much else.

I was in agony, convinced I'd broken my ankle. There was a cottage next to the lock and I wondered whether I should shout for help, or try to struggle to the front door. But I couldn't have got to the front door. At that moment I couldn't have got anywhere. I felt like throwing up. I felt like dying – anything to stop my ankle hurting. I must have sat there in torment for half an hour, longer. Gradually, though, after its first nauseous intensity, the pain began to ease a little and I pulled myself to my feet, gingerly testing my weight. The ankle was badly twisted but, as far as I could make out, in one piece. The main problem seemed to be the tendon up my leg which felt as if someone was trying to gouge it out with a paring knife.

After a moment or two's deliberation I limped back to the boat having decided to go on. Well, what else could I do?

What was the alternative? Moor up? Admit defeat? Concede that finally I'd got old? It's like falling off a horse, having an accident boating on your own. You need to get back into the saddle as soon as you can or you won't get back into it at all. Besides, I had this crazy idea that it would be better to keep the ankle moving so it wouldn't stiffen up. I took a couple of painkillers. Then I took two more.

I reckoned that it was only an hour or so to where I'd planned to moor, perhaps less. And if that meant a bit of discomfort, then it wasn't too much of a price to pay to be able to boast to myself that I'd confronted the years and won.

But this is no way to cruise the canals. As I've said before, canal cruising isn't about the arrival, it's about the journey. What I was doing now was just trying to get somewhere. Cruising so that I wouldn't have to cruise any more. In truth I'd lost interest in the game; I'd had enough of it. I was suddenly tired of waterways and everything to do with them. I was exhausted, totally spent.

At Sands Lock, the next one up, it was an effort of will simply to move around, and when I did I was ponderous and clumsy, too aware of everything I did, measuring out each step I took. Nothing seemed to be automatic; I couldn't get back into the routine. Every move I made had to be consciously thought out. Every familiar part of the locking process had to be painstakingly analysed before it could lead to action.

Bottomley Lock was soon followed by the two at Warland. Getting through them was excruciating. My ankle and leg were throbbing but everything else about me was beginning to ache too: my right shoulder, which always hurts after heavy locking; my right leg, which was the only one I could use opening the heavy gates and which I was putting under excessive strain; and of course my back, my damned back, which aches most of the time anyhow but which can sometimes be unbearable these days. Everything was taking so much longer now too. Partly it was my lack of mobility but mainly because I had no energy left any more. The tank had run out. Every step was an effort, every move a determined assertion of willpower, mind over matter. Really, I should have moored up. I should have stopped there and then and called it a day. There was no reason to go on, nothing to justify punishing myself like this.

Except me.

The light was fading fast now which didn't make it any easier. At first it was hardly noticeable, just a softness in the air, a gentle dimming of the world as if someone had turned off the central light and switched on the lamps instead. But dusk doesn't last long in these parts. Once the sun has fallen off the edge of the world, the curdling twilight thickens in minutes and soon what were once hills become shadows, and what was once was the stillness of the evening becomes impenetrable night, with only the quiet ticking of the boat engine to confound the silence.

Longlees was the last lock of the day and I closed the top gate with ineffable relief. Even feeling fresh and fit, locking alone in the dark on an unfamiliar stretch of canal is foolhardiness verging on stupidity. It was pitch black now, raven night, thick and oppressive, moonless, lightless. I switched on the boat headlamp. It was like laying a pale watercolour wash across the canal. A coot disturbed from its roost by it took fright and flapped across the towpath with a screech like dry chalk on a blackboard. In the distance, alarmed by the commotion, another bird fluttered in the trees.

Justice slid through the water, her engine barely louder than a sewing machine. We were in a world of our own, a thousand miles away, making a fantastic journey on some as yet undiscovered inland sea: magical, unreal, like a hallucination. I blinked my eyes and when I opened them again she wasn't floating any more – she was flying again now. Flying on those great wings of hers stretching out to the sky, her engine throbbing to their beat; and me mounted on her, clinging to her back as if she were a great bird, dipping and swooping among the black clouds on some mission to find the moon...

I think it must have been the painkillers.

They were stronger than I thought.

The summit is short here and as soon as I'd left the lock I was aware of a cluster of lights flickering ahead of me in the gloom. At first I thought it was a cottage on the moors, or perhaps the faraway streetlights of a village; but as I got closer it became apparent that it was another boat. It was moored and its curtains must have been open, for the reflection from its cabin shimmered in the black waters outside, becoming clearer as I approached. I saw the flash of an opening door. I saw a pale, thin figure emerge onto the bank and start walking up the towpath towards me. It was a man. He was carrying a torch, its beam dancing and darting about like an impatient flame in a newly lit fire.

He must have heard me coming. But I got the impression he was expecting me too.

'You all right?' he shouted, 'You looked as if you were limping.'

'I had an accident,' I said, 'a fall…'

'I thought so. I saw you a couple of locks down,' he explained. 'Midge is a retired nurse. She's told me to tell you to come aboard straight away, no excuses.'

She had already got out the first-aid box ready for business, and the kettle was crooning to itself on the stove. Before long I was sitting with my foot in a bowl sprinkled with some evil-smelling liniment she assured me she kept for this sort of thing. At the same time Don poured me a large whisky ('A well-known analgesic, old boy. Just look upon it as a medicine.')

Afterwards Midge took a packet of peas from the freezer and pressed it gently against my ankle. 'Hold it there for a few minutes and then I want you to put your foot back in the hot water again.

'I know what I'm doing,' she added. 'Believe me.'

And I did believe her. I'd have believed her if she'd told me it would make me feel better to soak my foot in the whisky and drink the evil-smelling liniment instead. I'd have believed her if she'd told me to pour it over my head and turn three times to face the moon. She had that sort of authority, Midge. That sort of command of the situation.

'You'll have some food, of course,' she instructed me. 'We've got some leftovers from dinner.'

I tried to protest but Jan silenced me. Jan, like Don, was Midge's friend. Like Midge she had a brusque way about her that thinner skins than mine might have thought rude.

CHAPTER TWENTY-THREE

'What else were you planning to eat this time of night?' she demanded to know.

'Well, I've still got some pie left…'

'Don't bother arguing,' she said. 'You'll only lose in the end.'

They were from Macclesfield, I learnt, a strange old place where the countryside was beautiful too, like this, and where the people were friendly and the beer cheap but could I please not go telling my friends about it down in London because they'd rather not be invaded by southerners since there were enough of them already, thank you very much, pushing up house prices and clogging up the roads…

The boat belonged to Midge but she hadn't been well. Jan, whose husband had died not long before, had agreed to travel with her for the summer. Don came up to see them both whenever he could. He'd been working in Leeds so it had been quite convenient for him recently.

'We're meeting some other friends tomorrow,' he said, 'or else I'd have suggested you travelled with us tomorrow. It's a shame, really. It would have made it easier for you.'

The leftovers were chicken curry, spicy and nourishing. I bolted them down. I hadn't realised how hungry I was. There was more drink too: wine, beer. I drank that fast too.

'You were lucky,' said Midge. 'You can't have been far off a fracture, but ankles are very resilient.'

'It hurts,' I said. Although to be honest, it hurt less with the drink inside me.

'It will do. But it'll hurt more tomorrow.'

When I left she pushed a plastic Co-op bag into my hand. Wrapped in it were the peas. 'You may need them later tonight,' she explained. 'Or in the morning. Either way, you'll be thankful of them, trust me.'

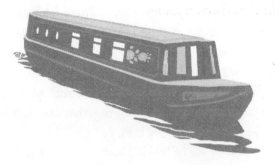

Twenty-four

saw him first running down the towpath towards me, arms flailing about like a windmill in a gale. I didn't know what to think. Once, years ago, when I worked for Barrow Urban District Council clearing the banks on country brooks, a bloke in my gang put his sickle through a wasps' nest. That's what this guy reminded me of. A bloke who'd just had a serious contretemps with stinging insects.

It turned out he was trying to attract my attention.

'I'm coming through!' he shouted. 'I'm coming through!'

Certainly something was coming through, something quite unpleasant actually. Probably from the region of his underclothing was my best guess. I could smell it at twenty paces. It had the same vile piquancy as the gunge I find in the bilges after *Justice* has been laid up for the winter. And there was another underlying odour there which at first I couldn't place. Then I had this flash of the recycling bin at home the last time we'd had a party.

'Wait for me,' he said. 'I'm at the top lock, I'll be with you soon. You could even give me a hand down, couldn't you?'

Despite the doubtful standards of his personal hygiene I was actually very pleased to see him once I'd worked out what he was after. He was travelling single-handed too, attempting like me to get through the swing bridge near Smithy Bridge before it closed later in the day. Travelling together through the locks would make it a lot easier for both of us.

It was the first stroke of luck I'd had that morning, a morning that had been a very long one. It had begun in the middle of the night about three hours after leaving Midge's boat when I attempted to turn over, the way you do when you're asleep. But someone had thoughtlessly nailed my foot to the bed. Or that's what it felt like. I woke up in agony. After that, there was no way I was going to get back to sleep again – despite the best offices of Midge's peas which weren't so much frozen as pureed by the time I'd finished with them. Not that it's fair to blame the peas. Frankly, it would have needed half the stock of Iceland to relieve the pain I was in. I didn't believe human beings could hurt this much without bleeding.

It made the going very slow when I finally started boating. Painfully slow, but I guess you'll have been ahead of me there. True, my ankle did begin to feel better the more I walked on it. But since I tried not to walk on it any more than I had to, that's not saying much. It began to swell up. By mid-morning most people seeing me would have concluded I'd got a tennis ball stuffed into my sock.

But my new travelling companion wasn't sympathetic. He ushered me back up the locks at Littleborough to where I'd only just come from by boat.

CHAPTER TWENTY-FOUR

'Yes, yes, I'm very sorry to hear about your accident but could you hurry up?' he said, ignoring my limp. 'I don't want anyone nicking stuff from my boat. I live on it, you see.'

Why he thought anyone would steal from it, I don't know. On first sight it looked like a tip. Its deck was covered in bags of rubbish and empty cider bottles, and its roof was piled high with odd bits of wood, long-dead batteries and fragments of broken engines. This was not a boat that spoke of untold riches locked away inside. The truth was, it would have been useless locking anything away inside since most of its windows were broken, and you could have stepped through them. In fact, stepping through them was probably the easiest way to get into the boat with all the clutter on the deck.

This was a man who was living in a world of his own, which I guess was OK since they knew him there. Out here in the real world, though, he took a bit of getting used to. He picked up a rusted bit of something or other as if was it was a piece of bone china.

'I would have been very sad to see that stolen,' he said. 'Very sad indeed.'

I worked the locks for him while he stayed on board so that we could get our two boats together as quickly as possible. But afterwards he seemed to expect me to continue to work the locks, even though I was now having to handle *Justice* at the same time. The sum total of his contribution to our progress was to stand between the two boats in the locks as they emptied, one foot on each, pretending to keep them apart.

'We don't want them scratching,' he explained.

Scratching? I don't think it would have been possible to have scratched his boat. Scratching requires paint and his hull was all rust.

It wasn't long before I'd had enough of him so I told him that if he didn't start pulling his weight I was going to stop for coffee and leave him to go on alone.

'Coffee? That's a great idea,' he said. Then he added, 'Three sugars for me, please.'

His problem was that he didn't really know how to handle a boat. He may have lived on a boat but he clearly hadn't spent much time moving boats about. As a result, some of the basics of cruising were totally alien to him. But then a lot of basics the rest of us take for granted seemed totally alien to him too. Like the concept of property, for instance. I ended up making him a cup of coffee, soft touch that I am. Afterwards he pinched the cup I served it in. I saw it later inside his boat.

He seemed almost offended when I wanted it back.

'This was my brother's boat,' he confided in me, as if it were somehow an excuse for his pilfering. 'He left it to me, you know.'

'What, in his will?'

'No, not in his will. He's not dead. He left it to me when he went to prison. Well, not exactly left it to me. But he owed me some money, you see. So I just took it.'

The two of us struggled down the flight to Littleborough, although doing the locks he was more of a hindrance than a help and I eventually sent him back to his boat where at least he didn't get under my feet. We passed through Thickone Lock (which must have an interesting story behind it if only it could be told in polite company) and finally arrived at the swing-bridge near Smithy Bridge where we'd been heading. Work was clearly about to start. It was already cordoned off with orange tape and a gang of disconsolate workers stood smoking around a Portacabin which had been dumped near the towpath.

I thought I might finally get away from my travelling companion at this stage, but he stuck with me like a herpes infection. I might not be travelling any faster teamed up like this, but he certainly was and he didn't intend to let me out of his sight until he was good and ready. We passed the seventeenth-century Clegg Hall, which is said to be haunted by the ghost or 'boggart' of a young boy who was thrown to his death over the ramparts by a wicked uncle. Occasionally the spectre is said to appear to warn passing travellers of danger.

A bit of me expected it to materialise as I went by. 'Beware of strong-smelling men in scruffy boats. They will promise progress but be as lazy as an overweight tabby cat and will steal your cups into the bargain.'

Although why would any apparition bother coming all the way from the other side to tell me this? This much I knew for myself without supernatural intervention.

Eventually, thank God, we parted at Rochdale where he'd decided to moor for the night. In one sense it was a shame because if he hadn't stopped there, I might have myself, if only for old time's sake. I used to work with a bloke from the town years ago and I know it well enough to know the good pubs. Most people over fifty have heard of Rochdale if only because it was the birthplace of Gracie Fields. Nowadays no one under fifty has heard of Gracie Fields or if they have they probably think it's an executive housing development in a posh suburb somewhere. It's a shame really. Rochdale's a surprising place. The DJ Andy Kershaw was born there and his mentor John Peel once worked in the town in one of its many mills. Singer Lisa Stansfield comes from nearby Heywood but isn't related to Gracie Fields whose real name was Grace Stansfield. Weird, huh?

The most interesting building in Rochdale is the domed Catholic Church of St John the Baptist which is modelled on Santa Sofia in Istanbul, of all places. It was built in 1924 and has an extraordinary blue and gold Islamic-style mosaic set in an arched recess that towers high above the altar, the work of Italian craftsmen from Manchester.

Now whose idea was that, then? A Catholic church looking like a mosque in a northern mill town which would end up almost a century later with a 10 per cent Asian population? You can't help but admire the vision. You can't help but admire the foresight. You can't help but smile at the mysterious ways in which God moves.

The waterway that takes its name after the town is actually two separate canals. From Sowerby Bridge to Littleborough, the way I'd come, it's almost completely rural, assailing the Pennines by a route that must make it the most beautiful canal in the country, far more impressive than the last mile or two of the Llangollen in Wales which is often cited as the most attractive canal in Britain. But from Littleborough southwards it is Mr Hyde to Dr Jekyll, chalk to cheese. It burrows into the Greater Manchester conurbation with such suddenness it's unsettling, without even the courtesy of a suburb to warn you what you're in for. One moment you're cruising through a bucolic idyll of stone cottages and twee humpback bridges; the next it's all red brick and concrete with railways and roads wrapping themselves around you like the damp on a foggy evening.

Everything about the canal changes. The first thing you notice is that the water becomes filthy, littered with flotsam from the hills and jetsam from the town, so that some locks are almost solid with rubbish: tree branches and old pallets, a sludge of last year's leaves, plastic bottles, old furniture and drinks cans. It begins to feel increasingly claustrophobic too, with industrial estates and housing developments closing in on you and only the occasional tract of waste ground, or sometimes even a field or two, punctuating the mounting urban inevitability of it all.

The section of the canal after Littleborough is where most of the restoration has taken place. Until just shortly before I made my trip, Littleborough had been the limit of navigation and travelling from there towards Middleton where I planned to spend the night, there was much evidence of the substantial work that had taken place. New bridges had been built to replace ones which had been levelled, fresh channels had been dug where the canal had been culverted and around Castleton, where the canal had been cut in half by the M62, it had been completely diverted to pass through a tunnel originally built for a road.

So much of it was new and pristine; so much of it was still incomplete. There were a lot of reinforcing rods about, a large number of soil banks awaiting turfing and there were lengths of new towpath under construction all over the place.

All around was concrete, everywhere you looked. Concrete culverts and concrete bridges and concrete banks, all of it white and freshly laid and so lacking in graffiti it was scarcely recognisable as concrete at all.

It felt very unwelcoming, like finding you'd strayed onto a building site when you were heading for the park. It felt unsafe too, with a lot of sullen kids wandering around looking for mischief. I put their mood down to the fact that until recently they must have seen the derelict canal as their territory, a place they could call their own and get away from adults. They hadn't yet got used to this thin trail of brightly painted boats which they must have known even then was only a prelude to an inevitable future in which they wouldn't have much of a stake. Every now and again I'd come across a gang of them furtively smoking something or other under a bridge and they'd eye me up in the manner of lions surveying a zebra at a bush watering hole.

One group greeted my arrival with a fusillade of rocks and half-bricks before scurrying away up the bank in fits of inane laughter. Some others gobbed on me from the top of a bridge. One of them even attempted to urinate on the boat from the parapet. But his intelligence quotient was so low he couldn't breathe and manage his fly-buttons at the same time so he finished up wetting himself down his leg. If I didn't know what Lancashire kids thought of narrowboats before, I did now.

I had more trouble at the top of the flight of locks at Slattocks which I wouldn't have expected, looking at the place. It seemed sedate and respectable, one of those semi-rural suburbs left over from the 1950s. But a posse of drunken twenty-somethings who were old enough to know better targeted me and once more I found myself dodging missiles. This time, to add variety, they started lobbing eggs too. Eggs? Did they just happen to be coming back from the shops with eggs? Or they had gone out equipped with them intending to find a boat to attack?

'Hey, we'll really put the frighteners on someone today. I've brought the extra large free range ones.'

I'd had enough of it. This was a new canal and there'd been a lot of this sort of minor trouble, so British Waterways had instigated a series of security measures, one of which was a team on emergency standby. I called them expecting they'd be hours turning up, if they turned up at all. Instead, within minutes, a Land Rover skidded to a halt and four guys got out looking like bouncers at a nightclub. I couldn't help but get the impression they were rather relishing the prospect of a dust-up.

What the drunken twenty-somethings thought, I don't know – they didn't hang around long enough for me to ask. The BW gang had scared them off. They'd put the fear of God into me too, as it happens.

One of them sauntered over, rolling his shoulders like the cops in *Life on Mars*. He was small and stocky, and although he lacked a pickaxe handle to complete the image, his impression of a thug was convincing enough. He was eighteen stone if he was an ounce, with a beer belly that wouldn't shame a morris dancer – although this was a man who'd kill rather than ponce about with bells on his ankles waving ribbons in the air.

'Sorted,' was all he said.

He got back in his Landy with his mates and accelerated off in a cloud of dust.

It had been another arduous day and dusk was already beginning to fall by the time I emerged from the bottom lock at Slattocks. I'd been on the go more than ten hours by now and my foot had become so numb it had almost stopped hurting. Occasionally it would deliver me a jolt of pain up my leg just to remind me it was still there; periodically it would give up the struggle and buckle under me. But most of the time we lived together in uneasy harmony: it agreed not to hurt me too much as long as in return I didn't ask it to do too much for me.

The fact that it was late concerned me. After the trouble I'd already had, cruising in this twilight made me nervous. The landscape made me nervous too. I couldn't work out whether I was in the country or the town. Beyond the towpath there were fields but the towpath itself was gouged with motorcycle tracks and the hedges were littered with old mattresses and abandoned electrical goods with their insides spewing out. On the grass were black marks, the scars of burnt-out fires.

On the other side of the canal I was aware I was passing an estate of some sort. But I'm not talking about Hampstead Garden Suburb. I could hear the sound of car tyres screeching and people shouting at each other. Occasionally I became aware of the sound of breaking glass. I didn't know what was happening that night but I knew I was somewhere close to Oldham, just a mile or two from where the year before there'd been the worst racial disturbances in Britain since the Brixton riots of 1981, with upwards of 500 youths confronting police with bricks, bottles and petrol-bombs in a pitched battle that lasted four days. A report commissioned afterwards by the Home Office concluded that deep-rooted segregation had been at the heart of what had happened. It had led to a fractured city in which there was profound mistrust between different communities – a problem the local authorities had failed to address.

But this was just one version of history. Travelling along the canal as I'd done, you could see the atrophy that lay of the core of it all. It was the economy, stupid. It was obvious in the amount of abandoned industrial land I'd passed, in the derelict factories and the crumbling old mills. Oldham had once been a rich town. Back then, 13 per cent of the world's cotton was produced there. Now no one wanted cotton, or at least no one wanted it at the price Oldham charged for it, despite the cheap labour from the Empire which it imported during the 1950s and 1960s in a desperate attempt to stem the rising tide of the inevitable.

I only had a few more locks to go now, and at one of them I saw a couple of teenagers eyeing me up as I approached. I was certain there was going to be trouble and I mentally prepared myself for it. But they turned out to be friendly enough and actually gave me a hand to help me on my way. Somehow this made me feel guilty that I'd pigeonholed them the way I had. But it's what you do when you get fearful. Fear propagates suspicion and that in turn generates more fear and so on in a continuing destructive cycle. It's what had happened to me; it's what had happened in Oldham during the riots.

'Where you heading, mate?' one of them asked and I explained to him that I had to be at the Rose of Lancaster pub that night. What I didn't elucidate was why that destination was so important to me. To have done that would have meant betraying the extent to which people like me – older people in expensive boats – were hostage to people like him – young people with not much going for them. For the truth was that in the early days after the Rochdale Canal reopened British Waterways were so concerned at the extent of vandalism directed against boats that they were assembling groups of us at the pub and convoying us down into central Manchester under guard. I was scheduled to be taken down the next day.

Narrowboat dreams, eh? They don't tell the newcomers this sort of stuff when they're looking through the glossy magazines deciding whether they want a blue boat or a green one.

But I knew about it. In fact, in a perverse way the menace of these urban canals had been part of what attracted me to the North in the first place. It reminded me of how canals used to be when I first started cruising the waterways and everything wasn't so damned chocolate-boxy as it is now, when things weren't always so twee and cutesy as today. When, as a way of spending your spare time, canals were a new concept; and to be on a boat at all you were a groundbreaker, a pioneer of a new leisure age. I'd wanted to see the North, hadn't I? Well, what had I expected the North to be? The South with funny accents? The Home Counties with mountains, and our industrial past reduced to heritage, packed away tidily for the delectation of tourists in museums? Had I not expected there to be any casualties from the changes that had happened over the years since canals were the motorways of their day? For God's sake, had I expected Jerusalem in this green and pleasant land of ours?

The next lock was open and ready for me when I got to it. And the two after that. So tired was I now that I wasn't thinking clearly and I don't know when it struck me that this wasn't just coincidence and that there was someone ahead preparing them for me. It was Don from Midge's boat. I saw him in the distance swinging his lock-key. By this stage I felt like crying with exhaustion. It was like the previous day, only worse. I could have kissed him.

'We were expecting you earlier,' he said when I finally got to the pub. 'You're eating with us again tonight – no, it's no use objecting, you know what Jan and Midge are like. Besides, Midge wants to look at that ankle of yours. She thinks you're overdoing it.'

Overdoing it? I had to smile. There were times that day when I'd wondered why I'd been doing it at all. But then there'd been many times during the trip when I'd wondered the same thing. Even now, looking back, I don't know if I've got a satisfactory answer to that question. Perhaps I was genuinely trying to find out something about where I belonged as I'd convinced myself when I was first planning the journey. Perhaps I really was trying to find the North. Or perhaps it was just a big boy's game, as Em always suspected, just an excuse to get away from London and the routine of normal life.

Either way, mooring up outside the Rose of Lancaster that night, I began to feel for the first time that I'd done what I set out to do, even though it had done for me in the process.

I couldn't do it now, I know that much. Not single-handed, anyhow. Physically, I wouldn't be up to it. I'm too old now, and older in my head too. I see things differently. I'm more cynical about what you can achieve by journeys like this. Or maybe I'm just more cynical, full stop.

'I need a shower,' I said to Don. 'Give me half an hour. Tell Jan and Midge I'll be along later.'

Twenty-five

It was over then, and I sort of knew it.

Early the next morning the British Waterways' SWAT squad arrived at the pub and marshalled us down through the outskirts of Manchester and into the centre. It was a quick and painless journey and I've hardly any recollection of it. Sharing the locks with Midge, Jan and Don would have speeded progress anyhow, but with the squad preparing the locks ahead and closing them behind us afterwards it seemed no time at all before we'd passed through the flight at Newton Heath and the tower-blocks of Piccadilly were coming into view above the roofline of the centre of the city. I spoke to Don about the trip recently and he reminded me that there had in fact been a final crisis in one of the locks when *Justice* had jammed on the wall and for a moment or two it had looked as if she might tip and sink.

But I have no memory of this. Whatever happened I have consigned to a part of my brain labelled 'The Rochdale and Other Potential Disasters'. In fact, there's only one thing about this section of the journey that I do remember with any clarity because in view of the hostility I'd met on the canal it touched me and I felt the need to take a picture of it to record it and remind myself of how I felt.

I have the picture in front of me now and in many respects it's a dull scene, taken at one of those featureless out-of-town junctions where a road crosses a canal. *Justice* is in a lock with Midge's boat. Midge herself is winding up a paddle with her lock-key and next to her Don sits on the lock-beam taking a breather. In the background is a scene that could be any drab high street in any undistinguished suburb in any city in the country. The Apollo Furniture shop is on the corner (Re-Upholstery Service Available); near to it is Church Street Carpets (Made and Fitted Within 48 Hours By Experts). Between them the Shuckel Tandoori House lies shuttered, too early in the day to be open.

Coming down the canal I had been spat at, sworn at, attacked with bricks and eggs and virtually peed on. That was what this section of Greater Manchester thought of its newly restored canal, a canal that I thought was a triumph of restoration, one of the jewels in the crown of the whole British Waterways' system.

But there's another view of these things and that's what I saw around the lock at that unpromising location that day, and which I found so moving. Boats were unusual then, so unusual that a couple of dozen people had gathered to witness my passage, interrupting their journeys, or their shopping, or whatever else they were doing with their lives, to stand and stare. There are old people in the picture. Teenagers. Young mothers holding up their children to see, pointing out to them these strange and gaudy creatures in the dark lock below. Creatures worth stopping to look at. Unusual creatures. Creatures to brighten this dreary suburb where, before this, the only people in generations to want to bring it colour were graffiti-artists.

One bloke asked me if it was true, had I really come all the way from Banbury by canal? And an elderly woman, almost in tears, told me about when she was a girl and the boats had gone through regularly. She'd never expected to see them back again in her lifetime, she said.

I supposed, pitched against some of the adventures other travel writers have, mine was a pretty modest affair. But then, I'm no adventurer and those narrowboaters who are – like the guy who went to the Black Sea a few years back – put the wind up me. But I guess most of us are like that, aren't we? It's terrific to read about journeys like that, or see films about them. But even if we had the inclination, we haven't got the money or the time or the youth to do that sort of thing. There's the kids and the family and the job to think about – those thousand and one clawing concerns that root us to the real world.

No doubt people will mock me for the size of my canvass. They'll accuse me of being cautious, conservative, dull. But as I potter through the English countryside, as I've done for the past thirty years, what unfailingly interests me about the canals is looking inwards, not out, observing the fine warp and weft of England that links its people to its landscape and its landscape to its past. Because whatever that past has brought us to, it is a part of us all and part of what makes us what we are. Journeys, as I've said before, are in the mind, not on maps.

They're about what's inside, not out. A personal CAT-scan, not a window on the world.

I cruised down to the junction with the Ashton Canal where what now seemed an age ago I had turned after that early morning cruise up the side of Canal Street. This time I was approaching it from the opposite direction so that I had to pull round hard to do a tight turn of more than ninety degrees. There are pictures of this too because a friend had come to record the end of my journey. I don't look too bad, all things considered; a bit worn, a bit tired and obviously in some discomfort because you can see I'm trying to take the weight off my bad foot. He wanted to take me out that night to celebrate, but I wasn't up to it. I had to get off early next morning, and first thing, before it was even light, I cast off en route for the Peak Forest Canal where I had arranged a mooring for the winter.

I was in the North for the next three years, during which I made a further three Pennine crossings, making a total of five in all. But never again would I do one entirely alone.

It was only when my mother became incapable of living at home on her own any more and it became apparent to my brother and me that we'd have to move her to the nursing home we'd arranged that I finally left. I took *Justice* to Barrow-upon-Soar near Leicester, just a few miles from the village of Rothley where I was brought up and which was soon destined to become the most famous village in the country after little Madeleine McCann, who lived there, was abducted from Portugal.

I got a temporary mooring behind the mill race near the Navigation pub and every day I travelled into Leicester where

CHAPTER TWENTY-FIVE

I spent a couple of weeks redecorating my mother's flat to rent out to pay the nursing home fees. My brother and I helped her move one weekend, and though by now her gently exploding brain was so damaged she forgot the flat as soon as she left it, she never settled in her new home and was dead inside the year.

I left Barrow for Banbury after the funeral.

I travelled across the summit of the Grand Union in a three-week window of blistering weather that opened unexpectedly in the middle of a wet English summer. It was still and sultry, not a breath of wind to relieve the relentless heat. Some days I could barely breathe with it. It passed in a dream.

Author's note

Nobody's real in this book, including me as the narrator. I'm nothing like I describe myself, and neither is anyone else I describe whether or not I give them their real name or make one up for them to protect them from themselves. Em in particular is not real. In fact, she is a total invention. I need to make this point very strongly since the woman I live with is sick to death of getting mistaken for her, something which is bound to happen since they do a lot of the same things and in many ways are very similar.

The Rochdale and the Huddersfield Narrow Canals aren't real either. Or at least not in the way I describe them in this book. I travelled the South Pennine ring (as the trans-Pennine circuit incorporating them has come to be called) the first year that it was possible in recent times. Although the book is a pretty faithful representation of the difficulties I encountered on that journey, time has gone by and things are very much improved, as I can testify, having done it again twice since.

They are terrific canals to explore by boat or foot. I would hate anything I have written to put people off them.

Thanks

To my old friend Miles Hedley who volunteered himself for the thankless task of correcting my wayward spelling and punctuation and finished up suggesting jokes.

Also to Martin Clark whose knowledge of the Pennine waterways is unparalleled. It has prevented me getting untold amounts of egg on my face. His website at www. penninewaterways.co.uk has to be the first port of call for anyone thinking of boating or walking canals in the North.

Finally to Jennifer Barclay, my editor at Summersdale, who made me believe I could write this book in the time available.

www.summersdale.com